THE EMERGING GOOD
IN PLATO'S *PHILEBUS*

SERIES EDITOR

John Russon

 REREADING ANCIENT PHILOSOPHY

THE EMERGING GOOD IN PLATO'S *PHILEBUS*

JOHN V. GARNER

 NORTHWESTERN UNIVERSITY PRESS • EVANSTON, ILLINOIS

Northwestern University Press
www.nupress.northwestern.edu

Printed in the United States of America

10   9   8   7   6   5   4   3   2   1

Library of Congress Cataloging-in-Publication Data

Names: Garner, John V., author.
Title: The emerging good in Plato's Philebus / John V. Garner.
Other titles: Rereading ancient philosophy.
Description: Evanston, Illinois : Northwestern University Press,
    2017. | Series: Rereading ancient philosophy | Revised version
    of the author's thesis (doctoral)—Villanova, 2014. | Includes
    bibliographical references and index.
Identifiers: LCCN 2017000576 | ISBN 9780810135598 (cloth :
    alk. paper) | ISBN 9780810135581 (pbk. : alk. paper) | ISBN
    9780810135604 (e-book)
Subjects: LCSH: Plato. Philebus. | Pleasure. | Ethics, Ancient.
Classification: LCC B381.G38 2017 | DDC 171.4—dc23
LC record available at https://lccn.loc.gov/2017000576

CONTENTS

Acknowledgments   vii

Introduction   ix

Part I: Basic Dialectical Concepts

Chapter 1. The Learning Procedure   5

Chapter 2. The Mixed Life and Its Causes   37

**Part II: Pure Pleasure and Knowledge in the
Order of the Good Life**

Chapter 3. The Intrinsic Goodness of Pure Pleasure   69

Chapter 4. Purity and the Sciences   103

Conclusion: Why Should the Good Come to Be?   141

Notes   145

Bibliography   167

Index   177

ACKNOWLEDGMENTS

I dedicate this book to the memories of my professors David Kangas and Helen Lang. Without their support alongside that of Martin Kavka, Gabriel Rockhill, John Russon, and above all that of my advisor Walter Brogan, neither this book nor philosophy would have been possible for me. I owe endless thanks as well to my family, and above all to my wife Carly, for their love and patience during my many years of study and writing. Finally, I would like to thank my dear friends, mentors, classmates, and colleagues at Villanova, in Florida, Philadelphia, Delaware, Georgia, and at the University of West Georgia. I owe Sherwood Belangia and Jedd McFatter a special thanks for their assistance in editing. I have gained enormously in the way of truth from all of you; any errors herein are strictly my own.

INTRODUCTION

What is it like to learn? The *Philebus* might seem an unlikely place to find an answer. For learning is not obviously thematic in the dialogue, whereas the themes it does explore—pleasure, knowledge, metaphysical kinds— are shifting and fragmentary. Unlike other dialogues of Plato, the *Philebus* is far from a dramatic masterpiece. And yet, as a measure applied to our familiar experience of what learning is like, the *Philebus* can discipline and deepen our understanding of what it means to learn. The *Philebus* is a lesson about lessons, a μάθησις that each of us can undertake. Studying its brief phenomenology of learning (52a ff.), I came to see that Plato's experience was my own experience. I was surprised to discover a kinship not specific to my time or place, and enjoyed a pleasure nearing what Plato describes. This experience guided me to a new hermeneutical approach to the *Philebus*: the dialogue's lessons, insofar as they are lessons about the learning process itself, should—despite all the critical questions regarding the textual transmission and history of the dialogues—remain accessible even as they were originally learned, or else they are not genuine lessons (μαθήματα). Reading the *Philebus* well and appropriating its teaching requires that we appropriate ourselves as learners.

Only late did I realize that this hermeneutics implies a response to the seemingly simple question: what is the topic of the dialogue? Other interpreters have given answers. For example, Damascius, who wrote the only surviving ancient commentary on the *Philebus*, raised several possible candidates including pleasure, intelligence, mixture, the unattainable transcendent good, the immanent good in animals and/or humans, the mixed good as such, and the mixed good for animals. He claimed the topic is the mixed good, that is, the good for living beings who are "naturally cognitive and appetitive."[1] Modern commentators typically select among options in a similar way, choosing the human good, or pleasure, or one among the many kinds of goodness.[2] My own experience, however, suggests a different thesis: the topic of the dialogue must not be any particular good or kind of good. It must be the good itself. The dialogue—and perhaps every genuine philosophical dialogue seeking to attain knowledge—must seek to share in this good if it is to illuminate any other topic. For to know is to understand a good version of the known. And to learn is likewise always to arrive at this ability to discern charitably, even if the context of the learning and the learning itself are local and temporary.

This hermeneutics opens the *Philebus* to the reader because it allows us to see the text as the effect of a relivable learning experience. All learning generates effects in our lives, effects that may appear, for example, as a book, a dialogue, a way of thinking, an institutional body, or a pleasant feeling. These effects can always bear witness to their source. They can always become a helpful aid to a serious learner who encounters the lesson again. Understood or reunderstood in light of their source, the effects are made new by the life of the mind. I believe the *Philebus* should be approached in just this way, as the artifact of an inquiry into the good itself. Thus, while the *Philebus* offers historically significant results (including classifications of pleasures, analyses of various sciences, comments on the nature of the soul, etc.), we cannot simply abstract the subject of the *Philebus* by working backwards from those results. For no one could even evaluate those results without first approaching them from within the lessons that inform them.

For this reason, my exploration of the *Philebus* has emerged as something more limited in scope than a general commentary. I have focused primarily on the dialogue's account of learning and the pleasure it brings. More specifically, I have aimed to show that, in the *Philebus*, the account of learning demands that at least some things essentially emergent—for example, the pure pleasures of the learning experience—can be at the same time intrinsically good.[3] In light of this interpretation, I therefore ask, what does this claim say about Plato's conception of the good, about his metaphysics of being versus becoming, or about his understanding of the good itself? How does this speak to our own experiences of learning?

Ultimately, if the pure pleasures are, as I argue, "emerging goods," then I will show that the *Philebus* must also hold that the good in itself transcends being or existence. This thesis implies further that all kinds of things, regardless of the extent to which they share in being, can admit of a wholly good version. In order to defend this claim, I show in chapter 3 that the nature of pure pleasure does indeed have this double character—as wholly good and as wholly emergent—for Plato. Prior to that, however, I show in chapters 1 and 2 that the dialogue's earlier, metaphysical passages are essential to the interpretation of the ontology underlying the later passages on pleasure. Thus, my own research proceeds from the prerequisite ontological concepts examined in part I to the central, phenomenological analyses of pure pleasure and learning in part II. In general, while part I's technical concepts are necessary, the reader seeking the more accessible, experiential implications of learning for Plato might benefit by turning first to part II, and in particular to chapter

3, where the analysis of the actual experience of learning occurs and the most significant conclusions are drawn.

I hope the following, more detailed overview of the structure of this book will aid the reader who might wish to jump right in to chapter 3 in this way. First, chapter 1 is about Socratic dialectic and the very principle or structure (λόγος) at work in any truth-seeking conversation. The core of dialectical practice is what I will call Socrates's "learning procedure," a procedure demanding from each interlocutor an openness to emerging into a new understanding. Such learning, however, requires that we allow the object of common inquiry to emerge as multiple or multifaceted; its appearance as multiple is necessary to reveal its proper being or nature. As I clarify later in chapter 4, the intellection of "each thing as truly itself in every way" is the pinnacle and essence of this dialectical practice. Chapter 1 shows, however, that this intellection depends on the good's power—as the source of our ability to grasp good and true versions of things—to transcend any single, particular perspective or kind of life. Plato makes this point dramatically when pleasure's war to claim the good life for itself alone is lost, and the interlocutors agree that no single life alone (μόνος) can capture the good itself. The good life is and must be a mixed life.

Chapter 2 flows immediately from the conclusion that the good life is "mixed," for it examines Socrates's concept of the cause (αἰτία) of such mixtures. Mixtures, he argues, emerge when a limit or measure is imported by a cause into what lacks measure. Socrates proposes to clarify his point through his famous analysis of "all that exist now in the universe." This analysis, as I argue, should be understood merely as an example or case study serving to exhibit the nature of a mixture as such. As Socrates shows, even the mixture nearest to us, that is, the whole world at present, is revealed, as a mixture, to require multiple explanatory factors. Above all, every mixture has a cause; and by showing that humans share in causation itself, Socrates thus shows that the emergence of this world is never a simple "given." Rather, causes like us have some control over it. Part I thus examines the core dialectical concepts—the limit, the unlimited, the emerging mixtures, and above all the cause—that serve, in any account (λόγος), to explain in real terms the emergence of the living present around us.

Part II follows and examines the lives of pleasure and knowledge in turn, showing that they can be combined well only by a soul that shares in the life of causing measure to emerge. In chapter 3 I show that this share in causation is an evident feature in Socrates's account of pure pleasures and learning.[4] All pleasures are bound by their nature to becoming and yet some of them come to be purely, as is exemplified in actual learning. In this experience, the psyche is fulfilled or assimilated to a measure or a norm that it engages for its own sake. This experience contrasts with pleasure-seeking, when the soul is pulled to try to remedy a need or lack of measure. The experience of learning, by contrast, implies that the soul's fulfillment is due precisely to its prior share in self-control. Chapter 3 thus contains the book's core phenomenological import in the way it links soul's experience of coming to a real measure in learning with soul's experience of coming to be self-measuring.

Chapter 4 expands on this thesis by linking the experience of learning to the encounter with the "lessons" offered by various scientific disciplines. That is, pure pleasure is the experience, either psycho-sensuous or simply psychical, of relating to pure instances or manifestations of forms. Certain sensuous pure pleasures serve as symbolic indicators of the way we can share in measure-giving. Other, purely psychical pleasures of learning bring us to share directly in the original importation of measures. Measure can thus be imported even into soul's sensuous faculties. Thus, Socrates's final ranking of "causes" in the good life can be understood as depicting this descending manifestation of measure. Pure pleasure, which is the last cause listed by name, is, as always something emergent in itself, a completely unique member of the order. For, as becoming, it shows us that being itself does not restrict or delimit the boundaries of the good itself. Rather, the good shares itself with, and is imported into a good life by, some this-worldly, emerging things. The good in itself must therefore have a scope that "transcends being in power and dignity."

In short, pure pleasure reveals to us that there can be good nonbeing. But this good nonbeing only emerges, so far as we know, for living beings who, in encountering measure itself and in bringing measure to themselves, allow this measure to reverberate through all levels of their lives. But this emerging measure, as completing the very definition of the good human life, must therefore be an ever-ongoing completion. For it is a process following from our participation in the ongoing self-definition of the human by the human. Thus, humans must be said to be, by definition, beings-in-the-making, that is, beings who are, above all, a learning experience (μάθησις).

THE EMERGING GOOD
IN PLATO'S *PHILEBUS*

PART I

Basic Dialectical Concepts

The Learning Procedure

The *Philebus* begins with a "restatement" in the sense that it begins with Socrates reporting on an already ongoing conversation. Socrates recounts two theses that have been offered about the nature of the good. And thus we expect that we are reading an "ethical" dialogue. This expectation, however, seems not to be fulfilled immediately. Instead this beginning leads the interlocutors to discuss what it is to give an account (λόγος) of something.[1] Indeed, after only a few pages outlining each candidate for the good life (i.e., the lives of pleasure and knowledge), the dialogue becomes entangled in a dense problem about the nature of accounts, a dense logical quandary about the one and the many. What I will show here is that this logical problem is not only connected to Socrates's vision of the good life but also provides us with a way to take part actively in constituting the good life as a one-many structure, or mixture.

First, however, we must ask, what is Socrates's argument for understanding the good life as a mixture? Socrates introduces this problem by way of pointing out an error inherent in the very kind of account (λόγος) the hedonists in the dialogue are giving. Indeed, from the opening line of the dialogue, different kinds of account-giving are represented by Socrates, on the one hand, and by his interlocutors Philebus and Protarchus, on the other. Philebus accounts for the good life as one thing alone (i.e., pleasure), while Socrates implicitly accounts for it as a life of an orderly plurality wherein some things, such as knowledge, are prior to others in the order of inclusion. But before Socrates can actually defend this structure, he must first argue that any account of the good life stating that the good life consists of only one kind of thing is always already a failed account.

As I will argue, Socrates shows that any account of something must involve a reference to that thing "as such and such." For this reason, a genuine account of something, for example, a definition, could never be true unless what it accounts for can be manifest as a multiplicity. If what we account for could not itself be genuinely multiple, then our definitions of it would

Context + premise

"falsify" and cover over the supposedly non-multiple reality they account for.[2] If the good were only one thing alone, no account of it could ever emerge as true. If we are to give an account of the good life at all, therefore, we must express the good as a multiplicity and account for the good life as a plurality. The very form of Protarchus's claim that pleasure is the only good—and that it cannot be differentiated into kinds—therefore precludes the claim's truth. Only by first exposing this logical difficulty can Socrates proceed to fully examine the claims of hedonism.

Still, while Socrates will engage in refutation here, he also suggests a kind of positive way forward out of the impasse he identifies in the hedonists' failed account-giving practice. To the extent that Protarchus (and Philebus, who refuses even to speak on his own behalf) allows neither that pleasure is itself multiple nor that the good life is multifaceted, Socrates diagnoses him with a fear of account-giving. To quell this fear Socrates introduces the "learning procedure," which shows how any genuine account of something posits that thing as a unity and, if it exists, also posits it as manifold in a way that does not conflict with the unity in question. By unfolding this plurality we come to grasp the specific nature of each reality in question. And while the dialectical learning procedure may not by itself lead us to a completely definite and final account of the good life, the procedure nevertheless sets us on the right track. It reveals the definition of the posited object as much as is possible for the inquirers. The realization that the good life itself must be treated in this way is what sets the dialogue on its longer path of discerning the right order of the good life's elements.[3]

1.1. The Two Candidates and the Two Kinds of Accounts

On close examination, the first lines of the *Philebus* reveal that the dialogue is not about the good life as separate from account-giving. Rather, the interlocutors are already implicitly engaged in an exploration of different ways of giving and receiving accounts (λόγοι). Socrates begins: "Well, then, Protarchus, consider just what the thesis [τίνα λόγον] is that you are now taking over from Philebus—and what *our* thesis [ἡμῖν] is that you are going to argue against, if you find that you do not agree with it. Shall we summarize them both?" (11a).[4] We discover Protarchus and Socrates in the middle of a dialogue in which two different accounts of the good life have already been given. Protarchus is charged with inheriting an account of pleasure as the good, an account already built and defended "once and for all" by Philebus, who is no longer willing to participate (11c5). Socrates by contrast explicitly speaks of the account he will defend as "ours" (11a2), as something shared, and, we shall see, as something that can be kept alive for us, can be restated, and will be resaid again and again through Socrates's continued presence with us. Socrates, of course, defends knowledge; but it is his mode of defense that stands out.[5]

The next passage offers additional evidence that different modes of account-giving are at stake in the introduction. For the characters embody their discourses very differently:

> SOCRATES: Philebus holds that what is good [ἀγαθὸν] for all crea-
> tures [ζῴοις] is to enjoy themselves [τὸ χαίρειν], to be pleased [τὴν
> ἡδονὴν] and delighted [τέρψιν], and whatever else goes together
> with that kind of thing. We contend that not these, but know-
> ing [τὸ φρονεῖν], understanding [τὸ νοεῖν], and remembering
> [μεμνῆσθαι], and what belongs with them, right opinion [δόξαν . . .
> ὀρθὴν] and true calculations [ἀληθεῖς λογισμούς], are better
> [ἀμείνω] than pleasure and more agreeable to all who can attain
> them; those who can [δυνατοῖς], get the maximum benefit possible
> from having them, both those now alive and future generations.
> Isn't that how we present our respective positions, Philebus?
>
> PHILEBUS: Absolutely, Socrates.
>
> SOCRATES: Do you agree Protarchus, to take over this thesis that's
> now offered you.
>
> PROTARCHUS: I am afraid I have to. Fair Philebus has given up on
> us [ἀπείρηκεν] (11b3-c6).[6]

Philebus does not simply defend pleasure. He accounts for the good life as consisting of only what agrees with one "kind" (γένος) (11b5). Protarchus is thus left to defend pleasure's kind as the sole good for all living beings. By contrast, Socrates's summary already shows important structural differences. First, he defends reason and intellection "and what belongs together with them [καὶ τὰ τούτων αὖ συγγενῆ]" as better for any of "those who are capable [δυνατοῖς]" of sharing in them. Presumably those capable may include any number of kinds of living things; and Socrates does not yet specify or delimit who is capable.[7] Second, Socrates's use of the comparative "better [ἀμείνων]" commits him neither to making knowledge the only kind of good nor to the claim that knowledge, as good, excludes goods other than knowledge. His account already makes room for others.

Furthermore, Socrates is depicted in the opening lines not simply as adopting the testimony of others regarding what is good but rather as seeking it originally for himself. By contrast, Protarchus defends an inherited account whose very source, Philebus, also himself appears to have adopted the account entirely from others.[8] This inheritance becomes clear in the closing lines of the dialogue, when Socrates and Protarchus expand on Philebus's sources:

> SOCRATES: In view of all the considerations laid out here and out
> of distaste for Philebus' position pronounced by countless oth-
> ers on many occasions, I maintained that reason is far superior to
> [βέλτιον] pleasure and more beneficial [ἄμεινον] for human life
> [τῶν ἀνθρώπων βίῳ]. . . . And did not pleasure turn out to receive
> fifth position, according to the verdict we reached in our discussion?
> . . . But not first place, even if all the cattle and horses and the rest
> of the animals gave testimony by following pleasure. Now, many
> people accept their testimony, as the seers do that of the birds, and
> judge that pleasures are most effective in securing the happy life;
> they even believe that the animal passions [τοὺς θηρίων ἔρωτας]
> are more authoritative witnesses than is the love of argument
> [λόγων] that is constantly revealed under the guidance of the philo-
> sophic muse (66e1–67b7).

Philebus appears to have inherited his vision of the good from his observation of animals' desires or from others who accept their testimony. As to whether there might be a specifically human element worth desiring, and as to whether each person must explore this element for him- or herself, he appears utterly indifferent. Rather, an imitation of others' desiring is enough for him. What he desires, he desires precisely because it is desired.[9]

By contrast, Socrates does not define the good life by what is already desired. He is not satisfied with imitation or inheritance of desire but seeks originally the "possession or state of the soul" that makes for a good life (11d4). And this element, in turn, will be "the one that can render life happy [τὸν βίον εὐδαίμονα] for all human beings" (11d5). Thus, instead of delimiting the inquiry to what we already desire, or to what others happen to desire, Socrates seeks the element that originally defines and measures desirability. In this way, the good that remains to be discovered in the forthcoming inquiry, if it can be discovered, will define the seeker and the happiness of the seeker; the seeker's nature will not define beforehand the good that is to be discovered.[10] This is perhaps why Socrates allows so much latitude when he says that knowledge offers a better life for any of those "capable" of it. The task of discerning who is capable remains an open inquiry; it is not something predefined. The question could only ever be decided in the course of the inquiry, that is, only if we first inquire. It is thus open to all who seek it. Only in this way—by first seeking the measure itself that accounts for the presence of goodness in *any* good life—can we come to discover the element that can make life happy for humans.

This order plays a vital role in Socrates's argument. For later, once both true and false pleasures have been examined, it becomes clear that knowledge is always good for the participant capable of it, while pleasure is not. For this reason knowledge has priority. Thus, the opening of the *Philebus* already suggests that the dialogue will be concerned not only with differing opinions but also, essentially, with a vision of the right order for account-giving, and with what is required for an account to be a good account. A Protarchus who inherits his vision of the good from Philebus, who in turn inherits it from the animals, is contrasted with a Socrates who originally inquires for himself into the original defining source itself. This original inquiry is the first prerequisite of truth in any account of the matter.

1.2. The Requirement to Distinguish between Pleasures

The floodgates have now been opened for the discussion of the requirements of account-giving itself. The issue arises explicitly for the first time when Socrates objects to Philebus's habit (noted at 12b7) of linking the name of the goddess Aphrodite to the name of pleasure. At 12c1–d5, Socrates says,

> I always feel more than human dread over what names to use for
> the gods—it surpasses the greatest fear. So now I address Aphrodite
> by whatever title pleases her. But as to pleasure, I know that it is
> complex [ποικίλον] and, just as I said, we must make it our start-
> ing point and consider carefully what sort of nature it has. If one
> just goes by the name it is one single thing [ἕν τι], but in fact it
> comes in many forms [μορφὰς] that are in some way quite unlike
> each other [ἀνομοίους ἀλλήλαις]. Think about it: we say that a
> debauched person gets pleasure, as well as a sober-minded person
> takes pleasure in his very sobriety. Again, we say that a fool, though
> full of foolish opinions and hopes, gets pleasure, but likewise a wise
> man takes pleasure in his wisdom. But surely anyone who said in
> either case that these pleasures are like one another would rightly
> be regarded as a fool? (12c1–d5).[11]

Socrates notices that to link pleasure to the name of Aphrodite generates at least an apparent conflict with the claim that pleasure is also many things (ποικίλος). Assuming pleasure is indeed pleasure, the problem is that, if we are to name pleasure with the name of another (i.e., of a goddess, and eventually of "the good"), then we must be assuming not only that different pleasures are all alike in their emergence as pleasures, but also that pleasure is, in each differing case, the same as some additional character (and never its opposite). Socrates is thus pressing Protarchus to see if the claim that "pleasure is Aphrodite" (or, later, "pleasure is good") is consistent with the claim that pleasures are manifold and unlike one another while still remaining pleasures. If each pleasure is different, and each is still a pleasure, then may we also consistently say that each of them is also called Aphrodite (or, later, called "good")? Or, rather, should only some of them be called thus?

Socrates initiates a familiar tactic here. He tests Protarchus for consistency. Typically an elenchus will show that an interlocutor who thinks of himself as holding consistent beliefs is actually holding (implicitly or explicitly) at least one belief that is inconsistent with one or more of the others.[12] This elenchus, however, proceeds differently. For Protarchus appears to predict that Socrates will try and identify a contradiction in his position. Protarchus's response, then, will be to deny preemptively that pleasure is indeed many (ποικίλος) things, and he will do so in order to save the identity of pleasure with the good. He will deny the very phenomenon of pleasure's plurality in hopes of saving himself from possible refutation. While this defensive tactic contains no logical inconsistency in itself, Socrates will treat it as a pre-dialectical and anti-dialectical retreat from honesty with oneself, one on a par with dialectical inconsistency.

Socrates is thus forced to engage in a kind of proto-dialectic with Protarchus to show that it is not necessary to deny the plurality of pleasures. To see this, we must analyze three elements from out of the concession Socrates is presently seeking (in 12c1–d5 above). First, he has asked whether, in linking the names of pleasure and Aphrodite (or by implication pleasure and the good), Protarchus intends to consider pleasures to be (1) alike one to another in some respect in addition to their being alike as pleasures. He then asks whether there really are pleasures that are (2) manifold and unlike one to another. Finally, he asks whether Protarchus believes (3) that to consider pleasures as unlike in some respect or another is to threaten the status of pleasures as being alike as pleasures. Protarchus's response clearly indicates that he holds (1) and (3); but while he admits that pleasures do indeed *seem* different from one another, he nevertheless takes the drastic route of denying a version of thesis (2) altogether. Pleasures are not really different from one another, he claims: "Well, yes, Socrates—the pleasures come from opposite [ἐναντίων] things. But they are not at all opposed to one another [οὐ μὴν αὐταί γε ἀλλήλαις ἐναντίαι]. For how could pleasure not be, of all things, most like [ὁμοιότατον] pleasure? How could that thing not be most like itself [τοῦτο αὐτὸ ἑαυτῷ]?" (12d7–e2). Protarchus not only denies that pleasures can be "opposed to one another [ἀλλήλαις ἐναντίαι]" insofar as they are all pleasures. He also insists that they, all being pleasures, are themselves "maximally alike to one another" (ὁμοιότατον). Any apparent differences stem from the opposite things that occasion them, or cause them to occur, but not from differences in the pleasures themselves.

We should note two points about Protarchus's denial of a version of (2). First, we find in this passage Protarchus's first use of the plural in the dialogue to talk about pleasure. Protarchus's very language thus contains the implicit concession that pleasure is not only one thing but also many (even though he still denies any unlikeness between pleasures). Second, Socrates had not in fact requested from Protarchus the concession that Protarchus in fact rejects in the above passage. Protarchus rejects, let us call it (2'), that is, the claim that pleasures may be "opposed to one another [ἀλλήλαις ἐναντίαι]." Socrates had in fact requested that he accept not the stronger (2') but the weaker (2), namely the concession at 12c9 that pleasures are "unlike each other [ἀνομοίους ἀλλήλαις]." These are importantly different concessions.

Socrates nevertheless proceeds to consider (2'), in order to see if this stronger claim would cause Protarchus problems. If not, then (2) will not cause problems either. Socrates argues that, in fact, even (2') is no danger. For some things might indeed be even opposite one to another while they still remain alike. "Colors," remarks Socrates, "certainly won't differ insofar as every one of them is a color, but we all know that black is not only different [διάφορον] from white but is in fact its very opposite [ἐναντιώτατον]" (12e5–7). He also mentions that figure remains figure, though some figures are opposites and that there are many more such examples (12e7–9). We might envision numbers which, while being one even and the other odd, remain numbers. Being alike is, at least in such cases, not necessarily threatened by being plural, unlike, and even opposite; that is, it is not threatened by the concession of (2'). This is so because pleasure may be, says Socrates, "all one in genus [γένει . . . πᾶν ἕν], [while] some of its parts are absolutely opposite to one another [ἐναντιώτατα ἀλλήλοις], and others differ [διαφορότητ'] in innumerable ways. . . . So don't rely on this argument [λόγῳ] which makes a unity of all the things that are most opposed [πάντα τὰ ἐναντιώτατα ἕν]. I am afraid that there are some pleasures that are contrary [ἐναντίας] to others" (13a2–4). If Socrates is correct, then Protarchus does not need to deny all differences or even opposition in pleasure in order to retain the likeness of pleasures to pleasures.

Socrates can here be understood as offering Protarchus a kind of pre-dialectical therapy. That is, he is not trying to "trap" Protarchus in argument by having Protarchus admit that there are opposite pleasures, thus causing Protarchus to deny that "pleasure is pleasure." Protarchus thought that was Socrates's direction, but he was misreading Socrates, acting as if Socrates is a common eristic. Socrates aims, rather, to free Protarchus from his (ungrounded) fear that opposite instances of a kind of thing destroy the self-identity of the kind and destroy the pro-pleasure argument. Socrates suspects that Protarchus really believes there are opposite pleasures. He suspects that Protarchus's denial of opposite pleasures is a defensive measure of hiding. But hiding is really just avoidance of the dialectical therapy that can save.

Even so, Socrates *is* cautioning Protarchus that the admission of a specific set of opposite pleasures would indeed challenge, not the alikeness of pleasure to pleasure, but the identification of all pleasures as good. This latter thesis is the core of the hedonists' position. It would be destroyed if pleasure truly admits of one specific set of extreme opposites, that is, the opposites of "good and bad."[13] For if there are good pleasures and bad pleasures, then, while the alikeness of pleasures would not necessarily be destroyed, the identification of all pleasures with the good would be destroyed. By analogy, using Protarchus's mythological language, if there are divine and non-divine pleasures, then the identification of every pleasure with the deity would be absurd.

Responding to the question of whether there are really opposite pleasures, then, Protarchus expresses hesitation: "Maybe so. But how will this harm our thesis [λόγον]?" Thus, here, he is initially willing to consider the idea of opposites. But not for long. For he will quickly withdraw again in fear.

> SOCRATES: [It will harm your thesis because] you call these unlike [ἀνόμοια] things, we will say, by a different [ἑτέρῳ] name. For you say that all pleasant things are *good*. Now, no one contends that pleasant things are not pleasant. But while most of them are bad but some good, as we hold, you nevertheless call them all good, even though you would admit that they are unlike [ἀνόμοια] one another if someone pressed the point. What is the common element in the good and the bad [ἐν ταῖς κακαῖς ὁμοίως καὶ ἐν ἀγαθαῖς] pleasures that allows you to call them all good?
>
> PROTARCHUS: What are you saying, Socrates? . . . Do you think he will accept it when you say that some pleasures are good but others are bad? (13a8–c1).

Socrates did not ask, "What is the common element in all pleasures that allows you to call them all pleasures?" He asked, "What allows you to call them all also *good*?" Socrates had already distinguished the thesis (2) that there are unlike pleasures from the more extreme thesis (2') that there are pleasures in extreme opposition to one another. With this new exchange we can now also distinguish another version, namely (2"), the thesis that there are specifically these opposite cases of pleasure, namely "good and bad" pleasures. Now, Socrates can show that even (2") does not necessarily conflict with the thesis that "every pleasure is pleasure." But the hedonists do not simply wish to argue that "pleasure is pleasure." After all, they wish to argue that "every pleasure is good," for pleasure is itself the good. Admitting opposite pleasures might not harm the kinship of pleasure to pleasure; but admitting the specific pair of opposites "good and bad" would harm it. Thus, while Protarchus was initially tempted at 13a8 to admit (2'), that is, that perhaps there are opposite pleasures, the threat of sliding into accepting (2"), that is, cases of bad pleasures, is too much for him to bear. Admitting bad pleasures would certainly cost him his treasured thesis that "all pleasures are good."

Now, we can surely notice that the admission of (2') does not seem to lead, all by itself, to (2"). Socrates recognizes the difference between these claims. For in this passage, he is merely asking whether there are cases of bad pleasure. He is not inferring their existence from (2'). Protarchus, on the other hand, clearly does not recognize the difference between these various claims:

> PROTARCHUS: What are you saying, Socrates? Do you think anyone will agree to this who begins by laying it down that pleasure is the good? Do you think he will accept it when you say that some pleasures are good but others are bad?

> SOCRATES: But will you grant that they are *unlike* each other [ἀνομοίους γε φήσεις αὐτὰς ἀλλήλαις] and that some are opposites [ἐναντίας]?

> PROTARCHUS: Not insofar as they are pleasures (13c2–3).

Protarchus needs to deny that some pleasures are bad. But his logical imprecision causes him to deny even more than he needs. Socrates, by contrast, knows that not all of these denials would be required for a person to reasonably try and defend all pleasure as good. Only a denial of (2") is required.[14]

Instead, Protarchus's defense of an indulgent hedonism is conducted with a remarkably defensive austerity.[15] The unrestrained hedonist is inadvertently too restrictive in his pseudo-reasoning, while the strict intellectualist is, in effect, more generous and open-minded. The hedonist, lacking the good use of reason, has in effect become the opposite of the permissive libertine he desires to be. An overarching theme of the dialogue thus comes to light: Socrates, by being committed to reason, can attain the true and good version of what the hedonist desires, without even seeking it. The hedonist misses out not only on the good in things other than pleasure but also on the worthwhile pleasures. This dramatic theme thus mirrors the dialogue's primary philosophical thesis that only the prioritization of reason will allow for the emergence of the good and true pleasures.

We should also notice here that Socrates has yet to criticize explicitly the Phileban moral claims. No critique or defense of an account of morality can be mounted if account-giving itself cannot first get off the ground. The defensiveness and confusions of Protarchus will have to be overcome before any real criticism of the moral claims can be leveled. In other words, the initial struggle with Protarchus is pre-dialectical. He must enter into genuine dialogue with Socrates if there is to be any hope of discerning the truth about the good life. As things stand, Protarchus irrationally fears the admission of any differences between pleasures. He is left only able to stipulate that "pleasure is the good," even though what this stipulation entails or requires in the way of defense escapes him. He is left confusing this claim with the claim that "pleasure is pleasure." He thus fails even to give an account, for stipulations and tautologies fail to "speak reality."[16] Protarchus's most pressing problem is therefore his logical, or rather dialogical, deficiency.

The dialogical problem dramatically displayed in Protarchus's character here can also be restated more compactly in the form of a logical dilemma. On the one hand, if the hedonist refuses the possibility of identifying pleasure with anything other than itself alone (because pleasures do not differ from each other at all), then this refusal contradicts the identification of pleasure with the good (or with "Aphrodite"). The hedonist can say nothing about pleasure except that it is pleasure. He or she cannot, then, account for the very practice of naming pleasure with another name, that is, with the name "good." On the other hand, if the hedonist resorts to stipulating dogmatically the claim that the self-identity of pleasure—pleasure's status as being just pleasure itself and nothing else—is synonymous with its being "good," then he or she is merely asserting baldly what is in fact being called into question in the inquiry. That is, the hedonist begs the question. He or she takes the assertion that pleasure is good as if it is evidence for the establishment of the same thesis, namely that pleasure is good. In either interpretation of the denial that pleasures differ in any way from pleasures, the hedonist gives no *account* of pleasure as good. In this way, Protarchus's fear of "differences" turns out to be not merely a fear of losing the battle over hedonism but a fear of giving an account (λόγον διδόναι). His resultant attempt to salvage pleasure's goodness ends up as either self-contradictory or circular.

Because Protarchus's most pressing problem is his failure in dialogue, Socrates thus criticizes, in the passage that follows, not the moral claims made by Protarchus but his account-giving strategy:

> SOCRATES: But really, Protarchus, this takes us back to the same old point. Are we, then, to say that pleasure does not differ from pleasure [ἡδονὴν ἡδονῆς διάφορον], but all are alike [ὁμοίας]? . . . Suppose I imitate you and dare to say, in defense of my thesis, that the most unlike [ἀνομοιότατόν] thing is of all things most *like* [ὁμοιότατον] the most unlike [ἀνομοιοτάτῳ]; then I could say the same thing as you did. But this would make us look quite childish, and our discussion would founder on the rock. Let us therefore set it afloat again. Perhaps we can reach mutual accommodation if each side accepts a similar stance toward its candidate (13c5–d7).

It might appear that Socrates has suddenly shifted the topic from ethics to logical accounts. However, as I have shown, Socrates has all along been criticizing a misguided view of account-giving. Socrates's appeal to treat each candidate fairly thus is not trivial. He merely reveals the way the irrational methods of Protarchus, unless we abandon them, leave us with no recourse other than to imitate one another in irrationality. Socrates thus pleads with Protarchus:

> SOCRATES: Let me be the one questioned in turn by you . . . [about] wisdom, knowledge, understanding, and all the things that I laid down at the beginning as good. . . . Won't my answer suffer the same consequences as your thesis did? . . . Taken all together, the branches of knowledge will seem to be a plurality [πολλαί], and some will seem unlike others [ἀνόμοιοί . . . ἀλλήλαις]. And if some of them turn out in some way actually to be opposites [ἐναντίαι], would I be a worthy partner in discussion if I dreaded [φοβηθεὶς] this so much that I would deny that one kind of knowledge can be unlike [ἀνόμοιον] another? That way our whole discussion [λόγος] would come to an end like that of a fairy tale—with us kept safe and sound through some absurdity [ἀλογίας] (13e8–14a5).

Immediately after this exchange, Protarchus changes heart and concedes that there are manifold and unlike pleasures: "But I am rather pleased by the fact that our theses are on the same footing. So let it be agreed that there can be many and unlike kinds of pleasures, but also many and different kinds of knowledge" (14a7–9). Protarchus's concession is not, however, won simply through a "trivial" device of appealing to the prospect of equal logical treatment of each candidate (though Protarchus could be expected to be attracted to the idea of equality).[17] Rather, Protarchus has independent reasons to assert that pleasures can be unlike one another, if only because he can observe the phenomena. Thus, Socrates's proto-dialectic has in fact helped free Protarchus to actually say what he believes about the phenomena. Whether he is right or wrong is less important than the fact that he has moved from an unstable ground, shifting between bald assertion and contradiction, to the more promising ground of account-giving. Protarchus now shares in more than a mere proto-logos. He has taken a share in the λόγος, in the voicing of shared phenomena, or in voicing itself as a sharing of phenomena. Socrates has thus, at once, helped free Protarchus not only from his irrational fears, but also from the ἀλογία of unmitigated hedonism. If Philebus is incurable, Protarchus is perhaps curable.

1.3. The Principle of Accounts and the Sources of Controversy

Protarchus's refusal to allow differences between pleasures was tantamount to a refusal to give an account. Socrates, however, has yet to explain his own, positive vision of account-giving. Starting at 14c1 he offers us some clues. There is, he claims, an amazing principle (λόγος) informing various accounts (λόγοι), a principle that should itself now be brought out into the open: "It is a principle that has turned up here, which somehow has an amazing nature. For that the many are one and the one many [ἓν γὰρ . . . τὰ πολλὰ εἶναι καὶ τὸ ἓν πολλὰ] are amazing statements, and can easily be disputed, whichever side of the two one may want to defend" (14c1–9). The problem of the one and the many cannot be avoided. It has already appeared in the preceding dispute, and it will continue to arise unless we take it on.[18] Thus, Socrates must try to explain this amazing source of difficulties.

Helpfully, Protarchus presents us with an instructive case of the kind of pseudo-dispute that misses out on the deep and serious one-many problem:

> PROTARCHUS: Do you mean this in the sense that someone says that
> I, Protarchus, am one by nature [ἕνα γεγονότα φύσει] but then also
> says that there are many "me's" [πολλοὺς . . . τοὺς ἐμὲ] and even

contrary ones [ἐναντίους ἀλλήλοις], when he treats me, who am one and the same [τὸν αὐτὸν], as tall and short, heavy and light, and endless such things [καὶ ἄλλα μυρία]?

SOCRATES: You, dear Protarchus, are speaking about those puzzles about the one and many that have become commonplace. They are agreed by everybody, so to speak, to be no longer even worth touching; they are considered childish and trivial but a serious impediment to argument if one takes them on. No more worthy is the following quibble: when someone who first distinguishes a person's limbs and parts asks your agreement that all these parts are identical with that unity, but then exposes you to ridicule because of the monstrosities you have to admit, that the one is many and indefinitely many [τό τε ἓν ὡς πολλά ἐστι καὶ ἄπειρα], and again that the many are only one thing [καὶ τὰ πολλὰ ὡς ἓν μόνον] (14d3–e8).[19]

These passages suggest that the pseudo-problems arise for two key reasons. First, the subject matter from which the example studied is drawn is a sensible thing (15a1). Socrates is not necessarily denying that sensible things may be unified; but he is saying that even if they have unity, they can be expected to take many predicates.[20] Second, taking many predicates would not be a problem unless one were to insist either that the object can take "indefinitely many" predicates while also at the same time remaining one thing, or that it can remain "only" one thing while being many. It is not even necessary to refute those who trouble over such problems since it is evident that the claims trivially contradict one another.

Socrates wants to focus not on these trivialities but on what he will now call the "genuine problem" of the one and the many. The trivial controversies arise when we take the unity "from the things that come to be or perish [τῶν γιγνομένων τε καὶ ἀπολλυμένων]" (15a2). By contrast, the genuine, meaningful disputes arise, says Socrates, when "someone tries to posit man as one, or ox as one, or the beautiful as one, and the good as one" and discussants then have a "zealous concern with divisions of these unities [ἑνάδων]" (15a1–6).[21] The key for Socrates is that these henads (unities) are posited by a serious inquirer neither as only (μόνος) a unity nor as only an indefinite (ἄπειρος) many.[22] For in the much-disputed passage that follows, Socrates says we must always pose a series of questions about each of the posited units, specifically questions about how they can be both one and plural. We must ask:

Firstly, whether one ought to suppose that there are any such unities truly in existence. Then again, how they are supposed to be: whether each one of them is always one and the same, admitting neither of generation nor of destruction; and whether it remains most definitely one and the same, even though it is afterwards found again among the things that come to be and are unlimited, so that it finds itself as one and the same in one and many things at the same time. And must it be treated as dispersed and multiplied or as entirely separated from itself, which would seem most impossible of all? It is these problems of the one and many, but not those others, Protarchus, that cause all sorts of difficulties if they are not properly settled, but promise progress if they are (15b2–c2, see endnote for the Greek).[23]

The exact number of the "genuine" questions listed by Socrates is highly controversial.[24] The problem of the exact number can be defused somewhat, however, by the consideration that Socrates may be listing mere examples of questions that can be asked. He may not be making an exhaustive or necessary list. Even so, we can distinguish several "moments" of a larger problem here. To see them, we must read the passage in light of the thrust of the whole surrounding inquiry. As I understand these moments, Socrates suggests that we might ask, first, "whether [εἰ]" units are or exist (15b1). This turns out to be a very important question in its own right, as I shall argue momentarily. Second, we might also ask "how [πῶς]" such a unity could—while being always one thing and not changing—remain steadily "this one [μίαν ταύτην]" (15b3–4). (This is the particularly controversial question for interpreters, and we will return to it.) Then, third, we might ask "whether [εἴτε]" the seeming impossibility arises—given that there are many "emergent things [τοῖς γιγνομένοις]" and "indefinite things [ἀπείροις]" coming to be this one thing—that this one thing might become "separate [χωρίς]" from itself. (This convoluted sentence has been my paraphrase of the core of question three.)

To begin, we should first ask in general, what makes this whole line of questioning different in kind from pseudo-questions that arise regarding sensible things that become? The first obvious difference is evident in the first question: it asks about the very "being" of the posited unities. I know of no interpreter who disagrees that the problem of their being is at stake there. Yet many interpreters overlook the importance in the way the question is posed as a question. For Socrates, I want to argue, is saying that genuine questions must not begin by presuming the being or existence of the unity to be a given. Socrates has avoided language implying existence or being of the *henads* in the passages when he first posits them, speaking of them only as "one ox," and so on. When he speaks of the "positing" of them, therefore, he is showing us that we should begin as uncommitted to the being or existence of each of these posited *henads*.[25] For the being or existence of a *henad* is precisely what is in question in the first question. No genuine first question would even arise if the answer were taken to be pre-given truth, guaranteed automatically in the initial positing.

Understood in this way, the subsequent questions can be seen to flow from this first question about being. If the very being of the *henad* already pluralizes that *henad*—because a "unity which is" is something that is not merely "unity" but is also more than unity (i.e., it also "is")—then the subsequent questions of whether and how a *henad* can "remain a unity while also having being or existing" must arise as well. Many interpreters struggle with the second question in the passage above because they miss this point. There seems to them to be no good reason for Socrates to "worry" about whether unities that are not sensible or becoming can also "be." (Because such worries about being, they think, only arise for sensible things, or things that become.) My reading shows that there is and must be such a worry about *henads*: there is a worry about how the posited *henad* can be because once we say that "the one-ox" also "is," then this *henad* is thereby spoken as pluralized.[26]

Thus, Socrates is showing that there is a genuine difficulty in saying that a *henad* is, and this difficulty leads to the real logical controversies. While we might typically ask questions only about things that we assume exist, here we are asking about some unity that we do not yet take to be or to exist. We take the very question of its being or nonbeing to be the real "first question." This is evidently a question that cannot even arise in the mind of someone who takes a unity unproblematically both "to be and to be one."[27] But this is a question without which the other questions, as well as the distinction between inquiry into *henads* and inquiry into sensible things, loses all significance. By positing *henads* in a way that is explicitly not yet committed to positing their being or nonbeing, we thereby raise the genuine question of their being and thus of their plurality. We thereby open a new ontological field of inquiry. We posit that their being is not a given but is something problematic, and we are thus free to inquire into the being of the posited one *X*, about whether it is or is such and such, and how it can be such a singular-plural reality. Thus, we become open to considering the question of being at the same moment we become open to positing each *henad* itself as a thing in question, as a unity-determinable-as-plural.[28]

This positive account of the principle (λόγος) underlying all accounts (λόγοι) justifies and explains Socrates's earlier criticism of the Phileban argumentative strategy. From the start, Philebus and Protarchus had posited the identity of pleasure with some other one thing, that is, with Aphrodite, or later with the good. Protarchus was as a result afraid to engage in any real account of pleasure's different parts, kinds, or instances, believing erroneously that these differences ruined the case for the unity of pleasure or for pleasure's goodness. But Socrates's parody of Protarchus demonstrated that the refusal to admit divisions of pleasure is both unnecessary for the defense of pleasure as good, and it is indeed destructive of the possibility of accounting for (either some or all) pleasure as good in itself. Now we understand why it was so destructive. Genuine accounts must involve an accounting for whether (and if so, then how) the *henad* in question can be multiple. For even the "being" of a *henad* multiplies it. Thus, we have a serious philosophical difficulty here.

Even before examining Socrates's response to this difficulty, we can already see that to give a genuine account requires attunement to this problem and the courage to question being. For Protarchus, by contrast, the question of the multiplicity of the unity was originally "out of the question" since he believed it implied that his candidate would be destroyed. Socrates has thus shown that genuine dialogue cannot arise if this fear of nonidentity drives us to preclude even the possibility that our candidate might be a differentiable unity, or something whose being unfolds only as a nexus of relations to other things. We must not fear differentiability, since it neither precludes the self-identity of X nor implies by itself that X is bad. Further, without differentiability, our candidate X could not be truly associated with another *henad*. We would be driven into silence. For we would hold that all accounts falsify the very things they account for when they speak them "as such and such."

Socrates thus shows that these absurdities are themselves masks and falsehoods. Their proponents fail to take account of the way the definite multiplicity of a truthful λόγος preserves and reveals the structure of the being itself. Any genuine logical inquiry must operate with a spirit of openness wherein the determining of the being of the *henad* is also a determining-as-multiple of what we seek to learn. Without this openness the very activity of account-giving is destroyed, and engagement in the speaking of things is rendered only a performative self-destruction or a cover over truth.

For this reason Socrates insists that his line of questioning must arise anywhere genuine discourses on reality emerge:

> SOCRATES: [It] is through discourse [λόγων] that the same thing
> flits around, becoming one and many [ἓν καὶ πολλὰ . . . γιγνόμενα]
> in all sorts of ways, in whatever it may be that is said at any time
> [καθ᾽ ἕκαστον τῶν λεγομένων ἀεί], both long ago and now. And
> this will never come to an end, nor has it just begun, but it seems to

me that this is an "immortal and ageless" condition that comes to us
with discourse [τῶν λόγων αὐτῶν] (15d1–9).

The translation of the last line could be even stronger, for the genuine controversy of the one and the many is here said to arise "from accounts themselves
[τῶν λόγων αὐτῶν]," from what it is to be an account. We noted earlier that
Socrates did not use the term αὐτός to refer to the being and plurality of
the *henads*. Here, however, he does use the term, not to speak of the unities
posited, but of the accounts themselves, which express the *henads*. To be a
genuine account per se is thus to be a realm in which each thing is allowed
to come to itself properly in its own being, that is, in its being opened to its
own multiplicity.

We have already observed the way the failure to account for this basic
principle of accounts has impacted the silent Philebus. For he has no time at
all for the complexities of accounts; he remains silent. We have also seen it
in Protarchus's denial of the differentiability of the subject of study, that is, in
the way he falls into the trap of moving endlessly between mere bald assertions and self-contradictions. Endless pseudo-controversy is the fate of such
persons.[29] The genuine accounts themselves, by contrast, must involve the
accounting for something "as such and such." And we must therefore face the
problem directly of how a posited unity can be both one and many.

1.4. Socrates's Response to the Genuine Controversy

To give an account of something is to face genuine problems about the
unity and plurality of the things about which we speak. Unless we are careful, however, we may misuse the one-many structure and fall into confusion:
"Whoever among the young first gets a taste of it is as pleased as if he had
found a treasure of wisdom. He is quite beside himself with pleasure and
revels in moving every statement, now turning it to one side and rolling it all
up into one, then again unrolling it and dividing it up. He thereby involves
first and foremost himself in confusion" (15e5–16b3). Protarchus takes some
offense at Socrates's subtle criticism of him here; but Socrates is not entirely
critical. For Socrates acknowledges that the novices are implicitly noticing
and manipulating the real one-many structure. If they are to overcome this
misuse of the structure, they need a more adequate response to this "ageless
and immortal" burden given us by accounts of being.

Socrates suggests that there is indeed a way to temper the tendency of
interlocutors to misuse the one-many structure and to slide into mere dispu-
tation. He says:

Indeed, there is not, nor could there be, any way [ὁδὸς] that is finer than the one I have always admired, although it has often escaped me and left me behind, alone and helpless. . . . It is not very difficult to describe it, but extremely difficult to use. For everything in any field of art [τέχνης] that has ever been discovered [ἀνηυρέθη] has come to light [φανερὰ γέγονε] because of this. . . . It is a gift [δόσις] of the gods to men, or so it seems to me, hurled down from heaven by some Prometheus along with most dazzling fire. And the people of old, superior to us and living in closer proximity to the gods, have bequeathed us this tale, that whatever is said to be consists of one and many [ὡς ἐξ ἑνὸς μὲν καὶ πολλῶν ὄντων τῶν ἀεὶ λεγομένων εἶναι], having in its nature limit and unlimitedness [πέρας . . . καὶ ἀπειρίαν] (16b5–c9).

The phrase "whatever is said to be consists of one and many" has provoked much controversy because it remains ambiguous between referring to things which always "are" or things which are always "said to be." A close look, however, shows that Socrates's phrase is perfectly adequate. Clearly he is responding to the previously mentioned "immortal and ageless" condition that comes with "the accounts themselves [τῶν λόγων αὐτῶν]."[30] But also, the one-many principle, as we have seen, does not arise in language alone, as if there were no reference to "what is" in that discourse. Rather, true accounts open onto the being of things. The positing of the *henad*—the discursive act of rendering being problematic—is the opening moment wherein the very unfolding, emergence, or coming-to-light of the genuine being of the posited *henad* can occur. The gift of the gods is thus a procedure opening both onto "what is" and onto "what is said to be."[31]

This accordance explains why Socrates suggests that the gift makes possible all discoveries in any art (τέχνη). For art is something based in discoverable, learnable principles in which many persons can share.[32] But these principles are not merely transferred from the teacher to the learner; rather, they are independent of the teacher or learner and are discoverable by different persons simultaneously in unconnected times and places. The gift of the gods thus shows us "how to inquire and learn and teach one another [σκοπεῖν καὶ μανθάνειν καὶ διδάσκειν ἀλλήλους]" not because it shows us how to influence each other, nor because it shows us how to manipulate language separately from reality (16e2–3). Rather, it grounds learning and teaching because, in the course of the public unfolding of the object of inquiry, it reveals the logical structure of the being itself *in* and *as* the ontic structure of the account itself.[33] The learning of any genuine art must involve an engagement with this public unfolding, though it is clear that art is just one of many genres of practices that do so.

Fortunately, Socrates gives us more insight into what this "learning procedure" involves in the passage that follows: "Since this is the structure of things [τούτων οὕτω διακεκοσμημένων], we have to assume [θεμένους] that there is in each case always one form [μίαν ἰδέαν] for every one of them [παντὸς ἑκάστοτε], and we must search [ζητεῖν] for it, as we will indeed find it there [εὑρήσειν γὰρ ἐνοῦσαν] . . ." (16c9–d4). Before finishing the passage, we must clarify that the initial line "τούτων οὕτω διακεκοσμημένων" has to be interpreted as referring back to "accounts of what is [ὄντων τῶν ἀεὶ λεγομένων]." Frede's "things" is a relatively neutral term, but it might suggest to the reader that this passage changes topics and begins to speak of some "things" other than those that share in the structure of accounts. Now, we can continue with the passage and examine its content more closely. Socrates continues:

> And once we have grasped it, we must look for two, as the case would have it, or if not, for three or some other number [ἀριθμόν]. And we must treat every one of those further unities [τῶν ἐν ἐκείνων ἕκαστον] in the same way [ὡσαύτως], until it is not only established of the original unit [ἀρχὰς ἓν] that it is one, many, and unlimited [ἓν καὶ πολλὰ καὶ ἄπειρά], but also how many kinds [ὁπόσα] it is. For we must not grant the form of the unlimited [τὴν . . . τοῦ ἀπείρου ἰδέαν] to the plurality [πλῆθος] before we know the exact number [ἀριθμὸν] of every plurality that lies between [μεταξὺ] the unlimited and the one. Only then is it permitted to release each kind of unity [τὸ ἓν ἕκαστον τῶν πάντων] into the unlimited and let it go (16d4–e3).

Some aspects of this procedure are uncontroversial. After positing the one-idea for each thing, we must seek not only this single idea but the two, or three, if needed. And for each additional *henad*, each of them is to be taken not merely as a one alone, as a many, or as an indefinite plurality, but also, finally, as a specific "how many [ὁπόσα]." The overall task, therefore, is to determine the original idea as being of some "number [ἀριθμὸν]" between what is indeterminate and one. Only then do we "bid farewell [χαίρειν]" to the account and allow the idea to pass into the indeterminate.

Several details of the passage, however, are more controversial for interpretation. First, Socrates appears to guarantee for us that we will "discover as being [εὑρήσειν . . . ἐνοῦσαν]" the single idea that we posit. And this passage makes explicit a strong analogy between being (as revealed in a λόγος) and the "number" of a *henad*. This analogy opens up two possible interpretations. First, one might argue that the discovery of the "being" of the unity is what propels us to posit, next, that the posited unity is therefore, for that reason, also a "two." The discovery of being is thus a primary discovery that then sparks subsequent discoveries that further reveal the added features, or "number," of the *henad*. Alternatively, one might argue that the full unfolding of the "being" of the unity occurs only when the unity is completely determined, in the end, as some final, determinate number. Being is not what makes any *henad* "two"; being is found only in the fully unfolded number specific to each *henad*. Importantly, both of these interpretations—call them interpretation kind (1)—assume that the discovery that the "unity" also "is" is already the discovery of something more than the original unity.

Yet, one might argue on the contrary that to posit the one-idea is already to posit implicitly that the one-idea contains an implied, yet-to-be-specified being. The being is not explicit or defined yet; but it is there implicitly. According to this reading—call it interpretation kind (2)—the procedure aims to connect this implied "one-being" to other ideas, but this process of connection is, at once, the process of making the implicit being of the original *henad* explicit. That is, the positing of the "two" or the "three" would have nothing to do with the notion that "unity + being = two." Instead, "two" and "three" would be some additional and separate ideas posited along with, or after, the original unity is posited. They would be separate ideas that, when posited, already imply that they themselves have their own being. For example, the search for the one-ox reveals that it is connected to and differentiable from other ideas (such as mammal or horse), and each of those then becomes an independent subject of study. We then have to posit the one-mammal, which itself contains an implied being that must in turn be made explicit. If we take this route, then the ultimate implied "being" of the original, posited "unity," once it is unfolded, will be discovered as inclusive of the implied being of mammal, and so on. Thus, discovering the implied being of ox will require several independent studies of each idea in any way connected to the study of the original unity. If so, then the "two" and the "three" could be seen to symbolize the practice of positing separate, discrete *henads*, each already having an implicit being. These other ideas need not be discovered through discovery of the "one as being" (yielding the "two"), but rather they are independently posited as distinct ideas that admit of their own proper multiplication and discovery in their own being. They could each be seen as wholly new "re-beginnings" of the learning procedure, even as they also unfold an original unity. We would restart the whole procedure for each idea we subsequently (due to our discovery of its connection with the original unity) posit, and thus we discover that we must diversify the original unity "into" its proper, ultimate connected plurality of beings. Here, the being of the original, posited being is always also the being of the beings into which the study of the original being unfolds.

The debate between (1) and (2) hinges on what Socrates means above by saying that "we must treat every one [ἕκαστον] of those further unities in the same way [ὡσαύτως]." Socrates may mean to say, first, that we should complete the whole procedure—showing each unity to be a determinate "how many"—by performing the procedure only on the single idea that we originally posited. Thus, the term ὡσαύτως would imply that, in any separate situation of learning, we should start again "from the top," by way of a discrete act of original positing. If today we seek to learn of oxen, then we begin with the one-ox. Tomorrow it may be humanity or justice. We do the procedure again and again for each separately posited idea on each separate occasion. Thus, we do not repeat the procedure "in the same way" back upon the results of the original division. If this is what Socrates means, then there is only one procedure that is undertaken each time, and it is repeated completely and separately anew in each separate instance. If this is the case, then whenever "we look for two, or three, or some number," we are already undertaking the same procedure we will undertake each time (in different ways each time). Each situation will call for the enactment of the same core procedure.[34]

An alternative to this first interpretation of ὡσαύτως is also possible. We can call it the "recursive" interpretation. For Socrates may mean that the procedure is not just one single method repeated on separate occasions, but that it is a vast, complex, and continuous procedure which, once begun, must be repeated and performed back upon its own results. It is one procedure that therefore differs in each implementation, since it is performed first on the *henad*, then again on what is implied as connected to the *henad*, then again on the next division and so on. For example: the one-ox is posited, divided, and discovered as a "two" (e.g., perhaps as two species, or as connected to the idea of "mammal," etc.), or as "three," and so on; and finally, this "ox-as-three" must be, in turn, subjected to a further division into kinds. If so, then we do indeed initially posit a single *henad*, followed by the seeking and discovering of two, three, and so on. But, here, the subsequent procedure adds overall complexity to the initial procedure by restarting the procedure, not by working on a newly posited idea, but rather by working on the division which has itself been discovered as a result of the initial division of the initial *henad*. The later divisions aim, in turn, to find the determinate "how many" for each of

those prior connected *henads*, that is, for two, three, and so on (each severally), and not merely for the original idea posited. Each determination thus
reveals a new complexity that is still a complexity proper to the originally
posited idea. If this is what Socrates means, then we are not already performing the whole procedure when we divide the initial unity and discover the
"ox-as-two" and "ox-as-three" and then we repeat the procedure on them.
Rather, we must also follow through with an additional task of applying the
procedure back to those results "in the same way." We apply the method
again to "each of them," showing how many *they* (i.e., the two, three, etc.
severally) are. Only then do we arrive at the ultimate "how many" of each of
them, and only as a consequence, in the end, do we thus arrive finally at the
fully involved "how-many" of the original *henad*. The procedures would thus
build upon one another, progressively determining, division by division, the
determinate number of the whole of wholes (or the number of numbers). The
whole procedure itself would thus be modified and modulated as the process
moves forward with each subdivision and sub-subdivision. Each procedural
division of each division would unfold a separate division which contributes
to, and modifies, the whole of the division.[35]

In short, the non-recursive interpretation suggests that the ultimate "how
many" to which we will arrive in the procedure is fundamentally "regional."
Each time we perform the same procedure on a new idea. The total number
could never be decided, since a new posit could always be made. The second
interpretation suggests that the ultimate "how many" of the original idea is
in fact the number of other unitary ideas (two, three, etc.) and the number of
kinds of each of those ideas and so on. Each idea would be independent and
yet constitutive of the unfolding of the original first idea. The total number
of wholes or numbers could never be decided, since a new recursive analysis
could always be made.

I believe that Socrates's ὡσαύτως can be interpreted in either way. And
while it might seem necessary to decide between these interpretations, I do
not think it is clear which one should be chosen. Furthermore, it is not clear
that these are exclusive options; Socrates is describing the procedure "in
outline," and he may even allow that the procedure itself admits of employ-
ment in multiple ways. No matter which interpretation we favor, however,
it is clear that for Socrates the learning procedure requires that any posited one-idea be subsequently determined as plural. One factor rendering
the one-idea plural may be, as in interpretation (1), the very being of the
idea (which pluralizes the unity). But even if there is some factor besides the
idea's own being that pluralizes the idea (and the being is only discovered
in the full unfolding of the other connected *henads*), as in interpretation (2),

Socrates's point would be basically the same: the complete being of an idea is discovered only in the determination process. Furthermore, in all acceptable interpretations, we must affirm that the "being" or "number" of the originally posited idea differs from the one-idea alone. The two interpretations differ merely with respect to whether the determination of each one-idea as plural is the determination of its being (which makes it plural), or whether the discovery of the plurality of each one-idea is just a necessary condition for revealing the final and complete being of the idea as it relates to other ideas. Thus, in any interpretation, the multiplicity inherent in the very fact that an idea also is, or is plural, does not falsify but rather reveals the idea's being-what-it-is (as ox, man, good, beauty, etc.). Either the discovery of the being of the idea is, sparks, or coincides with the determination of divisions; or the divisions make possible the revelation of what the thing is, insofar as it is bound to other ideas. In either case, what is revealed is not a one-alone (i.e., a "monad") but rather a one-determinable-as-multiple (i.e., a "henad"). To say a thing is one, say novice arguers, precludes its being many or vice versa. For Socrates, by contrast, we see that the dilemma posited in such eristical argumentation is a false dilemma. It is avoided by our recognition that the separation between the one and the infinite, while real, is not exclusive of intermediates. Furthermore, these are not exhaustive classes either, since a lone one or an absolute infinity cannot in truth reveal the "being" of any reality. The larger point is just that, for Socrates, the determination of the intermediate "how many" opens the *henad* to being. It does not obscure what each being is, as novices believe.

Even so, there remains another problem with the passage. For confusion might remain about what is meant by the "release" of the division "into the unlimited [ἄπειρον]" in the last step. The main interpretive conflict is, on the one hand, between interpreters who argue that it refers to an infinity of sub-kinds, divisions, or multiplications of an idea and, on the other hand, camps arguing that the reference to the unlimited refers to the infinite possible instantiations of each idea.[36] In both cases the assumption is that Socrates refers to a characteristic of the one-idea; the division, multiplication, or instantiation of the one-idea is in the end shown to be infinite. While that may be so, it would be difficult to adjudicate between these interpretations based on the passage. Furthermore, what does appear to me to be emphasized by the passage is the more important idea that the candidacy of the unlimited for answering the "how many" question—its candidacy for revealing the genuine being or number of the thing in question—is definitely rejected. To say that a posited *henad* has an element of indeterminacy is not an incomprehensible mysticism; it is an important admission. But it contributes nothing *specific* to understanding any *henad's* being. For the being of each *henad* has a determinable definiteness that extends only so far. Eventually, it must be "left to the indefinite." But this just means that, for all we know, this indefinition is a fate that is specific and proper to nothing (or, rather, to the indefinite in itself alone). Thus, it contributes nothing to the determination of being. This leads Socrates to say that the "sound that comes out of the mouth is one for each and every one of us, but then it is also unlimited in number. . . . Neither of these two facts alone yet makes us knowledgeable, neither that we know its unlimitedness nor its unity. But if we know how many kinds of vocal sounds there are and what their nature is, that makes every one of us literate" (17b2–8).[37] To say that "ox" is one or infinite is no real answer to the "how many" question. Such answers teach us nothing, because they do nothing to reveal the specificity of the reality; they treat each reality as a nothing-specific.

By contrast, the learning procedure demands an order. It demands that, before quitting the determination-process and releasing the task to the infinite, we must first discover the definite as much as possible. The definite number (ἀριθμός) is decidedly a number always between the unlimited and the one. This "between" is what reveals the true being of the unity, whereas the "boundless [ἄπειρόν] multitude . . . in any and every kind of subject leaves you in boundless [ἄπειρον] ignorance, and makes you count for nothing and amount to nothing, since you have never worked out the amount and number [ἀριθμὸν] of anything at all" (17e3–6).[38] Indeed, the bypassing of these "intermediates" is precisely the tactic employed in sophistics: "[The] clever ones [σοφοὶ] among us make a one [ἕν] haphazardly, and a many, faster or slower than they should; they go straight from the one to the unlimited [μετὰ . . . τὸ ἓν ἄπειρα εὐθύς] and omit the intermediates [μέσα]. It is these, however, that make all the difference as to whether we are engaged with each other in dialectical [διαλεκτικῶς] or only in eristical [ἐριστικῶς] discourse [λόγους]" (16c5–17a5). While both the eristic and the dialectician participate in discourse, the sophist abuses discourse and the possibility of accounts by refusing to admit any intermediates whatsoever.

This reference to the "intermediates [μέσα]" can also be taken to indicate that the learning procedure should not be interpreted as a point only about number forms, in the strict sense of "the two," "the three," and so on. Rather, number is just the paradigm case that leads us to learn what it would be to understand "each" on its own terms. Thus, the concept of an "intermediate" could be taken to encompass the example of numbers; or, alternatively, "number" and "intermediate" could be taken to be sub-kinds of some higher class. Either way, number's paradigmatic status does not mean that all other cases are variants of it. To exhibit this point, in closing this subsection I want briefly to approach Socrates's own non-numerical examples, namely the cases of determining and classifying musical intervals and of determining classes of elements of language (letters, consonants, vowels, etc.). These examples have been discussed extensively in the literature, and I will have opportunity in chapter 2 to discuss music in particular in more detail.[39] But there are two brief points that relate to the general outline of the procedure as I have depicted it here. The first pertains to the question of how the things that are "structured" as one-many first come to take on this structure. The second pertains to the relationship between the learning procedure and account-giving.

On the first point concerning structure, Harte has effectively emphasized the way mere "sound" is without an identity of its own. It gains its identity as it is involved in a structure that emerges in it, making it specifically voice-sound or music-sound. For sound to become music, a system or definite structure must be brought to it.[40] I agree that this is the content of Socrates's examples. Furthermore, the same thing holds true in Socrates's example of Theuth's discovery of letters and of the structure of vocalization. Harte expresses clearly the way the discovery of the entire field of study is a consequence of comprehending the entire imported structure. Socrates's method, she writes,

> is premised on the way in which its objects are ordered or arranged (διακεκοσμημένοι, 16d1). So, too, the method is linked with scientific discovery, both at the beginning, when Socrates associates it with everything that has been *discovered* (ἀνευρ σκω, 16c2) in the realm of any skill, and in the references both to the ancestors' discovery of music (17d2–3) and to Theuth's discovery of phonetics (18b8–9). Discovery is the making known of something that previously existed, but was as yet unknown. . . . The expert's grasp of a scientific domain is systematic, because no one of the elements of the domain can be understood on its own, in isolation from the system as a whole. . . . [To] understand what they are—to have a grip on their identity—*is* to understand their structural relations with each other. Each gets its identity only in the context of the structure as a whole.[41]

Harte's two main points here, as I understand them, are (a) no part can be understood as what it is without a grasp of the systematic relationship of parts to each other in and as a structure; and (b) the learning procedure Socrates has outlined in the *Philebus* helps us to discover an implicit structure that is always already there in the natural phenomenon. While I agree in part with both of these points, I want to suggest two ways in which I think they need to be qualified.

With respect to point (a), Harte goes on to say that the procedure of determining the one-many structure "should be thought of as an *analysis*; limit and unlimited are not, I suppose, actually separable; nor is limit actually 'applied' to something that might be described as undifferentiated sound."[42] With this point, I agree, but only if we understand that the analysis must follow from a prior synthesis. Limit and unlimited are inseparable in mixtures, yes. But in themselves, as I will argue at length in chapter 2, limit and unlimited are in fact necessarily separate from one another. They cannot be reduced to a third thing (mixture) nor to each other; and structured mixtures emerge only as a consequence of a cause that brings the absolutely separate limit to the unlimited.[43] Harte, however, regularly implies that the unlimited is a mere abstraction from mixtures, and not really something belonging to its own kind. I bring up this metaphysical point here not because I dispute Harte's insight about the nature of the learning procedure as in part analytic, but because limit and unlimited must be treated as originally ontologically distinct and separate from one another and not as abstractions from a common root.[44]

Second, in my view both music and voice—Socrates's preferred examples— must be understood as fields of study whose very structures depend on agents who structure them through causal practices, which practices are in some sense within those agents' own control. In chapter 2, I will therefore emphasize the way that for Socrates humans share in causing the very emergence of structured "fields" such as those of voice and music. We share in causing the very presence of limit or definition in sound, for example; and this sound would have been, without our causation, unlimited and without structure.[45] If this is so, then scientists are not only analyzers who begin with premade mixtures, though analysis surely has an important role in scientific practice. Rather, they must also be aware of their own intervention into the very structures of things, at least in certain cases. And they must be mindful, more generally, of all such instances wherein a cause must be invoked to explain the emerging structures of things.[46]

This point links directly to Harte's point (b). For while I also agree with her that the "learning procedure" is a procedure of discovery, I want to emphasize the way that Socrates has given examples of some fields of study that are indeed partly constituted by the very agents who are also their analyzers. Voice must be continuously created and re-created by those capable of bringing structure to sound. Only then can this structure or limit be "analyzed" from out of it. This means that we cannot simply accept natural phenomena as raw, uncaused, predefined givens from which limit and unlimited are premixed and can only be merely "abstracted." We must rather account for the original constitution—that is, both the structure and the act of importing structure—of the mixtures as mixtures. Indeed, as we shall see, this very causal, constitutional act is something in which we can and do sometimes share (see chapter 2).

Of course, we have no reason to believe that the learning procedure as introduced here must always intervene in the structures of each and every being, even as it unconceals the λόγος of that being. Yet we do witness, in examples like voice and music, the way that to engage in learning actively, through discovering the one-many structure of a field of study, is at least in some cases also at once to import structure, that is, a structure that would not have been manifest without this practice of learning. The learning procedure, therefore, is always already more than a procedure of accounting for givens; for it will also be, at times, creative of an order that would otherwise be absent.

Conclusion. The Initial Analysis of the Good Itself

The logical structure of beings themselves, and the ontic structure of accounts themselves, can only be revealed in the determinate multiplicity of accounts-of-being. This realization impacts Protarchus, for he can now begin to share in genuine dialogue. He can now come to see that the account of the good itself will generate, even as it discloses the good, a structured mixture of the good life, a mixture conducive to the emergence of multiple goods.[47] Socrates thus helps Protarchus move in stages from a position fundamentally focused on pleasure alone, and antithetical to account-giving, to a position that appropriates the proper ordering of the good's manifestation. Protarchus has learned to ask with openness, what is good?

This ethical development is not separate from the logical developments of the *Philebus*. For the inquiry into the good goes hand in hand with the ability to distinguish between kinds of lives.[48] Yet our concern is not merely to observe the multiple kinds of pleasure or knowledge. It is above all to discern the *value* in each candidate. Thus, we must first apply the procedure to the prize itself, that is, to the analysis of the good as such. For without seeking goodness in its proper unity-and-multiplicity—without asking "what is good?" originally and for ourselves—we will be left unable to discern whether all or merely some of each candidate life admits of goodness.

Thus, the good itself must be posited as something determinable in a one-many structure. For, if a definite account of it cannot be given, then it would

be futile to pursue anything instead of anything else; all of life would be aimless. The decision not to determine the good would therefore be, in effect, a
decision to live as if only indefinition is good. Furthermore, if the good itself
could not be manifest as multiple, then the good could not be manifest in
each distinct kind of life, that is, in lives that are themselves different in kind:
pleasure and knowledge. For to live as if the good is one thing alone—for
example, the indefinite—is always already to confine the good to one kind
of life and to exclude all others. It is possible for the good life to consist of
fundamentally different kinds of lives that can remain distinct in kind *only* if
it is possible for the good itself to be manifest as multiple.

For this reason, Socrates invokes a doctrine he claims to have acquired
from a mysterious source:

> SOCRATES: It is a doctrine that once upon a time I heard in a
> dream—or perhaps I was awake—that I remember now, concern-
> ing pleasure and knowledge, that neither of the two is the good, but
> that there is some third thing which is different from and superior
> to both of them. But if we can clearly conceive now that this is the
> case, then pleasure has lost its bid for victory. For the good could no
> longer turn out to be identical with it (20b7–c4).

Protarchus can only agree to this request to consider the good as a third
thing separate from pleasure because he has already come to appreciate the
power of and need for the learning procedure. We must consider the good
properly and on its own, that is, as something discoverable in itself and irreducible to another single kind of thing alone, if we are to learn specifically
what it is to be good. If we implicitly believe that the good originally belongs
to something else than to its own proper structure—for example, simply to
such and such party, tradition, church, or even to the universal aim for "happiness" among living beings—then we have yet to posit the good as its own
source. Thus, everything begins when we posit the good as its own proper
idea, that is, as distinct from any other kind of thing, even as distinct from
being. This procedure of considering the good per se can only be initiated
here, of course, and it is not yet completed. We do not yet know the "number"
or the "intermediates" relevant to the determinate manifestation of the good.
Rather, we have merely prepared ourselves to discover them. But unless the
preparation is initiated in this way, no proper discovery of the good's manifestation will be possible for us.

Thus, we must now attempt to determine the good as multiple, as "such
and such." Only then are we empowered to discern how each separate

candidate measures up with respect to the diversity of its aspects. Socrates and Protarchus thus agree to begin by considering the good as a "threefold":

> SOCRATES: There are some small matters we ought to agree on first, though. . . . Whether the good is necessarily bound to be perfect [τέλεον] or not perfect.

> PROTARCHUS: But surely it must be the most perfect thing of all, Socrates!

> SOCRATES: Further: must the good be sufficient [ἱκανὸν]?

> PROTARCHUS: How could it fail to be that? This is how it is superior to everything else there is.

> SOCRATES: Now, this point, I take it, is most necessary to assert of the good: that everything that has any notion of it hunts for it and desires to get hold of it and secure it for its very own, caring nothing for anything else except for what is connected with the acquisition of some good. . . . So let us put the life of pleasure and the life of knowledge on trial, and reach some verdict by looking at them separately (20c7–e2).

It is unclear from where Socrates derives just these three "attributes" of the good (completeness, sufficiency, and choice-worthiness), or how finally he intends to use this threefold characterization. Yet, what is clear is the way that, by expressing a set of attributes that flow from our own proper effort to discern the good as it is in itself, we are empowered to consider whether, how, and to what extent something else—say, the kind of pleasure or knowledge—is or is not consistent with the aspects of good we discern. By treating the good as separate; by expressing what we take to be its unfolded attributes; by positing it as having its own essence regardless of whether it "is" or "is not"; and by taking only this proper good in itself to be the standard by which to measure each of candidate lives' goodness, we thereby allow the candidate lives to remain independent of each other while they are measured vis-à-vis the good. In other words, the good itself, posited on its own, shows that neither of these kinds of lives is itself identical to the good. If the good were not separate from them and itself expressible in its own plurality, then it could not be a standard for measuring each candidate's goodness in a way that is distinctly proper to each.[49]

As a result, we can see that it is far less important for the reader to agree that these three attributes are the right ones than for the reader to see that only once an understanding of a set of attributes is established can each candidate kind of life be measured properly vis-à-vis the good. Certainly, nothing else lives up to the good's attributes in exactly the same way that the good itself lives up to those attributes. Yet, by judging each life by a set of attributes, rather than the bare, unstructured good, we can highlight to a greater extent the distinctness and difference of each of the kinds from the other.

Thus, for example, in respect of these three attributes of completeness, sufficiency, and desirability, each candidate falls short of the good for *different* reasons. Pleasure falls short because by itself it is incomplete, insufficient, and not choice-worthy without knowledge (21a8–d2). Thus, we learn that for pleasure to be more complete, sufficient, and desirable (i.e., for it to be more like the good's attributes) it has a particular sort of dependency on reason. Reason, by contrast, falls short of the attributes of the good for a very different reason: knowledge would not be worthy of "choice" (αἱρεῖν) to us unless it were accompanied by pleasure (22d7–e2). Protarchus is careful here to say that neither candidate alone would be "sufficient or worthy of choice for either man or animal" (22b1). Importantly, no claim is made here about the needs of a being that is purely rational and would not need to add pleasure to itself in order for it to find reason to be choice-worthy. But Socrates and Protarchus carefully admit that "for either man or animal" reason alone lacks choice-worthiness, that is, one of those core features of goodness. Thus, the way each candidate life alone "falls short" of the good is not an identical failure: pleasure depends on knowledge, if it is to be complete, sufficient, and desirable (like the good); knowledge, however, depends in no way on pleasure, except insofar as, and if, knowledge is to be chosen by us or other beings like us (who have needs and desires). Only the positing of the good as its "own" allows these differences to be unconcealed.

Thus, the comparison with the good has had the effect of emphasizing the distinction in kind between pleasure and knowledge, while allowing that they complement the complete good's emergence in the good life. The comparison can only emphasize this distinction in kind because the good itself has been posited in its own right and unfolded as a threefold. What thus comes to light is the way each candidate differs from the good in different ways. Thus, when Socrates and Protarchus agree, at 22a2–b8, that the good life must consist of a "mixture" of reason and pleasure, they already imply there that this mixture must be such that it is mixed from each element with different proportions. Each of the two candidates needs the other, but not in the same way, nor in the same amounts, nor for the same reasons. Thus, without such an "a priori" expansion of the idea of the good into a set of attributes, it would have been impossible for us to grasp that there is a proper difference in the way, the order, or the extent to which we must mix each separate candidate.

In the end, then, the refusal to count the good as multiple would have been a refusal to learn, that is, a refusal to allow oneself to come to an understanding of the different ways goodness will be manifest in the different kinds of lives that will be included in the good life. And if we cannot engage in this learning—if we cannot learn to distinguish between kinds of lives and to discern different kinds within each kind—then no matter what kind of life we think we live, we can be certain of only one thing, namely that our lives will be filled with nothing but "universal confusion" (20a3). We will have decided that the indefinite alone is valuable.

Thus, our remaining task must be to determine the precise mixture of and order for the mixing of the good life, taking into account the need to have a different analysis of each kind's proper character and proper manifestation of intrinsic goodness. This task requires that we specify more fully the differences between each kind, and thus Socrates's analysis of each kind is examined in chapters 3 and 4. Yet, in order to carry out this analysis, we must also determine whether some sub-kinds contribute more than others to the good life. This last question, therefore, concerning the very nature of a "contribution" must be examined first. Chapter 2 is therefore devoted to Socrates's analysis of "the cause of the mixture."

The Mixed Life and Its Causes

In the beginning of the dialogue Philebus wanted to show that the good is pleasure, and Socrates wanted to show that knowledge and its kin are "better than pleasure and more agreeable to all who can attain them" (11c1–3). The subsequent logical controversies drew out the way that the ethical problem of pleasure or knowledge is expressed, above all, as a logical problem of determining a one-idea as a definite manifold. Such a requirement is a prerequisite for the giving of any account and is necessary for learning. The illogical tactics (whether silence, circularity, or self-contradiction) of the hedonists fail to meet these conditions, and they fail to see that account-giving necessarily makes certain demands on us. The appropriate response to these demands is to recognize the inherent unity and multiplicity in any being's expression, that is, in any and all genuine ontology. The learning procedure then allows each and every being to open onto its own field, to become unconcealed for us as an intermediate. Of course, we cannot expect a final completion of ontology "once and for all." A remnant of indeterminacy always shows us that we must take up anew the task of ontology and engage again in the learning process, that is, in a kind of coming-to-complete-knowledge that is as good as complete, even in its coming-to-completion.[1]

Finally, by applying the learning procedure to the good itself Socrates has tried to show that a choice for the good life must be a choice to admit more than one kind of life. With knowledge and pleasure as our candidates, we have learned that each kind by itself falls short of the attributes of the good; and thus both can be good. The good life therefore emerges as a synthesizing of diverse kinds of lives. In a sense, we have already answered the driving question of the whole dialogue: the good life is a mixed life.

Nevertheless, the work of the dialogue is far from complete. For we must specify the right proportions of each candidate and the extent to which each candidate contributes. This task requires that we give an account of the very nature of contribution as such. Thus, Socrates now sets out to grasp the nature of causation, and he will argue that to cause is always defined as the bringing of a proper measure to what lacks measure. In light of this argument, Socrates's psychological and theological discourses can then be shown to serve as examples displaying such a responsible agency. The *Philebus* will thereafter focus its efforts on analyzing the psychological model and on the way we share in responsible agency. But it can do so only in light of Socrates's prior establishment of an account of causation per se.

2.1. The Dialogue's New Question

The learning procedure helped us arrive at the profound conclusion that the good itself is no single thing alone (μόνος), and thus Socrates concludes: "Enough has been said, it seems to me, to prove that Philebus's goddess and the good cannot be regarded as the same [ταὐτὸν]" (22c1–2). Philebus has mostly listened in silence to the arguments. But now he cannot bear the criticism. He speaks out in response to Socrates, insisting that the refutation of Protarchus has been false. For knowledge, he insists, can be refuted by the same strategy Socrates has used against pleasure. We could easily prove, he says, that "your reason [is not] the good, Socrates, and the same complaint applies to it" (22c2–3).[2]

We might expect Socrates simply to agree with Philebus that reason is not the good. Indeed, Socrates has admitted that reason alone is not the sole constituent of the good life; he has insisted on the need for mixture. Even so, Socrates rejects Philebus's attempt simply to turn the refutation against reason in the same way it was used against pleasure: "[The refutation] may apply to my reason [νοῦν], Philebus, but certainly not to the true, the divine reason [ἀληθινὸν ἅμα καὶ θεῖον . . . νοῦν], I should think. It is in quite a different condition" (22c5–7).[3] Now, importantly, Socrates does not say that some divine reason may simply be, by itself, the good itself. For an account of divine reason as alone the good would indeed violate his argument. Rather, he clarifies that some divine reason may be the "same" as the good in a very specific sense:

> SOCRATES: I am not arguing that reason ought to get first prize over and against the combined life; we have rather to look and make up our minds about the second prize, how to dispose of it. One of us may want to give credit for the combined life to reason, making it responsible, the other to pleasure. Thus, neither of the two would be considered to be the good, but it could be assumed that one or the other of them is its cause [αἴτιόν] (22c8–d6).

Socrates thus is not saying that reason wins the "first prize" or is alone the good. Rather, it is "responsible" for the good's emergence; that is, it takes part in causing the good life to emerge, even if it is not itself the good. Furthermore, this share in causation need not be exclusive to reason, for Socrates's language is comparative: "But I would be even more ready to contend against Philebus that, whatever the ingredient in the mixed life may be that makes it choiceworthy and good, reason is more closely related [συγγενέστερον] to that thing and more like [ὁμοιότερόν] it than pleasure" (22d). The new challenge is thus to determine which kind of life can be "more-of-a-kind [συγγενέστερον]" with the cause and can attain "second prize" (23b5). And since there can perhaps be many participants in this causation, and some participants may be preconditions for others, a decision about the proper order of inclusion is now what is truly needed.[4] Such an order needs a measure by which to establish the ranking, or else each candidate will simply claim that its own nature makes it more important than the other. To settle the matter, we must come to a common, shared understanding of "what it is to cause."

Thus Protarchus now concedes that Socrates's arguments against pleasure cannot simply be turned against knowledge by a sort of tu quoque. Both candidates fail to be the good itself; but they do not fail equally. The different extents to which each candidate imports goodness can be established even in this difference. Protarchus thus concedes: "By now it seems to me indeed that pleasure has been defeated as if knocked down by your present arguments [λόγων], Socrates. . . . And as for reason, we may say that it wisely did not compete for first prize, for it would have suffered the same fate" (22e5–23a1). It is true that Socrates has avoided from the beginning of the dialogue any defense of knowledge as being alone and by itself the "first prize." His original position stated only that knowledge and reason are "better." He will now show that this means reason has a kind of priority in causing a good order to emerge.[5]

2.2. The Decision to Analyze the Present

To arrive at a guiding idea of the nature of the cause, Socrates suggests that we can begin by carrying out a bold analysis of "everything that actually exists now in the universe" (which is an expression we may shorten into "the present"). Socrates's larger task here, as I will argue, is to show that the present exemplifies the nature of "mixture" (μίξις) and thus needs a cause. But what better way is there to discover the nature of mixture than to take hold of the case of mixture right before our eyes? Thus, we jump right into the analysis:

SOCRATES: Let us be very careful about the starting point we take. . . . Let us make a division [διαλάβωμεν] of everything that actually exists now in the universe [πάντα τὰ νῦν ὄντα ἐν τῷ παντὶ] into two kinds [διχῇ], or if this seems preferable, into three [τριχῇ].

PROTARCHUS: Could you explain on what principle?

SOCRATES: By taking up some of what has been said before. . . . We agreed earlier that the god had revealed a division of what is into the unlimited [ἄπειρον] and the limit [πέρας] (23c1–9).

What Socrates proposes to analyze here could also be translated as "all the presently existing things in the whole [πάντα τὰ νῦν ὄντα ἐν τῷ παντί]." Perhaps the most obvious thing about this formulation is its unclarity with regard to number: is Socrates referring to a unity or to a plurality? The variants of πᾶς and πᾶν appear in the formula first as plural and then as singular. We must not assume that this "singular-plural" formulation is accidental. For the whole point is to show that what is nearest to us at any time—this "now [νῦν]"—is of a "number" that cannot be evident simply at a glance. Socrates, I take it, is encouraging us to own up to this difficulty found in the most familiar. He is initiating in us a mindfulness with regard to the present, a mindfulness proper to one who is willing to learn.

Socrates also says here that we should begin by dividing the present by "two" or by "three." His indecisiveness indicates that he, like us, has not decided beforehand about the number of the present. He does not assume it to be this or that but rather seeks its number. And, even though he settles on an initial division into the twofold of the "unlimited [ἄπειρον]" and the "limit [πέρας]," this decision itself expresses a deep mystery. For the unlimited here serves as one of the initial "divisors," and thus one member of the initial number of divisors is not, in itself, any definite number at all. Honesty in counting the present demands that we account for the presence of this indetermination and uncertainty.

Even so, a rationale can be given for Socrates's beginning with the limit and unlimited as the "divisors." For, if any analysis must be at least a division of a subject into more-than-one, then it would make sense to try to begin, for simplicity's sake, with the smallest possible "number" of any division. That smallest possible division would surely be a division into something determinate, on the one hand, and into what is other than that determinate something, on the other hand. The most general name of this determinate something could be *A*, or limit, or the determinate, or whatever; the most general name of the other could be not-A, the unlimited, or the non-determinate, or not-whatever. In this way, not only do limit and unlimited together exhaust the field of possible logical alternatives, but also the divisors have the advantage of being incapable of reduction to one another. That is, even if they "hang together" in the present, they nevertheless cannot be reduced to being a one-alone. For if we know that "the present" is not only a definite one-alone (since we grasp it as manifold and analyzable), then we also know something else about the present: it is at least A as well as not-A. Thus, A and not-A—or, rather, limit and unlimited—are intuitively appealing; they stand for the smallest possible number—or rather "proto-number"—of divisors.

Even so, this division into the smallest possible "more than one" must also be counted as a division *of* something. That is, if limit and unlimited not only were exclusive of one another but also were exhaustive classes—that is, if there were no other distinct kinds that could help us grasp the present—then it would follow that there would be nothing at all "there" that is being divided in the division process. For the thing-divided cannot be simply either one of the opposite divisors alone. For if the thing-divided were only the limit, then it could not be truly divided except into limit and something else. But to divide limit into limit and something else would be to require that the thing-divided be not merely limit but also already both limit and something else (otherwise, the division would divide limit only into limit, which is not a division). By parallel, the thing divided cannot be merely unlimited; for to truly divide the unlimited requires dividing the unlimited into the unlimited and something else, and so on. Thus, what is divided, if it is indeed divisible and analyzable, is neither A alone nor not-A alone. It must also be something else, something composite, that is, a third kind of thing. Furthermore, since our logical opposites (or term negations) are irreducible to one another, they cannot be just one thing; each kind cannot be reduced to the other kind. But this means that they cannot be reduced to this new, third thing either. For to reduce them to the third thing would also be (per impossible) to reduce them to each other. There must therefore be a real third class to discover, which serves as the subject of division; but it itself must be irreducible to limit and the unlimited (and each of them irreducible to it). And it is for this reason, I would suggest, that Socrates accordingly posits the third class—a genuinely distinct mixed class—to account for the "togetherness" of the first two kinds in a divisible third something: "Let us take these as two of the kinds [εἰδῶν], while treating the one that results from the mixture [συμμισγόμενον] of these two as our third kind [τρίτον]. But I must look like quite a fool with my distinctions into kinds [εἴδη] and enumerations [συναριθμούμενος]!" (23c9–d1).

Thus, Socrates introduces the mixed class, but he also jokes that perhaps he is beginning to look like a fool. For he immediately notices that now, another, fourth class will be required to account for the features of the present. For how, after all, could the irreducible pair of *A* and not-*A* be "held together" as a third, divisible thing that would be reducible to neither and yet constituted from both? Something must bind these constituents together. This cannot be the work of the mixture itself, for it is a distinct, composite kind, composed in itself but not composing in itself. It cannot be either of the other classes, for limit alone or unlimited alone are powerless to bring about any synthesis with their opposite; they each have nothing of the opposite power in them. They could just as well remain in eternal separation. Thus, says Socrates, "[We] seem to be in need [προσδεῖν] of yet a fourth kind [γένους]. . . . Look at the cause [αἰτίαν] of this combination of those two together [συμμείξεως], and posit it as my fourth kind in addition to those three" (23c9–d6). Thus, our discovery of the third class has led us to still another "need," that is, a need to posit a fourth that explains the hanging-together of the hybrid third.

Furthermore, the justification for this fourth class can be reconstructed. For the original two classes, if they are logical opposites, evidently cannot be identical (since they exclude one another in themselves), and yet they also cannot be reduced to a third thing, for this would (per impossible) reduce them to one another. So the only conclusion, if there is any mixture to analyze, is that the third class—that is, the divisible thing in which limit and unlimited are held together and from which they can each be analyzed—must be some distinct kind of thing. But if this third is a distinct kind, while still being a combination of limit and the unlimited, could its own, distinct reality be dependent only on the limit, or only on the unlimited, or only on itself? It cannot be dependent only on the limit, nor only on the unlimited; for then, in either case, it would not be able to exhibit their combination, their togetherness. Furthermore, it cannot be dependent only on itself, for then it would lack its essential character as a combination, the very nature of which requires that the origins evident *in* it are in themselves other *than* it. And were the mixture dependent only on itself—were it simply a definite thing "itself by itself," entirely at one with its own self—then it could not be of mixed nature. For then, being an "itself by itself," it could only ever be this very same "itself by itself"; it could not exhibit the character of the hanging-together of both the "itself" and the "not-itself," of both *A* and not-*A*. It would not be a mixture. Thus, we must posit a fourth class that would be sufficient to account for the emergence-as-a-distinct-kind of the mixed class, that is, of the class that cannot all by itself cause itself to emerge as a distinct kind. Thus, the cause or producer of the third must be posited and sought out. For there is otherwise no reason to presume that limit and unlimited do not simply reside eternally by themselves, never mixed with one other. Why should there be a mixed class? Only the positing of a cause can initiate a search for the nature of the fourth.

Finally, even a possible fifth class is mentioned. For the mixture, made from limit and unlimited but always itself different from them in itself, has no features that empower it to account for the separateness of limit from unlimited. It has no power to offer separation. For it can only offer a mixedness. Thus, if the mixture can indeed be analyzed and divided back into its constituents, then none of the kinds mentioned so far can by itself do this work. Are we not "in need of a fifth kind that provides for their separation" (23d9–e1)? The number of kinds is, perhaps embarrassingly, expanding rapidly. Indeed, no matter what number of kinds we settle on, perhaps there will always be a remainder, and a new factor must be sought again each time. Thus, we must eventually simply release this remainder and let it remain indefinite. Socrates accordingly allows himself to work with just the first four classes for now.

Regardless of the number of classes, we should note that Socrates may have had another good reason for his embarrassment in the preceding passage. It may have stemmed from a troubling feature of his whole procedure so far, namely from the way he refers to both the limited and the unlimited as each an εἶδος (form) or γένος (genus or kind). We may wonder: how can "the unlimited" be an εἶδος at all, when (we might suspect) an εἶδος is always something determinate, that is, it is always definitely itself and never its own opposite?[6] Perhaps the unlimited should rather be called a "non-εἶδος," since it is the indeterminate itself, that is, something lacking definiteness? Socrates may therefore be embarrassed because he has moved too quickly. He has tried to begin his procedure by dividing the present "by" or "into" the unlimited. But in order to truly divide by the "form" of the unlimited, the unlimited must first be given some kind of form, some kind of limitation. Otherwise, there is nothing definite by which to divide.

This is perhaps why Socrates sets as his next task the work of "collecting" each of the kinds, and the unlimited must be collected first. The difficulty of expressing the distinctive character of each kind is most salient with the case of the unlimited, for it seems to defy definite form. In the subsequent sections I will address this problem by arguing that in order to grasp the εἶδος of the unlimited we must *already* be participating in the "fourth kind," that is, the cause (which is later identified with the intellect or νοῦς). For the cause will be defined as what brings limit to the unlimited, and only with this arrival of limit can the unlimited share in "being" any more than it shares in "nonbeing." But will Socrates succeed in revealing the proper character of the unlimited without falling into the trap of treating it as in itself limited and definite? I argue that Socrates rises to this challenge, and he can call the unlimited an εἶδος here, in the beginning, only because he foresees that the cause can "save" the character of the unlimited by collecting it and bringing it to mixture.

2.3. The Collection of the Unlimited

Socrates now sets out to "collect" certain of the kinds: "Let us take up three of the four, and since we observe that of two of them, both are split up and dispersed into many, let's make an effort to collect them into a unity again, in order to study [νοῆσαι] how each of them is in fact one and many" (23e3–8). Socrates suggests here that we must collect two of the three classes. These two classes turn out to be the unlimited class and the mixed class; each is "one kind [γένει ἓν]" and yet also multiple (26d3–7). (No doubt, the limit class is at times also depicted as a collectible class. Later, I will explain this seeming conflict as merely apparent, for the limit class can be collectible *into* the mixed class while, at the same time, it does not in itself need to be collected.)

First, then, we must find the common character of the unlimited. What is common to and characteristic of all things insofar as they are unlimited? In a long passage, Socrates links them to a characteristic of admitting "more and less":

> SOCRATES: Check first in the case of hotter and colder whether you
> can conceive of a limit, or whether the "more and less" [τὸ μᾶλλόν
> τε καὶ ἧττον] do not rather reside in these kinds, and while they
> reside in them do not permit the attainment of any end [τέλος].
> For once an end [τελευτάω] has been reached, they will both have
> been ended [τετελευτήκατον] as well. . . . Our argument forces
> us to conclude that these things never have an end [τέλος]. And
> since they are endless [ἀτελῆ], they turn out to be entirely unlim-
> ited [ἀπείρω γίγνεσθον]. . . . Wherever they apply, they prevent
> everything from adopting a definite quantity [ποσὸν]; by impos-
> ing on all actions the qualification "stronger" relative to "gentler" or
> the reverse, they procure a "more and less" while doing away with
> all definite quantity. We are saying now, in effect, that if they do
> not abolish definite quantity, but let quantity and measurement

[μέτριον] take a foothold in the domain of the more and the less, the strong and the mild, they will be driven out of their own territory [ἐκ τῆς αὐτῶν χώρας]. For once they take on definite quantity, they would no longer be hotter and colder. The hotter and equally colder are always in flux and never remain [προχωρεῖ . . . καὶ οὐ μένει], while definite quantity means standstill and the end of all progression [προϊὸν ἐπαύσατο]. The upshot of this argument is that the hotter, together with its opposite, turn out to be unlimited (24b8–d5).

The passage begins by proposing for us an example of relatives, that is, the hotter and colder. The thrust is, however, to argue that this particular case is just an example of the "more and less" character. It is precisely this characteristic relativity that all the examples suggest in the passage, and the examples clearly serve as mere aids for getting at this idea.[7] With this idea in mind, at least four specific characteristics of what is meant by "more and less" can be drawn from the passage. I will approach them one by one.

First, we must bear in mind that Socrates is trying to indicate the nature of what has no determinacy or definiteness in itself. The "more and less" character indicates that the unlimited is never properly itself. This impropriety can be analyzed into three senses. In one sense, the unlimited is always opposed to, or always opposes itself to, its own opposite. To be "more" is just to be more *than* something. But if this is all that "to be more" is, then to be more is nothing other than to be more than what is less than itself, that is, what is less than "what it is to be more." Thus, "to be more" has only what we might call a contrastive existence: it cannot be what it is without opposing itself to its own contrary. (The same would apply to "to be less.") Even so, in a second sense, "to be more" cannot have a merely extrinsic contrast with the less. Rather, if "to be more" only is what it is by relation to the less, then the more cannot truly exist separately from the less.[8] The contrast is thus intrinsic to its kind. (The same would apply to the nature of the less.) Therefore, the very nature of this relative "more" must itself contain at the same time the very nature of what it is to be intrinsically "less." Anything admitting this more-and-less quality thus admits of a truly radical relativity, that is, a relativity incapable of escaping its own opposite, even while it also can never simply be its own opposite, since it must contrast itself with it. The unlimited is at once contrastive and at the same time intrinsically and essentially that with which it is contrasted. The unlimited could thus be described equally well as a character that is "more-or-less," or "neither-more-nor-less," or "both-more-and-less." For each of these expressions says in a different way what it is to be the unlimited. While I will summarize these latter expressions with phrases like "more and less," Socrates thus really shows us that the unlimited cannot be found in any one expression. Last, in a third sense, it follows that the unlimited also cannot be found in any single characteristic "pair" of terms. For while the unlimited indeed has the "more and less" character, it also has the "neither-more-nor-less" character. And if it is found distributed into all the cases of comparative pairs such as hotter/colder, higher/lower, and so on, it also is not found in them, since it is just as much the negative of each pair; it is, for example, the neither-hotter-nor-colder. Thus, above all, the unlimited is always just as much the opposite of *whatever* characteristic—or characteristic pair—we might think of as characterizing it. This just shows us that, if we try to characterize the unlimited, we will be left saying that "it" (or "they," or "not-it," or "not-they") never attains any being at all, without also attaining the contrary of this being. It cannot be without its own other. In order to be what it is it must always also be what it is not. Above all, Socrates is trying to show, in the simultaneous success and failure of such expressions, that the unlimited itself exhibits precisely this success and failure to *be*, that is, a failure to be without also not being.

Thus, second, since the unlimited is always also opposite whatever it is, Socrates understands it as a character that is always a state of becoming, flux, or procession (προχωρεῖν). The flux of the more and less in itself never arrives at an end (τέλος), at any definite how-many (πόσον), or has any measure (μέτριον). The unlimited is thus always "becoming unlimited [ἀπείρω γίγνεσθον]"; it is an unlimited, ever-emerging process. Indeed, in the passage we find no shortage of variants of γένεσις that, unfortunately, are often translated into English with conjugations of "being."[9] The references to becoming should be retained because Socrates is clearly trying to indicate here that the unlimited cannot remain in any condition. The duality of the class—the inability of one opposite to escape from its own other or to be simply its own other—manifests itself as a constant shifting from one to the other. As soon as it is one (more), it is already also other (less). As it itself becomes more than itself, at once it also grows to be less than itself, for it is less than that which has grown to be more, which is just itself.[10]

Third, beyond its unstable becoming, the unlimited also is violently opposed by limit. Thus, Socrates is not merely claiming that the incessant flux and duality of the unlimited is like the duality inherent in a "set of two things." Rather, he is claiming that there is no intrinsic set-ability in the unlimited at all. For sets consist of definite elements; and no "set" can contain members that are themselves always changing into their own opposites, never attaining definite status, always violated whenever definiteness emerges.[11]

This is why the flux of the unlimited cannot be an "infinite number" (if such a thing is even conceivable); for it obliterates all quantity and all number.[12] To ask "how many" or "how much" about the unlimited therefore makes no sense; it is a fundamental misconception. This is an infinity that becomes without reliable pattern, order, end, count-ability, or set-ability.

Finally, fourth, we should reflect again on the idea that if the indeterminate things were to admit of determinacy, then they would be "driven out of their own territory [ἐκ τῆς αὐτῶν χώρας]."[13] The metaphor of violence raises the idea that we should resist the "philosophical" temptation to conceive of the unlimited as having in itself a definite character. If we conceive of the unlimited as in itself defined by limit, then we have always already only conceived, not of the unlimited, but at best of a mixture, that is, of something determinate in some way. We thereby bring something else from out of the proper realm of the unlimited, that is, from out of its intrinsic impropriety. Of course, Socrates wants to claim that there can be such a hybrid "limited-unlimited" class. But if I believe I grasp the unlimited when I am only grasping mixture, then I do conceptual violence to the unlimited. If instead I conceive of this mixture as a limited-indefinite—*and* I understand that it is not the unlimited but rather mixture I am thus grasping—then I avoid the philosophical abuse. For then I allow the unlimited to be other than the mixture that I think. I would then not predicate limit of the unlimited in itself but rather of the mixture, coming from out of the unlimited. Indeed, as we shall see later, Socrates holds out for something better than the expropriating of the unlimited, for he thinks that the unlimited is in fact salvaged or saved (rather than assaulted) when we make mixtures from it (thereby preserving the legacy of the unlimited within a new kind). What we learn here is that we must not confuse the mixture with the unlimited kind.

Above all, the argument for the separateness of the unlimited from limit serves an important function in a larger argument of the *Philebus*. For if we admit its separateness, then it becomes our responsibility to explain why anything that has a measured emergence should emerge with such limits at all. Once we grasp the radicality of what it would mean for there to be something in itself having no limit, we find that we can no longer simply assume that all things are pre-given with determinacy. Rather, the radical separateness of the unlimited demands that we explain how and why any such quasi-determinate things (mixtures) could come to be before us, could emerge as subjects for our analysis. We have discovered "the present" to be analyzable; it contains some indefiniteness but also some definiteness. If this is what we judge to be so, then we have already committed ourselves to the idea that it needs an explanation for how or why it should emerge thus, with such a quasi-determinacy. To admit that there is indeterminacy in itself, separate from all determinacy, is at once to recognize an exigency in all phenomena, that is, the exigency to explain why these phenomena come to be what they are, rather than becoming at once also what they are not.

Thus, the message here is that ontology cannot simply assume there is a determinate "furniture of the world."[14] Ontology must ask, rather, "Why is there something that is not at once also nothing?" Or: "Why is there being which is not at once nonbeing?" This question arises because we can recognize that, if all things were unlimited only, then there would always only be a war of being and nonbeing. All things would be irreparably at war with their own war against themselves. If things do not appear thus, then we must learn to respond to their exigency with inquiry. The inquiry they call forth, however, is not simply the classical question, "Why is there something rather than nothing?" For that question forecloses the possibility that there is something (the unlimited), the very being of which is also, at once, nonbeing. Socrates's question here, by contrast, does not rely on the thought that "without a cause there might have been nothing at all," that is, nothing at all either determinate or indeterminate. Rather, it relies on the intuition that there might be, or might have been, radical indeterminacy were there not some cause to bring limit to the unlimited. And if there is at present not only such a radical indeterminacy, but rather a restricted sense of indeterminacy in quasi-determinate things, then a reason for this quasi-regularity must be specified. If we think we typically find beings to be limited or limitable, sorted or sortable, determinate or determinable, and so on, then the possibility that things might not be so must be allowed to appear before us. It must occasion us to ask why things should emerge with some such determinacy or determinability. To be a phenomenon is to demand a cause.

Now, I should clarify: Socrates does not imply that the unlimited requires the invocation of a cause to explain its own, intrinsic impropriety. We only require an explanation for that which is in some sense limit*ed*, since the explanation, as we will see, will refer to a cause of the limit's presence. If there is no more something there to explain than there is nothing, then there is no reason to invoke a reason rather than not to. The indeterminate in itself is inexplicable. For in itself and by itself, it is the very nature of inexpressibility, of irrationality. No definition can emerge for it or from its nature. It defies the measure that a true cause always imports. It is the mixtures that demand inquiry into this cause.

Thus, we are left with the question of how this impropriety of the unlimited could possibly allow us to treat it as a kind of its own. While this task might seem impossible, Socrates does not balk at the challenge. For, though we may only be able to indicate imperfectly the character of the unlimited through examples or cases of things that are themselves partly limited, we can nevertheless treat the indefinitude indicated *in* the examples as its own γένος.

> SOCRATES: Whatever seems [φαίνηται] to us to become [γιγνόμενα] "more and less," or susceptible to "strong and mild" or "too much" and all of that kind, all that we ought to subsume under the genus [γένος] of the unlimited as its unity [ὡς εἰς ἕν]. This is in compliance with the principle we agreed on before that for whatever is dispersed and split up into a multitude, we must try to work out its unifying nature [μίαν . . . τινα φύσιν] as far as we can [κατὰ δύναμιν], if you remember (24e8–25a4).

Socrates does not say here that we can arrive at a perfectly unified idea of the unlimited. Rather, we must try to arrive at it κατὰ δύναμιν, that is, as much as possible. The cases of "more and less" and all of the others truly point to something we can consider "as one" or gather "as into one" (ὡς εἰς ἕν). In this sense the unlimited can still qualify as a γένος (or εἶδος at 23c9). It can qualify because, as a kind, it is like any other kind in precisely this way: it is not, in any way, the kind of thing that is opposite itself. That is, it is not the limit. This "negative comparison" with the kind of the limit assists us, for the unlimited, as we have seen, has an incessant and real negativity within itself. It is thus wholly appropriate to think of its negativity negatively. In doing so we withhold from it the arrival of the positive thought of limit; we employ a restrained thinking that withholds itself from its own characteristic activity of delimiting. This restraint yields for us a kind of negative conception of the negative class's self-negation.

Importantly, with respect to its status as thus gathered "into one" (ὡς εἰς ἕν) conception, Socrates does not say that the unlimited is in itself a unity. Rather, he says, very precisely, that the unlimited "preserved at least the appearance of unity [γένει ἓν ἐφάνη], since it was marked out [ἐπισφραγισθέντα] by the common character of the more and less" (26c9–d1). Now, we can perhaps understand this "marking out" to be a more positive way to think of the unlimited. But, as the passage suggests, we must mark out the unlimited "as one" only in an appearance or a showing (φαίνειν), that is, only in and as a phenomenon, not a thing in itself. And to think the unlimited as a "phenomenal one" is in truth to think of two things *together* in a mixture: it is to think the unlimited "as one"; and it is to think the limit "as not one." For in any phenomenon (mixture), the limit therein is never allowed simply to be itself. Rather, the limit in a mixture can only be "as not itself." This is a testament to the co-presence of the unlimited in this phenomenon. For example, equal sticks which appear as a phenomenon are never complete equals or the equal itself. Phenomenal space is thus a space of the "as not itself" for the limit class (e.g., for the equal), while it is also the space of the "as itself" for the unlimited class (e.g., for the not equal). Phenomena can show themselves, therefore, only because the unlimited does (in and for mixtures) this work of subtracting "being itself" from the limit class. The unlimited in itself therefore cannot be a mere abstraction we extract from features of extant phenomena. For it preconditions the very possibility of phenomena by the work of its own self-subtraction, that is, by the way it subtracts being itself from being itself when the cause introduces limit to it. The thought of this withdrawal-from-being in all phenomena is thus perhaps a positive conception of the unlimited "as a unity." But it is only a positive conception insofar as it is the thought of a phenomenon (mixture), not a thing in itself.

Thus, to "collect" the unlimited really means to gather it up into *another* kind, that is, to allow a mixture-phenomenon to emerge. Reason—what imports limit—is therefore already at work whenever we gather the idea of the unlimited "into a unity." Reason is at work there, generating the third class. Thus, its very act of respecting the originality and distinctness of the indefinite is also its creative work of generating the third kind. This work of reason therefore does not merely represent preexisting things or create abstractions from them. It actively presents things. It actively "saves" the unlimited class by (a) withholding limit from the unlimited so as to allow the unlimited to be itself, and by (b) applying limits to the unlimited, which allows the unlimited to exhibit its nature in phenomena (thus rendering the limit in them "as not one"). The phenomenal world's lingering indefiniteness is thus a testament to the reality of this unlimited class. But, above all, the world's emergence as a phenomenal mixture with measure is, as will become still more evident later, a profound testament to the operation of the cause.

2.4. The Limit and the Mixture

When Socrates proposes to collect the limit class next, he continues to treat the very act of collection as a generative work of reason. For instead of collecting the limit, he proposes instead a kind of substitution theory: "[Perhaps] it will come to the same thing even now [ἴσως καὶ νῦν ταὐτὸν δράσει] if, through the collection of these two kinds [i.e., limit with unlimited], the unity of the former kind [i.e., the limit] becomes conspicuous too" (25d4–6). That is, Socrates substitutes for the direct collection of the limit class by proposing instead to collect it indirectly by bringing limit together with the unlimited. As I will argue, this substitution occurs because limit in itself is already essentially unitary and does not need to be collected. This intrinsic unity does not contradict the "collectability" of limit with the unlimited, however, for the activity of generating mixtures can still yield for us an accurate conception of the limit. Thus, to collect the limit well will amount—at least for us—to the same thing as generating mixtures well.

Thus, while Socrates does offer examples of the limit, such examples are always mixed cases. We must therefore do conceptual work in order to grasp what they seek to indicate as the limit. The example of "the equal and equality [τὸ ἴσον καὶ ἰσότητα]," which I used above, is one case, and Socrates also adds others. He asks us to consider "things like 'double' [διπλασίου], and all that is related as number to number or measure to measure [πρὸς ἀριθμὸν ἀριθμὸς ἢ μέτρον ἢ πρὸς μέτρον]: If we subsume all these together under the heading of 'limit,' we would seem to do a fair job" (25a7–b3).[15] Socrates's statements are rather truncated here, but we may speculate on the content of some of his examples.

First, the contrast of limit with the other-dependency of the unlimited is clear. To be double per se is never to be "more or less" double, since it is a definite relation, that is, definitely not thrice. Furthermore, to be equal, double, or any other definite ratio does not require that the ratio is intrinsically opposed to any opposite. Whereas less is what it is only in contrast to the more, double is what it is without any regard to equal, more, less, blue, five, or square. Double differs from these ideas, but it is not opposed to any of them.

Furthermore, the examples suggest that the limit is not essentially contrastive and not engaged in incessant struggle with itself and others. Equal and double can each be thought as a completely distinct idea: equal does not contain double in its definition; double does not contain equal in its definition. Nor do they oppose one another. They simply do not make reference, necessarily, to one another. Even so, both ideas can still come to be sufficient explanations of one and the same phenomenon. For we can easily imagine a single line that is divided into equal segments. Each line can then be properly understood to be a double of the other. Alternatively, if we double a length, then the original and the new segment are equals. Yet, to be double does not depend on equal for its own nature (or vice versa); they are distinct ideas between which peace can also be established.[16] Similarly, we can imagine an octave as something that can be attained—disregarding whether we are moving higher or lower in pitch—by either doubling the length of a string or dividing (e.g., fretting) a string into equal halves. The thought of an octave can be sufficiently attained through both or either thought. Since, however, they are ideas that are originally distinct and independent of one another, and one does not have to be invoked simply because the other is, it follows that equal and double are not first defined as mere features belonging to any generated octave. For it can always be characterized by both or either.[17] Their own nature does not depend on the fact that they can both constitute the octave.[18] Thus, they are independent not only of each other but of anything they explain.[19] This power to be independent, while also working together in the peaceful co-constitution of a third, does not belong to the members of the unlimited class.[20] For they are ever in a state of self-opposition.

Barker has helpfully examined Plato's various discussions of limit in this musical context and has argued that Plato follows primarily the Pythagorean tradition of grasping sensible phenomena in terms of what Socrates here calls limit.[21] He argues that the scale of musical notes expresses for the Pythagoreans nothing other than numerical ratios. The octave, for example, is a perfectly definite relation of 1:2. Further, they found there to be no need to establish a categorical difference between the realms of "quantity" (or such ratios) and, for example, the realm of the phenomenon of "sound." There is no categorical difference between quantity and quality, for all phenomena admit of quantitative explanation or reduction. All phenomena (like music) are, in themselves, not merely expressible as numerical relations; rather, they *are* numerical relations.

Barker contrasts this strict Pythagorean vision with the "empirical" tradition culminating in the writings of Aristoxenus, which he suggests also had some influence on Plato. For this tradition, argues Barker, sound constitutes a continuum of possible ranges that in itself must be experimentally divided into various scales. Using the ears, one "hears" these scales and divides the range of possible pitches into classes and kinds. Ratios alone thus do not in fact sufficiently express the essence of music since they belong to the category of the quantitative, while music is sensuous, sonic, and thus in some sense nonquantitative.

Now, Barker argues that Plato shows influence from both Pythagorean and experimental traditions, though he shares more with the Pythagoreans. While I find this argument generally persuasive, my emphasis going forward will be to argue that the *Philebus* distances itself specifically from the reductionist features of the Pythagorean tradition. Music must be able to make reference to a class other than the limit alone.[22] Music is not simply a system of ratios. It is an expressible system. Indeed, as I will now argue, grasping the limit requires from us an active engagement of the mind that, in effect, expresses a mixture as a medium for understanding.

This idea that to understand limit is to produce mixtures actively is in fact dramatically presaged when Socrates prods Protarchus to get involved in the discussion. If you are to grasp the limit class, says Socrates, then you must "take the next step and mix [the unlimited] with the class of the limit" (25d). That is, we must share in bringing them together—even if only through a kind of imaginal enactment—if we are to understand limit and discern its presence. Only by doing so do we in turn grasp things around us as mixtures, and only then do we grasp the need for a cause. Thus, like Protarchus, we must share in bringing about order if we are to attune ourselves to how commonplace this mixing activity must truly be. Indeed, this sharing reveals to us the way limit shows up in all kinds of familiar domains we may have previously ignored:

> SOCRATES: Is it not true that in sickness the right combination [ὀρθὴ κοινωνία] of the opposites establishes [ἐγέννησεν] the state of health? . . . And does not the same thing happen in the case of the high and low, the fast and the slow, which belongs to the unlimited? Is it not the presence of these factors in them which forges a limit and thereby creates the different kinds of music in their perfection [τελεώτατα]? . . . And once engendered in frost and heat, limit takes away their excesses and unlimitedness, and establishes moderation and harmony [ἔμμετρον καὶ . . . σύμμετρον] in that domain? . . . And when the unlimited and what has limit are mixed together, we are blessed with seasons and all sorts of fine things of that kind? (25e5–26b5).

The examples are of many common kinds, encompassing what we think of as human-performed (music), as natural (seasons), or as both (health). Yet all of them come about due to the emergence of limit or measure. The structure of musical examples suggests to us this feature of the nature of the seasons, and seasons reveal to us this feature of healthy bodies or musical sound. Thus, as distinct realms, each realm nonetheless shares more than a metaphorical commonality. Each field exhibits a different species of "right combination" of measure into a domain that would otherwise be an aimless process. The fact that unmeasure could always have been the norm there, but is not the sole factor present, means that a right mixing is ongoing.[23] Importantly, this wording also suggests that not all ways of combining are equally "right."[24] If the right mixing of a domain depends on the co-contribution of multiple causes instituting different levels of mixings (as when both the soul internally and a whole city together must both be harmonized), then the varieties of more or less adequate mixings of the whole will proliferate, depending on whether the mixing is conducted well at all levels.[25]

Socrates's statements about music in the preceding passages also emphasize clearly the way limit is an *expressible* defining factor, that is, a something that, while separate in itself, can always commune with its opposite. For Socrates says that the arrival of limit "creates the different kinds of music in their perfection [τελεώτατα]," thus indicating that music's completeness remains intact even as it emerges in the "high and low [ὀξεῖ καὶ βαρεῖ]" of unlimited pitch (26a2).[26] The definition of music—its expressible limit—therefore must not be restricted to residing exclusively in the limit class. This is not because the limit by itself lacks the completeness of music's musicality and expressibility. Rather, it is because any genuine completeness must also be able to be expressed not only in itself but also with another when the cause joins them. Thus, to say that music in mixture expresses in synthesis "the same thing as" the limit class—which is the basis of Socrates's whole substitution method here—is not to say that limit lacks something or needs the unlimited. It is just to say that limit's completeness is so complete that it does not lack the power also to emerge-as-complete. And the mixed class alone is the site where we find this emerging-completeness.[27]

Importantly, despite our need for an actual expression of limit in such mixtures—that is, by the substitution method—nothing suggests that the unity of limit in itself depends on any mixtures. Limit as a class is independent. This also does not mean, however, that our need for synthesis is a weakness on our part. While the unity of limit in itself is necessarily different from mixture, a mixture is not for that reason automatically a false or illusory manifestation of limit. Certainly, the sufficient mixture that can express limit in its emerging-completeness will have to be a special and even a rare kind of mixture, that is, one that brings sufficient containment to the all-too-common disharmony of the unlimited element. Yet Socrates is at least showing us what is possible here: he introduces us to the third kind precisely by showing us that it is the very kind wherein the shining-forth of the unity-of-limit-as-it-is-in-itself can come to appearance, indeed a true and right appearance. This descent of limit can be justified if for no other reason than to "save" the unlimited κατὰ δύναμιν (according to what is possible) through the generation of the mixture.

Thus, Socrates is already suggesting a thesis we will explore more later: our intellects, when we engage with intellect's objects, will inevitably be generative. And there is no reason to try to avoid this generativity. There is no reason to restrict the science of music to study by itself as opposed to practice or performance. Even the purest theoretical inquiry will in practice yield instructive performances of some kind; and honest practical decisions must always involve inquiry into the limit that grounds the orderly life that results.[28]

Finally, this thesis that limit's completeness is expressible in mixtures and practical performances can also be restated in the terminology of "being" and "becoming." For limit can be understood to mean precisely this: it is something that is determinately what it is and is never other than itself. By contrast, the unlimited is something that is never determinately what it is but is always also its own opposite. Thus, to say that limit can emerge through the making of mixtures, as is Socrates's hope here, is just to say that what is truly itself can also emerge truly as itself, even in this emerging. Thus, Socrates describes the mixture in just this way, as "the joint offspring of the other two kinds" and "as a unity, a coming-into-being [γένεσιν εἰς οὐσίαν] created through the measures imposed by the limit" (26d3–9). The mixture emerges-into-being (γένεσιν εἰς οὐσίαν), and thus we must not reduce this phenomenon of becoming-into-being to the limit class alone, that is, to always-being-itself.[29] To understand mixtures as reducible to limit alone is precisely to fail to understand their distinctive kind. So too here: to understand becoming as reducible to being is to fail to understand what is proper to its kind. Reductionists are ultimately committed to the contradictory proposition "limit itself is unlimited." They are no less committed, thus, to the claim that "being itself is nonbeing." The reductionist is thus reduced to the absurd.

To avoid the reductionist absurdity, while preserving the evident analyzability of phenomena—that is, of phenomena that have order but are not order itself—we must respect the distinctness of the irreducible third kind. The "all that exists now in the whole" has been shown to be precisely such a phenomenon of this third kind. And thus any such singular-plural mixture— such as this "all" from which the analysis began—is in truth always also a "not all." For as mixture it cannot be all things by itself. No subject of analysis includes all of ontology. For that subject is always both an independent kind of thing *and* something that is dependent on independent other kinds. Thus, what Socrates offers in the analysis of "the present" is not a classification of the preexisting, eternal "furniture" of the world, but rather a case study of an emerging reality that has become, through the intervention of reason (as cause), a helpful occasion for us to discover features of *any* mixture, of their preconditioning kinds (limit and unlimited), and, subsequently, of the need for a cause to explain any mixture's emergence as something definite.[30]

2.5. The Cause of the Mixture

With limit and mixtures now established as their own kinds, we have completed the "long road" leading up to the account of the cause. My main argument now will be that the analysis of the present has shown us that we need a cause; but the nature of the cause per se nevertheless cannot be found *in* any mixture. We will only be able to grasp the nature of the cause by sharing, for ourselves, in actual causation. To show this, I will quote Socrates's introduction of the cause in full before analyzing each statement separately. (I have elided Protarchus's replies of confirmation.)

> SOCRATES: But now we have to look at the fourth kind we mentioned earlier, in addition to these three. Let this be our joint investigation. See now whether you think it necessary that everything that comes to be comes to be through some cause? . . . And is it not the case that there is no difference between the nature of what makes and the cause, except in name, so that the maker and the cause would rightly be called one? . . . But what about what is made and what comes into being, will we not find the same situation, that they also do not differ except in name? . . . And isn't it the case that what makes is always leading in the order of nature, while the thing made follows since it comes into being through it? . . . Therefore the cause and what is subservient to the cause in a process of coming-into-being are also different and not the same? . . . It follows, then, that what comes to be and that from which it is produced represent all three kinds. . . . We therefore declare that the craftsman who produces all these must be the fourth kind, the cause, since it has long been demonstrated sufficiently that it differs from the others? (26e1–27b3).

We can sort out several theses from this passage, treating each of Socrates's statements independently.

Statement 1: "But now we have to look at the fourth kind we mentioned earlier, in addition to these three. Let this be our joint investigation." In this passage Socrates reiterates his commitment to the status of the cause as "something else" that is distinct from the previous three kinds mentioned. For while those kinds are discovered through the analysis of the present, by contrast the cause is introduced by an act of "positing" at 23c9–d6: "[We] seem to be in need of yet a fourth kind. . . . Look at the cause [αἰτίαν] of this combination of those two together [συμμείξεως], and posit [τίθει] it as my fourth kind in addition to those three" (23d3–6). The analysis of the first three kinds has revealed the need to posit the fourth; but we have not discovered the fourth as included in the subject of analysis. The discovery of a need is not an insight into reality.[31]

Statement 2: "See now whether you think it necessary that everything that comes to be comes to be through some cause?" Socrates asks Protarchus, and implicitly us, to confirm his insight that whatever emerges emerges through some cause. Importantly, Socrates does not ask us if we believe, for example, that the unlimited—sheer indeterminacy—comes to be through some cause. For we cannot even hold beliefs or make claims about the unlimited unless it is present to us and unless we conceive of it through mixture. Thus, Socrates instead asks us here whether we think there is something with *some determinacy* to opine about at all. And if we think there is, then we are committed to opining about a mixed, emerging thing. And thus, if we opine (δοκεῖν)—that is, if we are attuned to something that seems to us to be thus—then we must posit a cause for this opinion-object (mixture), for emergent mixtures need a cause.[32] Nothing forces us to admit, from the start, that things seem mixed in this way; we may refuse to confirm Socrates's insight. Yet, dialectically, we cannot remain indifferent; we must admit that things do seem thus, that is, that they emerge as themselves but also as different than themselves. The sticks appear as equals but are not the equal itself. This admission commits us to a theory of emerging mixtures and the need for the cause. By contrast, if we wish to claim that "limit alone is" or "limitlessness alone is," then we must also admit what follows from those views: limit alone cannot be said to "be" unless we admit that limit is truly expressible as multiple. For "limit (which) is" already is not "limit" alone by itself. To think limit with being is to think it in mixture. What is unlimited, on the other hand, is always in incessant self-opposition; it is never any more "thus" than "not thus" in all respects. Thus, if something "seems thus" any more than not, then we assume mixtures; and then we are left with the last question: why does this mixture come to be "thus," rather than being a radical, chaotic, measureless unlimitedness? A cause of the presence of limit must be sought. It is thus "necessary [ἀναγκαῖον]" to posit the idea of cause, if we admit mixtures.

Statement 3: "And is it not the case that there is no difference between the nature of what makes and the cause, except in name, so that the maker and the cause would rightly be called one?" Here Socrates reduces the distinction between maker and cause to the status of a mere verbal difference. The nature (φύσις) of the maker is not distinct in reality from what it is to be the cause (αἴτιον) of what emerges.

Statement 4: "But what about what is made and what comes into being, will we not find the same situation, that they also do not differ except in name?" Socrates argues that the thing-made and what emerges from the cause are likewise different only in name. The thing made by a maker is just an emergence that results due to the work of the cause. That is, he identifies the product (ποιούμενον) with the process or emergent (γιγνόμενον) that emerges. No product is ever in a state of final, non-becoming; nothing emerging in an ordered process is itself a non-product. No product is ever fully complete, precisely because it is a product; and no ordered process is itself a cause that is not also an effect, since all ordered processes are products.

Statement 5: "And isn't it the case that what makes is always leading in the order of nature, while the thing made follows since it comes into being through it?" Socrates introduces the concepts of leading (ἡγεῖσθαι) and following (ἐπακολουθεῖν). He identifies causing/making with the former and process/product with the latter. There is no indication here of a temporal sense of priority. Rather, the priority appears to be logical and ontological. We may imagine, for example, a musician whose song appears as united with his or her own creative act since they happen at once. Socrates's argument is that they are nevertheless really distinct: the maker leads, while the music-made or music-in-the-making follows. The "temporal" simultaneity, precedence, or posterity of the leader's "appearance" vis-à-vis the resultant process is thus unimportant. Indeed, any of these appearances in a temporal order would never themselves be the cause anyway. For they would, as appearances, always be merely emergents or mixtures, not causes. Priority in time thus is no sign of ontological or etiological priority.

Statement 6: "Therefore the cause and what is subservient to the cause in a process of coming-into-being are also different and not the same?" This passage presents the most difficulty for interpretation, since the reference of "what is subservient to the cause [δουλεῦον] in a process of becoming" is unclear. It would seem plausible to assume that statement 6 is a restatement of statement 5. That is, Socrates only means to say that process/product is different from maker or cause. However, while δουλεῦον may indeed refer to the product or process that emerges (i.e., the mixture), it is more likely, I think, that Socrates's "therefore [ἄρα]" is indicative of the presence of a new point in this statement. That is, δουλεῦον refers not to the product/process, but rather to the ingredients or instrument that the cause employs *in* the making. A servant or "subject" is thus said here to enact into becoming (εἰς γένεσιν) the cause's work of leading. The subject should not be understood as the becoming itself, therefore, but rather as either (or both) limit or the unlimited insofar as they are put to work in a mixing. If this reading is correct, then statement 6 adds to statement 5 an additional distinction: the cause of the working is also not the same as the subjected elements or instruments that are at work. Thus the passage is reaffirming that the cause is not identical to anything in the mixture, including the limit and unlimited as they are working in the mixture.[33]

Statement 7: "It follows, then, that what comes to be and that from which it is produced represent all three kinds." This passage provides further support for my reading of statement 6, for it mentions the difference between the process/product and "that from which it is produced," calling them all together "all three kinds [πάντα τὰ τρία]." If the preceding passage had not made reference to the difference between product (becoming) and subject (the ingredient/ingredients that condition the possibility of the emergence and are being employed in the emergence), then this summary conclusion would not make sense as a summation. As it stands, however, it clearly summarizes the previous thesis. It makes reference to not merely the process or product (i.e., the emergent mixture) but also to the other two kinds. Further, since "that from which they emerge [ἐξ ὧν γίγνεται]" definitely refers not to the cause but to the ingredients or constituents used in the production, those constituents must be the limit and the unlimited, while the emergents (γιγνόμενα) are the mixtures for which these ingredients are being employed. Thus, Socrates's reference to "all three kinds" in one summary statement adds to our conviction that a sharp distinction is intended between (a) the three "analytic kinds," which are discovered through the analysis of the analyzable thing (albeit discovered as in themselves separate from it, in the case of limit and unlimited), and (b) the "cause of the mixture." The cause is just what causes analyzable things to emerge in the first place. It is not something that is put-to-work in the process of working, nor is it the process/product itself.

Statement 8: "We therefore declare that the craftsman who produces all these must be the fourth kind, the cause, since it has long been demonstrated sufficiently that it differs from the others?" Finally, Socrates gives another name to the cause or maker, that is, δημιουργός. He states that this craftsman "differs from the others." The reference to "the others" adds to our conviction that Socrates aims to distinguish the fourth kind in a special way from the other three. They can be discovered through analysis, while the cause cannot; only the need for it can be discovered there. Furthermore, the craftsman is said here to "produce all these" others. Despite appearances, Socrates does not say here that the limit and the unlimited are themselves products of the cause. This is confirmed in his subsequent statement at 27b7–c2: "As the first I count the unlimited, limit as the second, afterwards in third place comes the being which is mixed and generated out of those two. And no mistake is made if the cause of this mixture and generation [τῆς μείξεως αἰτίαν καὶ γενέσεως] is counted as number four." The καί in the last line is explicative rather than conjunctive; and the cause is thus said to be the cause of "the mixture, that is, of the emergent." When Socrates says that the cause "produces all these," he therefore means that the cause makes them all to emerge *as a product* (i.e., together as a mixture), not that they are each nothing at all before or without the cause. The cause does not produce the limit or unlimited in themselves ex nihilo.[34] Limit and unlimited are conditions of the mixture's possibility, and are employed in the making, and thus they cannot be in themselves products of the cause. The emergent mixture, in turn, is not a necessary precondition for any of the other three kinds. Rather, the mixture's existence follows from the existence of cause's relation to ingredients, a relation without which the mixture would not emerge. In other words, there would be or would have been only limit and/or only unlimited were there no cause.

Finally, to bring all of the concepts together, we can say that while "to cause" must mean to produce some mixture or another (i.e., some process-product), Socrates nowhere suggests that any possible becoming that happens to emerge, simply by emerging, would be rightly called a product of the cause's imposition of limit. For the unlimited emerges in itself in its own way; and yet the unlimited in itself cannot be said to be caused by the cause.[35] For the cause brings limit, and the unlimited in its own nature exhibits precisely a lack of limit. And thus, since mixtures are distinct from the cause and always have this unlimited co-ancestry, it is always conceivable that disorder, in a mixture, can "happen" to the mixture and traces of its unlimited co-condition can arise. But the cause cannot be said to be responsible for that chaos, for the cause's very definition is to bring limit and to always hold the mixture in harmony κατὰ δύναμιν.

Thus, we conclude that while any analysis of the process or product resulting from the cause's activity can yield for us an awareness of the a priori and necessary distinctness of the constituent kinds conditioning the emergence of that mixture, such an analysis cannot by itself make us aware of the nature of the cause. For the analysis shows us only that we "need" to posit this cause if we are to account for the nature of the analyzable thing. The cause is not in the analyzable thing. Of course, none of this follows unless we admit that the mixtures "seem thus." Socrates is merely showing us what we must posit, in the end, if we are attuned to the presence of some intelligibility in the phenomena.

2.6. The Candidates for the Cause

The relatively abstruse analysis of the "kinds" could easily lead us to lose track of the dialogue's larger purpose. Socrates is aiming to determine which life we should lead, which life is most akin to the cause of integrated harmony in the good life, and what is the proper mixture of intelligence and pleasure that

will constitute the well-mixed life. Happily, Socrates himself shifts the discussion back to these explicitly ethical topics. "We were wondering whether
second prize should be awarded to pleasure or to knowledge, wasn't that it?"
(27c). Which life is "more akin" to this "cause"?

Philebus cannot help but emerge from his silence at this point, for he
predicts the conclusion Socrates will draw, namely that the life of the mind is
most akin to the cause. Thus, to try to preempt Socrates, he forcibly restates
his cherished thesis that pleasure is best:

> SOCRATES: Do pleasure and pain have a limit, or are they of the sort
> that admit the more and less?
>
> PHILEBUS: Certainly the sort that admit the more, Socrates! For
> how could pleasure be all that is good [πᾶν ἀγαθὸν] if it were not
> by nature boundless [ἄπειρον ἐτύγχανε πεφυκὸς] in plenty and
> increase [καὶ πλήθει καὶ τῷ μᾶλλον]? (27e6–9).

Philebus insists that pleasure is unlimited, and since it is unlimited it must be
better than knowledge or reason. It must be what makes the good life good.
Of course, Philebus has not taken part in the dialogue as Protarchus has. He
has not openly examined his own commitments for consistency. He has not
related his commitments to the phenomena. He has remained silent while
Socrates and Protarchus have engaged in inquiry. Thus, we should not expect
him to be particularly moved by arguments. Even so, Socrates charitably tries
to remind Philebus that the "boundless" is just as much characterized by
"more" as it is by "less." The unlimited cannot escape from its own opposite.
Its nature is to be self-opposed. But the point is lost on Philebus, who cannot see that if pleasure were "boundless in plenty and increase," as he insists
it is, and if it were the good, as he believes, then the good itself would be
maximally bound to pain and badness. This point is not lost on Socrates, who
replies that "we have to search for something besides its unlimited character that would bestow on pleasures a share of the good. But take note that
pleasure is thereby assigned to the boundless" (27e8–28a4). If the good itself
were unlimited pleasure, then it would be just as much boundlessly pleasant as painful; and the good would also be boundlessly bad.[36] Therefore, the
unlimited is not and cannot be the good itself. Pleasure, of course, can still
be something that always contains an unlimited element or belongs generically to the unlimited kind, as Philebus claims (and Socrates agrees). But
if so, then it cannot be, all by itself, what makes a good life good. Rather,
it can only contribute to the good life if it is salvaged by another, rescued

from the boundlessness of its bind to its own opposite. Without this rescue, the unlimited can reliably generate neither goodness nor even regular pleasures-without-pains. Something else, something totally distinct in kind from pleasure or the unlimited, must be what accounts even for pleasure's good "share [μέρος]."

As for the nature of what accounts for this share, Socrates offers a suggestion: "It is the goddess herself, fair Philebus, who recognizes how excess and the overabundance of our wickedness allow for no limit in our pleasures and their fulfillment, and she therefore imposes law and order as a limit on them [νόμον καὶ τάξιν πέρας ἔχοντ᾽ ἔθετο]. And while you may complain that this ruins them [ἀποκναῖσαι], I by contrast call it their salvation [ἀποσῶσαι]" (26b6–c2). While Protarchus and Philebus may believe that pleasure, as unlimited, can only be "salvaged" by being left alone by itself, Socrates argues that nothing good (but only a flux of infinite pleasure and pain) can come from a life devoted to the unlimited alone in isolation.[37] Thus, the bringing of limits and measures to a life is far from destructive; it is the salvation of that life from its own inherent self-destruction. Thus, Socrates brings the ethical point of the analysis of kinds back to the forefront: if pleasure is to emerge as itself and not as its own opposite, and thus if it is to emerge as something good, we must infer that it is accompanied by a cause of the presence of limit, that is, by "wisdom, knowledge, and intellect [φρόνησιν δὲ καὶ ἐπιστήμην καὶ νοῦν]" (28a8).

Conclusion. Exemplars of the Cause

While the details of the order of the good life's mixture still remain to be worked out, Socrates has provided the basic outline of his account. The idea of the cause he associates not with the life of pleasure but with the life of the mind, that is, with "wisdom and intellect [σοφία καὶ νοῦς]" (30c6). This unification of the concepts of cause and intellect means that the life of the mind has priority. Yet, Socrates must still clarify where intellect, or νοῦς, can be manifest. Who or what can engage in this intellection? In the way of conclusion I will briefly examine Socrates's account of the way νοῦς, as the source of the emergence of measure, does not show up in one region of life alone but rather finds manifestations in many orders.[38]

Socrates begins by allowing the views of "the wise" to take the lead. "For all the wise [σοφοί] are agreed in true self-exaltation," he say, "that reason [νοῦς] is our king, both over heaven and earth" (28c6–8). Socrates finds no reason to oppose the claims of the wise regarding this king.[39] However, we should also notice that his contribution to the theological discussion will not resemble anything like a proof that there is such a king. Rather, he adopts a discourse about this intelligent cause that is already in circulation, and he inquires into the way this intelligence should be reconceived, if it is to be understood as harboring any truth. He thus asks, first of all, whether the world should be conceived as ruled "by unreason and irregularity, as chance would have it," or whether it is not "as our forebears taught us, governed by reason and by the order of a wonderful intelligence" (28d5–9). As it turns out, the stories of a wondrous intelligence giving order to things, Socrates notices, perhaps really do describe in images precisely what he has just now been accounting for conceptually. Cause is just what brings good order to things, and something like causation is spoken of by the tradition that insists an intelligent cause is king.

Yet, we must also notice that in Socrates's final ordering of the goods in the good life, νοῦς will not take the top ranking; it will take only third place (see the introduction to chapter 3). Why does intellect not take first place if it is here depicted in image-form as "king"? For one thing, Socrates admits that the talk of reason as "king of heaven and earth" should be understood as a playful "release from seriousness" (30e7).[40] Indeed, Socrates even lightly mocks the tradition that speaks this way, suggesting that we must "go into the discussion of this class itself at greater length" before simply agreeing to the traditional view: "Is this what you want us to do, that we should not only conform to the view of earlier thinkers who professed this as the truth, repeating without any risk what others have said, but that we should share their risk and blame if some formidable opponent denies it and argues that disorder rules?" (28e9–29a3). Socrates can only accept the traditional stories of the wondrous reason if he first examines them for himself in light of his own use of reason. If traditional accounts fail to grasp the very nature of the cause's activity of causation—if they depict the cause as arbitrary or as importing destruction—then they are not acceptable images. Cause must be understood, Socrates has argued, as what brings limit and measure; it does not yield chaos, pain, evil, or disorder. Socrates is in truth showing us that, if we are to adopt the traditional discourse on this divine cause, then the true concept of causation must guide this adoption. The traditional discourse must be read in light of the true nature of the cause.

Even so, Socrates does not leap directly to talking about a "divine" instantiation of causation. Rather, his method involves a more nuanced movement from the "fragmentary" instances of the work of cause (e.g., the psychical instance of the cause in us) to the possibility of a larger analogue. Thus, Socrates in effect hints that our forthcoming examination of causal psychology—an examination carried out for the remainder of the *Philebus*—will be a helpful exercise not only for psychology, but also for envisioning causation in any field, for example, in theology. Even so, we must bear in mind that psychology can examine only a "fragmentary" instance of causation. The cause "in us" must not be taken to be the paradigm of all causation. We exhibit a mere instance of this power.

In order to emphasize the fragmentary nature of our participation in causation, Socrates begins by comparing the "elements" in us to those in the whole:

> SOCRATES: [Each] of these elements in us is small and insignificant, [and] it does not possess in the very least the purity or the power that is worthy of its nature. Take one example as an illustration representative for all. There is something called fire that belongs to us, and then again there is fire in the universe. . . . And is not the fire that belongs to us small in amount, feeble and poor, while the fire in the universe overwhelms us by its size and beauty and by the display of all its power? (29b5–c3).

By constructing several such analogies, beginning with material elements in us and then moving ultimately to elements in the cosmos, Socrates demonstrates to us more about how analogies function (by "moving" from a selected example to another example which instantiates the same concept) than he does about the existence or nature of these macroscopic instances in themselves. If we inquire about the nature of any of the traditional elements as they are found for us, we can at least grasp this much, however: these elements as they are "for us" are not definitive examples. They are instances analogous to greater possible instances. In this way, Socrates's own analogies "move" from the fragments in us—that is, our analogical base concepts—to the large-scale targets of the analogies. And this move serves to limit any pretension we may have to being ourselves the model for all things.

Socrates uses this same procedural movement in the analogies regarding the nature of causality:

> We surely cannot maintain this assumption . . . : that this cause is recognized as all-encompassing wisdom, since among us it imports the soul and provides training for the body and medicine for its ailments and in other cases order and restitution, but that it should fail to be responsible for the same things on a large scale in the whole universe (things that are, in addition, beautiful and pure), for the contrivance of what has so fair and wonderful a nature. . . .

> But if that is inconceivable, we had better pursue the alternative account and affirm, as we have said often, that there is plenty of the unlimited in the universe as well as sufficient limit, and that there is, above them, a certain cause, of no small significance, that orders and coordinates the years, seasons, and months, and which has every right to the title of wisdom and reason [σοφία καὶ νοῦς] (30a9–c7).

Socrates thus progresses from the elements to more complex analogies concerning soul's activity, and finally to a regulative intelligence in the universe, analogous to that intelligence fragmentarily present in us.[41] Ultimately, however, his claims are guided not by imitation of tradition, nor by a projection of human features, but rather by the prior concept (which he himself has posited through his own engagement in inquiry) of what it is to be intelligent and ruling per se. The traditional accounts, all along, have always implicitly and unconsciously used such analogies. But in the past "the wise" tended to project a conception of divinity based on their prior conception of the human instance of intelligence. Socrates, by contrast, first develops an account of the very εἶδος of the cause and intelligence per se (i.e., of what intelligence must be); and only then does he make an analogical movement from fragment in us to the greater cause, strictly in light of that prior grounding. Moreover, his method is a wholly transparent and explicit appropriation of a practice of analogizing, not an unconscious anthropomorphizing or wish fulfillment. That is, we must understand ourselves explicitly and lucidly as causes, only because we share in and immediately grasp what it is to cause. We know ourselves to be engaging in a practice of analogizing, as persons who are engaging in moving from instance to instance in light of the per se idea of the cause. We must own up authentically to this use of our own projective analogizing or else we will fail to see that this procedure must remain within the bounds of the prior analysis of the concept of the cause.

If this is so, then a true idea of causation can be manifest even in regional discourses such as philosophical theology or philosophical psychology. Both can be helpful, and yet neither can function rightly without a prior philosophical examination of causation per se. In this way, Socrates says of the ancients that we should "share their risk and blame." We must appropriate for ourselves a share in the building of the original account of the cause for ourselves. To share thusly is already to engage in a self-causation. It is immediately to recognize that one is not and cannot be merely subject to the tradition but one must share in leading it; one must appropriate the active interpretation of it in light of a prior, essential inquiry.[42] Therefore, a causal practice—our participation in the practical use of reason understood in light of the inquiry into causality per se—must always ground any truth that might become expressed in the traditions of theology or psychology.

While it may seem incredible, this "practice of reason" is actually much more common than we may realize. Even a mundane science can only begin if we own up to our share in causation. For any science grasps a phenomenon not as something arch-original all by itself but as an original mixture, that is, as something expressing a demand for explanation. This sense of exigency is not *given* in the world—as is sometimes assumed—but rather it can only come to light for one who already shares in causation or intellection, that is, for one who brings to presence the measure that measures any mixture "as (not) itself." Without this share we cannot attune ourselves to the exigency of phenomena, that is, to the way they call for explanation.

Graciously, this power of attunement is available to each and every person in a way that is wholly sufficient for a first understanding of causality. Available to all is the ability to explore causation as it is instantiated in oneself and for oneself. For our own lives are emerging mixtures and indeed mixtures whose good governance is up to us κατὰ δύναμιν. Socrates, therefore, will now explore in more detail this life of the mind—this life of bringing good order—as it is available to us. In this way, he will reinforce the conviction that if the emerging world is to emerge well in all of its levels, then no matter who or what else may contribute, we too must share actively in its generation. For we ourselves can bring about an intrinsic goodness that would in no way arise without our contribution.

PART II

*Pure Pleasure and Knowledge in the
Order of the Good Life*

The Intrinsic Goodness of Pure Pleasure

The *Philebus* contains Plato's most thorough treatment of the question of pleasure's value. Even so, disputes arise concerning whether Socrates concedes in the dialogue that some pleasure is valuable in itself.[1] Interpretive debates focus largely on Socrates's summary statements in the conclusion. From 62c to 64b Socrates lists the segments (τμήματα) of knowledge and of pleasure which are to be included in the mixture of the good life (61e5). All knowledge is included, while only some pleasure is included. In a second list, elaborated from 64c5–66d2, Socrates ranks the possessions (κτήματα) that bring goodness to the good life (66a6 and 64c9).[2] Socrates's two final lists can be summarized in tabular form as follows:

THE INGREDIENTS IN A WELL-MIXED LIFE	THE RANKING OF "POSSESSIONS" CAUSING GOODNESS TO EMERGE IN THE MIXTURE
1. All kinds of knowledge (ἐπιστῆμαι) are explicitly included (62c). 2. Some pleasures (ἡδοναί) are explicitly included*: those that are true and pure (62e; 63d-e); those that are necessary (62e); those relating to health and temperance (63e); those attending upon virtue in general (63e). 3. Finally, we must mix in truth (ἀλήθεια) (64b). *Note: Other pleasures are explicitly not included: the most intense pleasures (63d); the pleasures going with folly and evil (64a).	1. "measure, and the moderate, and the timely [τὸ μέτρον καὶ τὸ μέτριον καὶ καίριον]," and like things (66b); 2. "what has measure, the fine, the final, and the sufficient [τὸ σύμμετρον καὶ καλὸν καὶ τὸ τέλεον καὶ ἱκανὸν]," and like things (66b); 3. "reason and intelligence [νοῦν καὶ φρόνησιν]" (66b); 4. things "of soul [ψυχῆς]" such as "sciences, arts, and right opinions [ἐπιστήμας τε καὶ τέχνας καὶ δόξας ὀρθὰς]" (66c); 5. soul's painless and "pure pleasures [ἡδονὰς . . . καθαρὰς]," which follow (ἔπειν) sciences (ἐπιστῆμαι) or perception (αἴσθησις) (66c); 6. the "ordered song [κόσμον ἀοιδῆς]" ends with the unnamed "sixth generation [ἕκτη δ᾽ ἐν γενεᾷ]" (66d).

Since only some pleasures—in fact, only the "pure pleasures"—appear in the second list, it has become a pressing task to discern where these pleasures stand with respect to goodness. Matters are complicated for interpreters because pleasures, throughout the dialogue, fall into the class of deficiency-dependent phenomena, which are thus always becoming. Despite this fact, pleasures are both included in the good life and ranked as a possession causing goodness. Do not these two aspects of pleasure—becoming and goodness—conflict with one another?

Readers who would solve this problem have fallen into two discernible camps. On the one hand, some interpreters have suggested that for Plato generally it must be the case that pleasure "rightly estimated and abstracted from all evil consequences" is good.[3] Indeed, some take the appearance of pleasures in both lists as the vital piece of evidence showing that pleasure as such, when "properly understood," is good.[4] On the other hand, some have argued that the *Philebus* concedes nothing at all to pleasure, for Socrates's inclusion of some pleasures in the order does not suggest that those pleasures are intrinsically valuable.[5] While pleasure appears in the good life, they say, it is at best extrinsically good. Frede, for example, argues that even pure pleasures are not good per se because their emergence depends on the process of fulfilling some deficiency. In short, a perfect life would not involve pleasure, because a perfect life would be, in the first place, without any deficiencies in need of fulfillment.

In response to this dilemma in the scholarship—and in particular to this latter, "perfectionist" view—I shall examine the pure pleasures themselves as the key to showing why pure pleasures are the only pleasures appearing on the list of causes in the good life.[6] Armed with an understanding of the account of pure pleasures, we can discern that each side of the interpretive dilemma above contains an aspect of truth. Pleasure, taken generally, is indeterminate with respect to value, and it depends on other conditions that would make possible its emergence as valuable. In this respect, the perfectionists are correct. Even so, some specific pleasures—namely the pure pleasures—emerge as intrinsically good and are in no way deficient with respect to their proper value.[7] Here those who claim that Socrates allows for an intrinsic goodness of pure pleasure are correct. However, we must remember that this applies only to pure pleasure and not to all pleasures. The goal of this chapter is to show how both of these theses hold true.

The impact of this argument is significant. Above all, if some pleasure is indeed intrinsically good in the way I argue, then Plato's account of the good is given a distinctive nuance. For if pleasure's occurrence always implies that there is an ongoing fulfillment of an ontological deficiency, and if a pure pleasure is intrinsically good, then we cannot claim that what is deficient in being is automatically deficient in goodness. Thus, the Platonic account of being must diverge from its account of the good. My strategy for defending this divergence is to argue in 3.1 and 3.2 that the *Philebus*'s pleasures are indeed in each case instances of becoming; they depend on ongoing "deficiency-fulfillment" of body or soul. However, more importantly, pleasure's emergence depends on the being of the soul that experiences it. Without the soul, even bodily motions would not attain the status of pleasure or pain. Thus, in order to study pleasures we must analyze the psychical states making possible their emergence. In the end, I focus on the psychical experience during learning. By arguing that for Socrates learning is a process of coming to knowledge and its measure, I show how such a self-aware experience of learning can be at once an emergence and also an intrinsic good. In particular, soul's condition during pure pleasure, as the experience of this coming-to-be into a measured condition, is partly an experience of soul's self-causation. It occurs in part due to the soul's participation in the act of causing measure to emerge for itself. The pure pleasure of this experience endures as long as the awareness and the process of coming-to-measure continue, that is, as long as we are still learning. Thus, the pleasure reveals itself to be a temporary and dependent phenomenon, ontologically speaking; it is a process that must come and go. Even so, it contributes a unique expression of goodness to the good life through its importation of measure into the good life as "measure-in-emergence." Thus, this chapter argues that the very possibility of such a completely good becoming, as is displayed in pure pleasure, sheds a new light on the relationship between Plato's account of the good and his ontology. Above all, it shows that the good is not being, and this very idea gives new significance to the expression that the good "transcends being in power and dignity."[8]

3.1. Pleasure as Dependent on Soul

At *Philebus* 32a9–b7 Socrates provides a general account of the pleasures of living beings. The passage initially reads as if it is restating without modification the deficiency-condition doctrine made famous by Socrates's refutation of Callicles in the *Gorgias*. There, Socrates argues that while a good such as health has a career that outlasts the recovery process from sickness, this fact does not hold true for pleasure; pleasure does not outlast the process that fulfills deficiency.[9] Here again, in the *Philebus*, Socrates argues that pleasure emerges only when a deficiency is in process of being fulfilled:

SOCRATES: To cut matters short, see whether the following account seems acceptable to you. When the natural combination of limit and unlimitedness that forms a live organism [ἔμψυχος], as I explained before, is destroyed, this destruction is pain, while the return towards its own nature [τὴν δ᾽ εἰς τὴν αὐτῶν οὐσίαν ὁδόν], this general restoration [ἀναχώρησιν], is pleasure.

PROTARCHUS: So be it, for it seems to provide at least an outline.

SOCRATES: Shall we then accept this as one kind [ἓν εἶδος] of pleasure and pain, what happens in either of these two kinds of processes? (32a9–b7).

While the passage seems to define pleasure as bodily fulfillment, this is not quite so. First, it mentions that pains and pleasures, such as the pain of "the coagulation of fluids in an animal through freezing" and the pleasure of the "return" to normal (32a3), belong to just one class of pleasure and pain.[10] Furthermore, this passage admits to describing pleasure only in brief "outline." For, as we shall see momentarily, Socrates does not think that bodily processes of fulfillment are by themselves sufficient for pleasure or pain to emerge. He also will not limit pleasure to experiences involving bodily motions. Thus, the passage turns out to be not an entirely general account of all pleasures.

Prior to this passage, however, Socrates gave a somewhat more general account (which he will need to clarify later) describing pleasure as something occurring for a soul-endowed (ἔμψυχος) being as it "goes back to its natural condition [εἰς τὴν αὐτῆς φύσιν ἀπιούσης]," or to its "harmony [ἁρμονία]," after a disruption (31d5).[11] This more general passage, we shall see, importantly does not tie all pleasure to bodily processes. It only specifies that pleasure is, in this natural instance of returning to a norm, a kind of going-back which is experienced by beings with soul.[12] Indeed, there is no mention anywhere in the *Philebus* or elsewhere of pleasures for a being without soul.

An additional qualification of Socrates's general account of pleasure arises in a later passage concerning the way a living being undergoes bodily flux. This later passage suggests that body's integrations and disintegrations are always ongoing.

SOCRATES: It has now been said repeatedly that it is a destruction of the nature of those entities through combinations and separations [συγκρίσεσι καὶ διακρίσεσι], through processes of filling and emptying [πληρώσεσι καὶ κενώσεσι], as well as certain kinds of growth

and decay [τισιν αὔξαις καὶ φθίσεσι], that gives rise to pain and
suffering, distress, and whatever else comes to pass that goes under
such a name. . . . But when things are restored to their own nature
again [εἰς δέ γε τὴν αὐτῶν φύσιν ὅταν καθιστῆται], this restoration,
as we established in our agreement among ourselves, is pleasure. . . .
But what if nothing of that sort happens to our body [σῶμα], what
then? . . . If in fact nothing of that sort took place, I will ask you,
what would necessarily be the consequence of this for us?

PROTARCHUS: You mean if the body is not moved [μὴ κινουμένου
τοῦ σώματος] in either direction, Socrates? . . . This much is clear,
Socrates, that in such a case there would not be either any pleasure
or pain at all.

SOCRATES: Very well put. But I guess what you mean to say is that
we necessarily are always experiencing one or the other, as the wise
men say. For everything is in eternal flux [ἀεὶ γὰρ ἅπαντα . . . ῥεῖ],
upward and downward?

PROTARCHUS: They do say that, and what they say seems important
(42c7–43a3).

In this passage, Socrates restates the deficiency-fulfillment doctrine of the
earlier passage and then considers the view that perhaps all things always
"flow [ῥεῖ]." This view appeals to Protarchus generally, and it is "held by the
wise." Yet, Socrates asks Protarchus to consider a strictly hypothetical case
of a body that would not be in flux. While (in a segment of the passage
I excluded) Protarchus was initially hesitant, he eventually decides in the
passage above at least to consider it as a counterfactual. If there could be a
stable state of body, he admits, then the living beings experiencing the state
would have to be described as remaining at "their natural condition [τὴν
αὐτῶν φύσιν]" without the processes of disintegration or replenishment. This
view remains consistent with the earlier, general claim that pleasure and pain
occur when a living being is disrupted or fulfilled. For Socrates and Protarchus agree that if one could be without bodily flux, one would altogether
lack a necessary condition for bodily pleasure.[13] Such a state without any flux,
however, does not seem possible for an embodied living being since, against
the counterfactual, bodily flux does always appear ongoing.

These passages by themselves would appear to suggest that living beings
must always undergo pain and pleasure, never arriving at the harmonious

mean, precisely because they are always undergoing bodily flux. This conclusion would therefore seem to imply that we could never experience a state without either pain or pleasure (nor could we ever experience pleasure without pain or pain without pleasure). But this is not so. For both of the passages I have so far analyzed are just parts of larger arguments that advance to a wholly different conclusion. Socrates has yet to clarify, as he soon will, that soul's proper experiences need not arise from, or exist in parallel with, the bodily flux. A living being will not, for Socrates, be necessarily bound at all times to a flux of pleasure and pain even if the body *were* to be always in flux. For soul's condition is not necessarily correlated with or ordered to body's condition. The argument for this conclusion depends on Socrates's eventual discovery of a striking non-parallelism between body and soul generally, and this non-parallelism must be taken into account in the analysis of pleasure and its kinds.

Advancing toward this new point, Socrates next examines a range of psychical states involving pleasure. Importantly, these conditions or states of soul allow for different kinds of pleasures than just soul's pleasures taken in bodily processes. Socrates's tactic is to explain, first, two extreme cases of the psychical condition in general and then, second, he fills out additional activities in between. The first extreme is the case we have already seen. A living being has a psychical relation to some bodily flux (i.e., perceptions) (32c-d). (Socrates also includes in this first group the living being's capacity to anticipate or retain bodily affections.) Second, at the opposite extreme, he deems "the life of wisdom and intelligence [τὸν τοῦ νοεῖν καὶ φρονεῖν βίον]" to be a divine condition by comparison to other possible lives. Such a condition has no relation to bodily flux at all, neither to present nor to anticipated or remembered bodily motions (33a6–9 and 21d8–e2).[14] Finally, Socrates fills out the intermediate range of soul's states in between these extremes. He distinguishes and defines soul's state of perception as the conjoined shock of body and soul in common motion, at 34a4. He defines memory as the preservation of perception, at 33a9, or preservation of a lesson (μάθημα), at 34b9. Finally, at 34b9–c1 he defines recollection as the regaining of a lost memory by the soul itself, that is, of a memory of a perception or of a memory of a lesson (μάθημα). Socrates is defining these psychical states, we shall see, because he is arguing that the psychical condition is what provides the sufficient condition for determining whether there is a pleasure and what kind of pleasure is experienced, even in cases of pleasures that involve bodily fulfillments.[15]

Now, examining the psychical state of perception more closely, Socrates claims that only those bodily affections which are in fact held in common with soul truly count as perceptions: "You must realize that some of the various affections [παθημάτων] of the body are extinguished within the body before they reach the soul, leaving it unaffected. Others penetrate through both body and soul and provoke a kind of upheaval [σεισμὸν] that is peculiar to each [ἑκατέρῳ] but also common to both [ἀμφοῖν] of them" (33d2–5). In the case where the affections do not reach soul, there is no perception at all, only unperceived flux. There is also, therefore, no bodily pleasure in this case. Socrates insists on calling this condition non-perception (ἀναισθησία) in order to distinguish it from forgetting (λήθη), which is departure of memory (33e–34a1). What has never yet been perceived or learned is not something that has been forgotten. When a memory of a perception, or separately a memory of a lesson (μάθημα), has "not yet emerged [νῦν οὔπω γέγονε]," we cannot say that memory is "lost"; for in truth it has yet to arise (33e3–6).[16]

With this general account of a set of psyche's activities in hand, Socrates can now connect the account of these psychical conditions to the accounts of various kinds of pleasures. The account of psyche's non-perception (ἀναισθησία), in particular, is important. For, when we return to the passage at 43a–b (where Socrates and Protarchus have discussed the possibility that all things bodily are in flux), we see that Socrates continues his argument there by invoking just this earlier concept of non-perception:

> SOCRATES: . . . But I guess what you mean to say is that we necessarily are always experiencing one or the other, as the wise men say. For everything is in eternal flux [ἀεὶ γὰρ ἅπαντα . . . ῥεῖ], upward and downward?

> PROTARCHUS: They do say that, and what they say seems important.

> SOCRATES: But as for me, answer this question: whether all living creatures in all cases notice it [αἰσθάνεται] whenever they are affected in some way, so that we notice when we grow [οὔτ' αὐξανόμενοι λανθάνομεν] or experience anything of that sort, or whether it is quite otherwise.

> PROTARCHUS: It is indeed quite otherwise. Almost all of these processes totally escape our notice [λέληθε].[17]

> SOCRATES: But then what we just agreed to was not well spoken, that the changes "upwards and downwards" evoke pleasures and pains. . . . But if stated in this way, it will be better and become unobjectionable[:] [Great] changes cause pleasures and pains in us, while moderate or small ones engender neither of the two effects (43a1–c4).

Since Socrates has already developed his concept of non-perception at 33e ff., he is now free to invoke it in this later passage. Indeed, if he had not already developed the concept, we might have expected him to reject the whole argument of the "wise men" and to deny that there is any radical flux. For radical bodily flux would seem to imply that there is never a state without pleasure or pain. Instead, Socrates uses the concept of non-perception to argue that, even though bodily motions appear as always in flux, there are at least some unperceived bodily motions, that is, there are occasions when real bodily motions do not affect soul.[18] But unperceived motions of body or soul are precisely not bodily pleasures or pains. Rather, if there is to be an actual pleasure of body, this pleasure is dependent on the motions of body being held in *common* with soul, just as Socrates argued earlier that sensation is dependent not only on bodily motion but also on soul's awareness of them.[19] Fulfillment of a deficiency of body, therefore, is not a sufficient condition for pleasure of body, as the initial, rough "outline" of pleasure's nature had seemed to suggest (at 32a ff.). Rather, only when those bodily motions "register" psychically, that is, when they are perceived, is there bodily pleasure (or pain, in the sensation of lack). Bodily pleasure (or pain) thus depends on soul, not merely on body.

Thus, as the passage continues, Socrates argues that the psychical condition, which determines whether there is or is not pleasure or pain, is not necessarily bound to bodily motions or processes. Even if there are always ongoing bodily processes, nevertheless a third condition, besides that of this flux of becoming-deficient or becoming-fulfilled, is possible. Socrates thus describes the "neutral state" of neither pleasure nor pain:[20]

> SOCRATES: [Great] changes cause pleasures and pains in us, while moderate or small ones engender neither of the two effects. . . . But if this is correct, then we are back with the same kind of life we discussed before. . . . The life that we said was painless, but also devoid of charm. . . . So we end up with three kinds of life, the life of pleasure, the life of pain, and the neutral life. . . . [Thus, that] the middle kind of life could turn out to be either pleasant or painful would be the wrong thing to think, if anyone happened to think so, and it would be the wrong thing to say, if anyone should say so, according to the proper account of the matter? (43c5–e9).

When a flux is not noticed, the condition of soul is neither one of bodily pleasure nor one of bodily pain, even if there is for body an ongoing bodily "flow." Thus, the question of soul's being in such a neutral condition is separate from the question of whether there is bodily flux. The absence of bodily flux would indeed guarantee an absence of bodily pleasure or pain as Socrates explicitly says at 32e and 42e. But there can still be a lack of bodily or psychical pleasure or pain, even if the body remains in flux. This last point is vital, for it allows Socrates to say, later, that while pleasures are dependent on a deficiency fulfillment of some sort (i.e., of body or soul), an unperceived emptying can be combined with a psychically perceived filling. Soul can therefore experience bodily (or purely psychical) pleasure that is unmixed with pain, that is, aesthetic (or purely psychical) pure pleasures.[21]

Importantly, the initial, "outline" account of pleasure and pain, linking them to bodily changes, was not wrong. When soul perceives the bodily restoration, there is indeed pleasure. Rather, the earlier account is merely an account of certain examples of pleasure; it is merely a description of a narrow kind of pleasure, that is, psycho-bodily pleasure, and this is all Socrates ever claimed it was (32a5). When soul senses or perceives bodily fulfillment, then there is a pleasure of bodily fulfillment. This account thus explains why the earlier passages (and the *Gorgias*) insisted that bodily pleasures were kinds of fulfillments. While there are indeed no bodily pleasures without bodily fulfillments, we now see that the latter are not sufficient for pleasure. Thus, this second group of passages has shown that the initial account cannot by itself serve as the general account of pleasure. While such motions are required for there to be bodily pleasures, the motions must be psychically relevant if there is to be pleasure. Not all motions of body are, however, psychically relevant.

Thus, between our two passages, we learn that Socrates places a psychical precondition on even the bodily pleasures. Bodily flux must be held in common with soul if bodily pleasure or pain is to result.[22] Thus, the very pleasures that might seem to some thinkers to be soul-independent pleasures—the most bodily of the pleasures—are in fact soul-dependent. This psychical precondition allows Socrates to examine anew the kinds of pleasures living beings can experience. Whether in cases of soul's perceptions (51a ff.), of its memory of a different condition vis-à-vis its present condition (35b ff.), or of its experiences of learning all by itself (52a–e), the psychical condition determines whether the condition of the ensouled being is pleasing or not. Indeed, in 3.3 I will show that not all fulfillments and deficiencies are even body-related. Rather, soul has its own deficiencies and fulfillments to worry about, that is, the experiences of ignorance and forgetting.

The exposition of the psychical precondition for pleasure leads us to see that pleasure, taken generally, is broader than the initial description of the "natural pleasures." If soul's activity were strictly bound to noticing bodily motion, then soul's experiences, by parallel, would be in a constant motion of corresponding pleasure and pain, since we have no known cases of bodily processes ceasing to flow. Instead, soul has the capacity to perceive or to not perceive these bodily motions. Thus, soul's neutral state (and, later, its pure pleasure) will not depend on body's arriving in a happenstance way at a neutral condition (or, later, at a fulfillment without simultaneous deficiency). Arriving at such conditions depends on soul. Socrates's deeper analysis of pleasure thus reframes the initial, outline account of the natural pleasures, which would otherwise seem to bind body and soul. Socrates here argues that bodily (i.e., psycho-bodily) pleasures are just a narrow kind of pleasures.

While the psychical dependency of the bodily pleasures reveals to us that they are just one narrow kind of pleasure, it does not yet specify for us the actual psychical condition in soul's various pleasures, above all in its pure kind. Happily, Socrates specifies the psychical conditions for the emergence of these various pleasures from 34e to 52e. By the end of this analysis, Socrates's question has become: if a wholly choice-worthy and valuable pleasure—pure pleasure—were to emerge for body or soul, what would be the psychical condition involved? This question will be the focus of section 3.3.

3.2. Pleasure as Becoming

Before moving to the account of pure pleasures, we must examine how the *Philebus* treats pleasure as belonging essentially to the world of becoming and change.[23] It is important to raise the point here because studies have linked pleasure's nature as "becoming" to the fulfillment-of-deficiency condition of body or soul (which is merely a necessary condition for pleasure's emergence). Furthermore, pleasure's status as becoming would be the most obvious piece of evidence one might try to use in arguing against its intrinsic goodness. After all, Socrates's arguments in the *Gorgias* in particular require that the pursuit of pleasure is harmful because that very pursuit would require the pursuit of a deficient state of being.[24] I will now argue that the *Philebus* confirms this prohibition on taking pleasure as an object of pursuit, precisely because pleasure is a kind of becoming and requires a fulfillment of lack.[25] However, the fact that even pure pleasure should not be pursued will not imply, as I shall argue, that pure pleasure lacks intrinsic, complete goodness.

The thesis that pleasure is becoming is stated in two distinct ways in the *Philebus*. First, at 27d and 31a9, Socrates and Philebus agree that pleasure belongs to the class of things which are indefinite. Indefinite things, however, endlessly change without any proper measure or stability (24b8–d4).[26] Pleasure's belonging to this class in which everything is what it is only by relation to its contrary would imply that pleasure is doomed to "becoming more and less [μᾶλλόν τε καὶ ἧττον γιγνόμενα]," that is, doomed to a kind of endless change from opposite to opposite. For example, just as a purely relative "more than" (i.e., a "more" defined only as more than what is less than itself) immediately requires a "less than" for its own existence (since to be more than itself it must be less than itself), so too does pleasure, insofar as it is unlimited, logically require the existence of its opposite, pain.[27] Socrates conceives of this co-emergence of opposites as implying an inability to arrive at an end (τέλος), a measure (μέτριον), or a definite how-many (πόσον); and he sees this inability as something positively harmful to whatever has this unlimited character (24b8–d4). For this reason, when Philebus claims that pleasure must be unlimited if it is to be best ("For how could pleasure be all that is good if it were not by nature boundless in plenty and increase?"), Socrates responds by quipping that if pleasure's value comes from its "unlimited" nature, then pleasure's goodness is equally badness.[28] For, insofar as pleasure is "unlimited emergence [ἀπείρω γίγνεσθον]," it stands no chance of escaping its own opposite (24b7). Thus, pleasure left to itself in the unlimited kind would be nothing but an ongoing procession (προχωρεῖν) of opposites without end or measure.

Socrates, however, also links pleasure to becoming in a second way, for pleasure also appears in the class of things having some definiteness, that is, the mixed class (forged from the limit and unlimited). Any determinate becoming, for Socrates, is a mixture of the definite with the indefinite; and it results from an introduction (ἐντιθέναι) of limit into the endless flux by a cause (αἰτία) (25e2 and 26e7–9). Socrates refers to such mixtures as harmonious conditions which "emerge into being [γένεσιν εἰς οὐσίαν]" given the cooperation of the limit (26d7). The "natural pleasures and pains" of living beings, which we have previously examined, "show up together [φαίνεσθον]" in just this mixed class, according to Socrates (31c5). They arise for ensouled beings who, as themselves quasi-ordered mixtures, have a relatively delimited condition. But since this condition is not totally "limited" (or totally "limit"), the relative order or structure of these living beings is subject to both disruption and return to order (31c9). Thus, for a mixed being whose order is disrupted, the return to the order is pleasing if it is noticed (32b1–4). Pleasure is therefore still a becoming (in this second sense), but it is no longer a radically unlimited becoming. It becomes in relation to an order in which it becomes.[29]

Thus, pleasures are depicted by Socrates as becoming, but in two ways. On the one hand, pleasure becomes indefinitely; on the other hand, for beings who are already somewhat delimited and ordered, pleasure becomes somewhat definitely, that is, relative not to its own opposite but relative to a somewhat determinate order. Bossi has argued, rightly in my view, that there is no contradiction in maintaining both accounts.[30] She argues that pleasures generally retain a tendency to unlimitedness, even when they emerge in the mixed class. Her argument is supported by the fact that only a few lines separate Socrates's affirmation of the indefiniteness of pleasure at 31a7–8 ("[Pleasure] is itself unlimited and belongs to the kind that in and of itself neither possesses nor will ever possess a beginning, middle, and end") and his account of it as emerging in the mixed and quasi-determinate class at 31c7–32b4. Bossi thinks this double account stems from the fact that pleasures have to be, so to speak, continuously "cared for" by a soul or a cause, which has to continuously impose or reimpose limits and order on the indefinite tendency. Otherwise the unlimited tendency of pleasure would become manifest, and those pleasures would inevitably destroy themselves and the living beings for whom they occur (26b7). Indeed, Socrates dramatically depicts the "goddess" as engaging in an activity of delimiting the unlimited pleasures, precisely so that those pleasures are "saved" (ἀποσώζειν at 26c1), that is, prevented from immediately destroying themselves and dissolving themselves into their own opposites.[31] While Philebus thinks the imposition of limits destroys the unlimited, Socrates thinks it saves the unlimited (27e9). For Socrates, we too ought to act as such causes, saving pleasures by delimiting their unlimited tendency. In both accounts, then, pleasure becomes. The difference concerns only whether becoming is delimited and salvaged by soul or cause (which brings limit), or whether becoming is left alone to its internal tendency to become indeterminately and self-destructively, that is, to be nothing separate from its own opposite.

Becoming, of course, has an important history in the dialogues. The notion of pleasure as becoming and never attaining whole being recalls the famous distinction between becoming and being at *Timaeus* 27e:[32] "What is *that which always is* [τὸ ὂν ἀεί] and has no becoming, and what is *that which becomes* [τὸ γιγνόμενον] but never is? The former is grasped by understanding, which involves a reasoned account. It is unchanging. The latter is grasped by opinion, which involves unreasoning sense perception. It comes to be and passes away, but never really is." Readers of the dialogues often take Timaeus's distinction between becoming and being to be equivalent to a value-distinction, that is, being is to be identified strictly with good, whereas becoming is to be identified with deficiency of goodness. If this were so, then if pleasure becomes, it is not good to that extent.[33]

Indeed, perhaps the most lucid presentation of such an argument for devaluing *all* becoming is located within the *Philebus* itself. From 53c to 55d

Socrates considers the arguments of some "clever friends," or the κομψοί (henceforth, the "subtlers," following Gosling and Taylor). The subtlers present a "teleological refutation" of anyone who would consider pleasure as both becoming and good. The argument is: (i) to become is to become for the sake of some being; (ii) being is always the good in this relationship, while the becoming is deficient of being/good; (iii) pleasure is a becoming; (iv) therefore, pleasure is not good.

It is worth noting that the subtlers' argument is very similar to the one Aristotle uses in book X of the *Nicomachean Ethics* to argue that pleasure is not essentially γένεσις (becoming), κίνησις (motion), or πλήρωσις (filling). Both the subtlers and Aristotle purport to show that γένεσις is dependent on the good/being relative to which it emerges (and, for Aristotle, it is dependent on the distinctive ἐνέργεια). Aristotle's point is to prove that pleasure is, or accompanies, actual being; it is not essentially becoming or in process. Indeed, he is opposing the radically anti-hedonistic implications of subtlers-style arguments by rejecting premise (iii). Even so, Aristotle still holds in common with the subtlers premises (i) and (ii), that is, the premises stating that all becoming or process is normatively subordinate to being or actuality.[34] Following this Aristotelian line of thought, Carpenter has argued (following the debate of M. Frede and Code) that Plato himself generally equates "becoming" with "metaphysical *and* normative deficiency."[35] That is, Plato posits that becoming is that which is deficient with respect to being; and ontological deficiency and normative deficiency (i.e., deficiency in goodness), says the argument, go hand in hand.

There is certainly an economy to Carpenter's argument for equating becoming with ontological dependency. Socrates has already agreed that pleasure is generally dependent on a deficiency-fulfillment, and separately he argues that it is a becoming.[36] Carpenter's thesis simply allows us to consider one claim as implying the other. If we keep this link in mind, and if we notice that the subtlers' argument is presented with some approval by Socrates in the *Philebus* itself, then we might be led to think that pleasure's status as becoming is thus also fatal to its bid for intrinsic goodness. For if deficiency in being is equivalent to value-deficiency, as the subtlers' argument says it is, then we have only two options: either we may deny that good pleasure becomes like the other pleasures; or we may deny that any pleasure is intrinsically good at all because all pleasures become.[37]

While most commentators choose one side or the other, I do not think we have to accept these two options as, in truth, exhaustive. Rather, while Socrates really does find the subtlers' argument to be helpful—and interpreters are right to notice Socrates's friendliness to these thinkers—at least four arguments could be adduced showing that their views are not actually embraced by the *Philebus*. If these arguments succeed, then we can reject each horn of the dilemma. We can argue, in the end, that all pleasures come to be and yet some pleasures still could come to be as intrinsically good. Grasping this possibility, however, will require rejecting the subtlers' perfectly strict identification of being with the good, that is, their identification of the scales of being and goodness. In my reading, Socrates is indeed asking us to reject this identification.

First, against the subtlers, we can argue against the first horn of the dilemma and reaffirm that all pleasures, including good pleasures, are becoming. The most general strategy would be to argue that the cost of allowing that some pleasures (i.e., the good ones) do not become is too costly from a textual-interpretive standpoint. The *Philebus* links even pure pleasure, that is, the good pleasures, to the fulfillment process model found also in the *Gorgias* and *Republic*. Even these pleasures involve πλήρωσις. The *Gorgias* in particular depicts pleasure as necessarily ceasing to exist when the process of fulfillment ends (487e).[38] The same view is reflected by *Republic* 583e9, which treats even the true pleasure of learning as a πλήρωσις which eliminates one's own ignorance. If ignorance is eliminated, so is the possibility of the learning process. These dialogues thus support the *Philebus*'s position. Pleasure essentially involves fulfillment and thus becoming.[39]

There is a second argument against the view that Socrates accepts the subtlers' position. For Socrates nowhere—apart from in his exegesis of the subtlers' views—even entertains the view that good pleasures are good "for the sake of" something else.[40] Yes, 21d ff. describes pleasure generally as part of a "choiceworthy" life, but never as choice-worthy "for the sake of [something else]." Likewise, the final order describes the good pleasures as "following" the sciences; but it does not define any goods that may follow from good pleasures or to which they lead, nor does it claim that, were there such goods, pleasure should be chosen as a means to them. While reasoning, for example, could be conceived as good for itself and for its making possible goods that follow from it, if by contrast there are good effects of pure pleasure, then they are not mentioned and they are not the purpose of pure pleasure. The depiction of pure pleasure as a valuable "accompaniment" to other goods, but not something chosen as a means, is supported by themes in other dialogues. The *Gorgias*, for example, depicts the good pleasures as the ones following from one's orientation to the good.[41] *Republic* 357b is likewise explicitly invested in denying that the "harmless pleasures" are good "for the sake of what results from them [οὐ τῶν ἀποβαινόντων ἐφιέμενοι]"; a harmless pleasure is "welcomed for itself [αὐτὸ αὑτοῦ ἕνεκα ἀσπαζόμενοι]."

With this special phrasing, Socrates clearly states that they are not good for whatever else comes from them; yet it also does not deny that pleasures are, ontologically speaking, themselves consequences.[42] (The passage also does not say we should pursue harmless pleasures but that we should "welcome" or perhaps "appreciate" them.) Given this balance of evidence, since the *Philebus* entertains the idea that good pleasures are good "for the sake of" some other good only in its exegesis of the subtlers' views, we have no reason to conclude that Socrates is explicating his own views there. He does not accept the subtlers' view that all becoming, and thus all pleasure, is only ever extrinsically good and "for the sake of" being.

Third, Socrates explicitly tells us in what respect he finds the subtlers' argument helpful. It is helpful, he says, just because it shows us that if pleasure is a becoming and involves deficiency-fulfillment, then it is absurd to pursue pleasure as a goal (i.e., as something for the sake of whose occurrence we should take an action or manipulate preconditions to serve as means). Socrates values the subtlers' argument because it provides leverage against another group of thinkers; let us call them the *désirants*:

> SOCRATES: It is true then, as I said at the beginning of the argument, that we ought to be grateful to the person who indicated to us that there is always only generation [τὸ γένεσιν] of pleasure and that it has no being [οὐσίαν] whatsoever. And it is obvious that he will just laugh at those who claim that pleasure is good.
>
> PROTARCHUS: Certainly.
>
> SOCRATES: But this same person will also laugh at those who find their fulfillment in processes of generation [τῶν ἐν ταῖς γενέσεσιν ἀποτελουμένων] (54d4–9).

Socrates's gratefulness thus stems from the fact that the subtlers' argument displays a relation of nonidentity, and of ontological dependency, between becoming and being: becoming depends on a deficiency of being. It becomes only so long as it still remains nonbeing. Becoming thus is not itself "[independent] being [οὐσίαν]."[43] As a result Socrates is grateful for the subtlers' decisive refutation of those who pretend to "find their goal or purpose in becoming [τῶν ἐν ταῖς γενέσεσιν ἀποτελουμένων]." For such persons who pursue any pleasure are clearly misguided. In finding their "purpose" in becoming they would also inadvertently be finding their purpose in, and seeking, a "deficiency of being":

PROTARCHUS: How so, and what sort of people are you alluding to?

SOCRATES: I am talking about those who cure their hunger or thirst or anything else that is cured by processes of generation [γένεσις]. They take delight in generation as a pleasure [χαίρουσι διὰ τὴν γένεσιν ἅτε ἡδονῆς οὔσης αὐτῆς] and proclaim that they would not want to live if they were not subject to hunger and thirst and if they could not experience all the other things one might want to mention in connection with such conditions.

PROTARCHUS: This is very like them.

SOCRATES: But would we not all say that destruction is the opposite of generation?

PROTARCHUS: Necessarily.

SOCRATES: So whoever makes this choice would choose generation and destruction [τὴν δὴ φθορὰν καὶ γένεσιν αἱροῖτ' ἄν τις τοῦθ' αἱρούμενος] . . . (54d9–55a6).[44]

The fault of these desire-addicted types is that they confuse the pleasure that emerges (e.g., when an observed fulfillment is taking place) with being the very purpose of life. Some of those pleasures may even be intrinsically good; but as soon as they take them for their reason or goal, they thereby take becoming itself to be a purpose. They therefore seek to bring about a state of affairs in which becoming (which they take to be a goal) is sustained or more becoming is created. Not only do they thereby inadvertently seek destruction (since deficiency is a necessary condition for becoming), but they are also confused about the nature of becoming/pleasure. For if pleasures are emergent things, then pleasures depend on a deficiency of being. So, Socrates is saying that the error of these *désirants* resides in the way they treat becoming, and pleasure, as if (ἅτε) it were independent being. They treat pleasure wrongly as if it were independent of the fulfillment of a deficiency of being or as if it were itself some kind of "being itself [ἡδονῆς οὔσης αὐτῆς]." In truth—as Socrates and the subtlers can agree—emergent things are not being, that is, they are not independent of deficiency-of-being (or becoming). As a result, Socrates and the subtlers can agree that the particular confusion of these *désirants* is twofold: (i) they take what is essentially dependent on deficiency-of-being to be independent of any deficiency-of-being whatsoever; (ii) they take this becoming (which they think is in fact being) to be a goal. Therefore, when the *désirants* set pleasure as a goal to attain they are, unawares, each time also setting as their goal "deficiency of being."[45] The *désirants* elect, unwittingly, to create or sustain destruction (φθορά) "for the sake of" pleasure's emergence.

Socrates can accept the subtlers' idea that we must not try to take becoming, since it is deficiency-dependent, as a purpose like these *désirants* do. But Socrates cannot agree with the subtlers when they set as their own end-goal a life rejecting all becoming and taking "being alone," or independent being alone, to be by itself definitive of the good (see, e.g., 22d and 66a).[46] Unlike the subtlers, Socrates has another option besides those of either the subtlers or the *désirants*, that is, besides either (a) pursuing deficiency-of-being (i.e., like the *désirants*) or (b) living a life of being-alone, apart from becoming altogether (i.e., like the subtlers). For Socrates, as I will argue in 3.3, good pleasure emerges precisely when that very pleasure is not desired as an end-goal. It must emerge, instead, as a surprise, in a sense. These pleasures are choice-worthy in the sense that they show up in a life worth choosing. They are the welcome ones, good for their own sake and nothing further. But the deficiency implied in the fulfillment process (which is indeed required for their emergence) indicates that they must never be desired or pursued as a goal.[47] If we desire them as goals in themselves, then in the same act of desire we would also desire deficiency-of-being (which is their precondition). Therefore, the subtlers are certainly correct to reject the *désirants*; and the subtlers' argument must be taken seriously, exactly as Socrates suggests. Not all aspects of it, however, are acceptable. For the subtlers reject all becoming as bad in a way, simply on the grounds that it depends on deficiency-of-being and should thus not be pursued. They fail even to ask whether some becoming could be good in itself, despite its deficiency of being (and thus despite not being something we should seek). For their a priori identification of goodness and being precludes this possibility. This implies that they fail to understand that the good's character is not only expressed in things suitable to be end-goals but also in some things unsuited to be pursued as end-goals. They fail to see that some intrinsic goods should perhaps be appreciated but not sought out.

Before turning finally to the account of this pure pleasure, we should suggest a fourth argument against taking the *Philebus* to endorse the subtlers. As I have already begun to indicate, the subtlers' argument is committed (in no subtle fashion) to identifying the goodness of what becomes with non-becoming, that is, with being. The subtlers' complete identification of being with the good would logically necessitate that no mode of nonbeing, such as becoming, could share in its own proper kind of sufficient goodness, unless it were to become the same as being. But being, as we know, does not become. Thus, if becoming were always "for the sake of being," in such a way that becoming's ultimate *good* were for becoming *to be*, then in that case there could be no such thing as becoming which is intrinsically good as becoming.[48] For then "good becoming" would be synonymous with "being." Something would (a) become well only inasmuch as that thing (b) does not become. The only good becoming would be dead becoming. Socrates disagrees. For in the following section, I will show that Socrates gives us a positive example of good becoming. From it we will learn that the proper good of becoming is not not-to-become. We will see that Socrates's friendly but ambivalent attitude toward the subtlers is no grounds for assuming that he supports their identification of being and the good.

3.3. The Emergence of "Pure" Pleasures

We recall that pleasure occurs as, and only if, there is a psychically relevant (e.g., perceived) process of filling a deficiency. The psychical condition is essential, and pleasures are bound up with psychical states ranging from perception to memory and recollection (33a–d). Furthermore, the psyche is no blank slate but always encounters perceptible things and bodily motions (if it encounters them) while already being capable of beliefs, memories, and so on. Such capacities allow some souls to perceive or to not perceive bodily occurrences, depending on the soul's activities of attention to perceiving and preserving perception of bodily processes, and depending on its other cognitive activities, some of which have no reference to bodily processes at all (34a5 ff., 32a9, and 41a ff.). Soul's own capacities condition its experiences to such an extent that even the basic desires are soul-dependent. According to Socrates, "every impulse and desire, and the rule over the whole animal is the domain of the soul" (35d2–3); and "we will, then, never allow that it is our body that experiences thirst, hunger, or anything of that sort" (35d6).[49] Furthermore, since soul has activities that are proper to itself as soul, and not merely activities in relation to bodily events or processes, Socrates can argue not only that soul's state conditions the possibility of perceptual pleasures, but also that soul is capable of independent pleasures of its own, which are neither sensual nor perceptual (because they involve no relation to bodily motions) nor bound to occur in parallel to bodily processes.[50] In order to examine the psychical condition at work in the pure pleasures—both psycho-bodily and psychical—however, it is helpful first to examine an account of the psychical condition in at least one impure pleasure.[51]

As an example of an impure pleasure Socrates mentions a person rav-
aged by thirst who desires to be filled with water (34e–35d). Soul is here
perceptive that body is emptying-out (and thus we have necessary and sufficient conditions for thirst and pain) while, at the same time, soul takes
pleasure in the act of anticipating fulfillment with water (which fulfillment
is not presently fulfilling the bodily deficiency). A source of replenishment
would bring about the body's return to a prior measure (health), though this
desired filling-with-water is not now arriving. This distinctively psychical
"accessing [ἐφάπτειν]" of a yet-to-come fulfillment is a pleasing encounter
for soul.[52] However, this pleasure merely adds a psychical pleasure on top
of a perceptual pain of thirst.[53] Soul's "memorial" access to the filling with
water thus produces an overall experience that is a "mixture" of pleasure and
pain (36b5).[54] The important point in this example is the idea that soul can
access and experience the psycho-bodily kind of fulfillment as anticipated,
regardless of whether the fulfillment (i.e., the bodily motion) is now occurring for body.

Even so, soul is not truly self-motivating in cases when it desires a source
of fulfillment because it perceives a deficiency (as when a desert traveler
projects a mirage-oasis when thirsty). In such a case, soul's "projection" of
water-flowing-in is motivated by soul's perception of deficiency, for example,
by the pain of thirst. This pain sometimes leads soul to invent false anticipations. This case is perhaps akin to what Feuerbach meant by an "imaginary
projection," that is, a projection created by a subject as a result of its awareness of finitude, neediness, or death and its revolt against it.[55] Likewise, for
Socrates, whenever soul creates anticipations because soul is motivated by
deficiency, soul has at best an impure, mixed pleasure-pain experience (36b5).
Even if soul's imaginary projection were to happen to be accurate (as when
a thirsty desert traveler imagines an oasis at the exact moment he or she
collapses into a real oasis and drinks from it), soul's hopeful and pleasant
projection is at best still part of an overall mixed condition of soul. For here
soul is still motivated by awareness of deficiency, that is, by pain.

The importance of "pure pleasures" (51a–52e) comes to light precisely at
this junction. For they are the pleasures that are altogether separate from
lack-driven desire (but not from lack-fulfillment, in effect). The desire for
them coincides with and is generated as the pleasure already emerges for us.
In "pure pleasure," soul accesses some source of fulfillment. But it experiences
that fulfillment because that fulfillment is actually arriving, not because soul's
notice of lack has generated the desire (as often occurs). Thus, during the
purely pleasurable experience, the deficiency that is becoming fulfilled goes
unnoticed:

PROTARCHUS: But, Socrates, what are the kinds of pleasures that one could rightly regard as true?

SOCRATES: Those that are related to so-called pure colors and to shapes and to most smells and sounds and in general all those that are based on imperceptible and painless lacks [τὰς ἐνδείας ἀναισθήτους ἔχοντα καὶ ἀλύπους], while their fulfilllments are perceptible and pleasant [τὰς πληρώσεις αἰσθητὰς καὶ ἡδείας] (51b3–5).

Without noticing any lack in either body or soul, soul's orientation is free of pain and lack-motivated desire.[56] In this case, in contrast to the case of the thirsting traveler in the desert, there is decidedly no corresponding perception of any deficiency that could be motivating soul's orientation or desire. Socrates's technical account of such occasions, when they occur perceptually, is thus to say that there are "perceptible fillings" that fulfill "imperceptible deficiencies" (51b). Such a perceived fulfillment can, for one, occur in relation to the actual bodily process that soul perceives, as when soul engages with body in the act of smell, thereby perceiving a fulfillment of the senses (51e2). The smell example implies that when we enjoy fine smells, we do not enjoy them because we notice deficiency for them in ourselves. Rather, a perceptible coming-to-a-norm is perceived as taking place and is thus pleasant, though we do not really long for it in its absence.[57] The example of fine odors thus helps us imagine how pure pleasure is taken in an experience that brings the desire to us; it is not an experience desired because we notice a lack of it.

Similarly, other perceptual pure pleasures come about in relation to (πρός) colors or sounds. Socrates is careful to specify, however, that these beautiful things are not "beautiful relatively [οὐ . . . ἕτερον καλὰς]" but rather are beautiful "absolutely [ἀλλ᾽ αὐτὰς καθ᾽ αὑτὰς]" (51d6–7). We encounter these "beauties themselves"—beauties in the plural—and the pure pleasures "follow [ἕπεσθαι]" from this encounter. The plurality involved in this experience is essential to it. For Socrates also gives the example of the experience of enjoying the pure musicality of a note (51d7). The sense of μέλος (note or musical phrase) here refers not to an isolated tone existing by itself but rather to something that emerges in a "structure" of interrelated constituents, as in a melody. The soul enjoying it is not driven by a desire to make the musical structure into a simple "one" (nor to dissolve it into indefinite sounds). For the note then would not emerge in its completeness. Its plural relations are integral to what it is as an emerging note.[58] This is perhaps why the enjoyment of the note is both a pleasure and it is pure. It is a pleasure because the condition of soul is one of attentiveness to pitch as it emerges into a discernible system. The μέλος becomes manifest through the contribution of multiple constituents emerging-into-the-norm of the note.[59] The experience is pure because the experience is not missed or sought before it emerges; the norm to which the note is emerging is announced in its very emerging.

If my reading of the aesthetic pure pleasures is correct, then they are conditioned by a psychical relation—perception or sensation—to a determinate manifold, that is, to beauty as emerging in a manifestly plural way. The form expressed is revealed in its completeness as an ongoing coming-to-completion.[60] Soul, during the pleasing experience, is neither disturbed by the prior absence of the emerging order; nor is it pained by the possible disappearance of this order. We do not miss the note before it occurs (unless, that is, we are appreciating a memory of a melody rather than the present song); nor do we lament the fact that the sounds are each flowing and plural. Soul does not desire to eliminate this process or this distinctive multiplicity; for then the note's emerging expression would be abolished. Soul is rather taking pleasure in the new emergent order as that emergent order emerges.

The account of the pure pleasures of soul by itself has analogies and disanalogies with the account of the aesthetic pleasures. As with aesthetic pure pleasures, when we experience a pure pleasure of soul, we are in no way motivated by awareness of a prior insufficiency or need. We are seeking neither to be impressed by an experience of an infinite otherness nor to reduce what we encounter to a one-alone. Rather, just as we must come to grasp the exact "how many" of a multiplicity before we can know its being, so too in learning experiences do we actually come to experience the definite, expressed being of something in its ongoing expression. We approach the learnable object in its mode of learnability.[61] Our experiences of distinctive, learnable lessons (μαθήματα) thus offer the paradigmatically pure pleasures for the soul itself:

> SOCRATES: Then let us add to these the pleasures of learning [τὰς περὶ τὰ μαθήματα ἡδονάς], if indeed we are agreed that there is no such thing as hunger [πείνας] for learning [μανθάνειν] connected with them, nor any pains that have their source in hunger [πείνην] for learning [μαθημάτων].

> PROTARCHUS: Here too I agree with you.

> SOCRATES: Well, then, if after such a filling with knowledge [μαθημάτων πληρωθεῖσιν], people lose it again through forgetting [λήθης], do you notice [καθορᾷς] any kind of pain?

PROTARCHUS: None that could be called inherent by nature [οὔ τι φύσει], but in our reflections [λογισμοῖς] on this loss when we need [χρείαν] it, we experience it as a painful loss.

SOCRATES: But, my dear, we are here concerned only with the natural affections themselves [αὐτὰ τὰ τῆς φύσεως μόνον παθήματα], apart from reflections on them.

PROTARCHUS: Then you are right [ἀληθῆ] in saying that the lapse [λήθη] of knowledge [μαθήμασιν] never [χωρὶς . . . ἑκάστοτε] causes us any pain.

SOCRATES: Then we may say that the pleasures of learning [τὰς τῶν μαθημάτων ἡδονὰς] are unmixed with pain and belong, not to the masses, but only to a very few?

PROTARCHUS: How could one fail to agree? (51e7–52b9).

Like the cases when body is in disorder but soul is unaware of that fact, so too here with soul itself: we are often unaware that we lack what is most proper to the soul itself. That is, we are unaware that we lack the learnable lessons (μαθήματα). Thus we often do not even yearn for such learning. Indeed, we are not even sufficiently able to yearn for the lesson in a case of actual, original learning like Socrates describes here. For we must first begin to learn the distinctive lesson we lack if we are to be able, subsequently, to recognize that we lack it. This is because in learning we undergo a fulfillment to knowledge. A subsequent lapse in the knowledge to which we are now coming—that is, a case of forgetting (λήθη) which follows a prior case of learning—really goes unnoticed unless one day we need once again to call up the lost knowledge. But Socrates's main point is that whenever we are *actually* learning, not reflecting on learning, then the fulfillment (πλήρωσις) with the specific lesson (μάθημα) is an immediate, pain-free pleasure.[62] Indeed, in this learning experience we are surprised not only by what we are learning but also, just as much, by the fact that we previously lacked this knowledge. *"I couldn't have known what I was missing!"*—that is the familiar phenomenon that arises when we reflect back upon what has happened. How could I have failed to foresee that this arriving measure would be my measure, and that it would arrive to measure me "as (not) myself"?

The response, in a way, is evident: an original experience of learning is a precondition for any such subsequent recognition of the lacking-self. Socrates thus notes that it is only in our "reflections" (λογισμοί) after the learning that we realize we had never yet encountered this lesson or had forgotten it.[63] But such a realization does not happen, and thus we have no pain, while we are actually learning, since our present awareness in the learning experience is only an awareness of the lesson itself, that is, of the ongoing fulfillment-to-knowledge. It is not an awareness of being deficient, of becoming deficient, or of making ourselves empty. There are no feelings (παθήματα) of the lack now becoming filled. Rather, learning itself involves us only in the awareness of the lesson, that is, only in the attunement to the positive, ongoing fulfillment (pure πλήρωσις). Thus, this pleasure is in effect utterly painless and pure.

Learning, again, is depicted in this passage as making possible a subsequent noticing of the need (χρεία) for the thing learned. Thus the learning makes possible the pain we feel when we notice subsequently that we have come to lack, or still lack to some extent, what learning brings. Thus, two important points can be drawn from this situation. First, if one lacks a μάθημα (lesson) because one has previously learned it and then lost it, then this present learning recovers the forgotten μάθημα. In this case, the lack can be attributed to λήθη (forgetfulness). Even in this case, if I am able to feel a need for this forgotten lesson, this ability just indicates that I must have already begun to relearn the lesson, or to reaccess the fulfillment (even if this is achieved through a relation to a remnant memory of the lesson). The direct pleasure of learning, as either accessing or reaccessing truths, is thus always prior to, separate from, and makes possible any subsequent pain of recognizing that one has forgotten or otherwise lacks a lesson.[64]

Second, and most importantly, we must also note that there are cases of lack that are not cases like this forgetting. For when one is learning a μάθημα, if one (previously unknowingly) lacks this μάθημα but one has *never* previously learned it before (and thus one cannot possibly sense its absence), then this present learning process is not a recovery from forgetting (λήθη) but is, rather, a case of what we might call "original learning." In this case, the soul that is becoming fulfilled must have been in a state of a more general ignorance regarding this new condition to which it ascends; it was not in a state of forgetting. The fulfillment of this original, more general kind of ignorance (ἄγνοια), rather than of a more specific, forgetting-based ignorance (λήθη), is analogous to the psycho-bodily cases of a non-sensate (ἀναίσθητος) condition, which is opposed to psycho-bodily forgetting (λήθη) of a perception. Remember: we cannot forget the yet-perceived, though we can be non-sensate with regard to it. So too here: we cannot forget the yet-learned, though we can be generally ignorant of it.[65] Just as with the case of a forgetting-based ignorance, however, the pleasure of original learning here is prior to, separate from, and first makes possible any pain of recognizing that one has been ignorant (ἄγνοια). In all cases, we can recognize a lack of measure only if that measure has to some extent come to presence, or is coming to presence. We can recognize the lack only if the measure is already announcing the lack as a lack to us.

Above all, the fact that there are such cases of ἄγνοια that are not also cases of the λήθη suggests that the "recollection myth" in Plato's epistemology must be read as an imagistic representation of what truly happens when we "originarily learn." If we are not careful, we can fall into treating original learning as if it is always a case of re-original learning, that is, of relearning what has "once" been known but now has become forgotten. The more precise conception of original μάθησις as depicted here, by contrast, suggests that the myth is a helpful but non-exhaustive interpretation of only some specific cases of learning. For not all ignorance has to be ignorance due to forgetting of what we "once" already knew. When a specific case of "original learning" proper occurs, the ἄγνοια gets measured-as-a-lack for the very first time in the learning of the new lesson.[66] This original learning experience thus introduces us originally to something we have never forgotten. It could now become forgotten, however, if we do not preserve the force of its truth through active memory, which is to say through a practice of always being prepared to learn and relearn, and to actively cultivate memories and memorials.[67] This requires staying practiced in dialectics, which in turn requires that we dwell in a truly dialectical community.[68]

Thus, for Socrates, a lesson moves me away from my unforeseen ignorance into a still-emerging order of knowledge, that is, into a new measure that measures me as a whole. Thus, perhaps the most important thing we learn from such a reflection on learning is a truth about "how to learn." To approach whatever we encounter as a lesson—that is, to prepare ourselves to learn—we must not presume erroneously that we are all-knowing, that is, that we are already the measure. That would be self-deception. But we also must not strive "to have our minds blown" at each event. For to seek out the indefiniteness of the mind-blowing experience—as when we become addicted to experiencing "the new for the sake of the new"—would be to seek to be deficient in knowledge so that we could learn. That would be the vice of the self-induced leaky jar scenario, for it would mean that we would seek to *need* to learn. Even so, it is still a wholly good thing to learn if one lacks knowledge. The learning is not an unfortunate event. Far from it, since the "lesson" is just an experience of coming to the measure that will be, and already has begun to be, definitive of oneself as the good version of oneself.

Pure pleasure, thus, is a vital component in the good life, due to the way it accompanies both the sensuous presentations of measures and the pure psychical encounters with lessons (as cases of a directly psychical coming-to-measure). These are two distinct kinds of the "coming-to-presence" of measure, and thus all of these pure pleasures can be assigned "to the class of things that possess measurement" (52d1–2).[69] Importantly, however, pure pleasure would not be included in the list of causes of the good life if it simply were to "have" measure. Rather, it must also contribute measure. To see how it shares in a genuine contribution, we must recall the condition of the soul in the pure pleasure experiences. First, soul does not hereby empty itself in order to experience this fulfillment. Only a pleasure-seeker—that is, someone controlled by the lacks in themselves—would do that. Further, if soul were to empty itself of knowledge, in order to be able to regain knowledge, it would thereby understand itself to lack this knowledge, since it itself would be responsible for generating the lack in the first place. And thus soul would feel pain at the absence which it itself has generated in itself. So, in general, if pure pleasures of soul or soul-body are to emerge, soul must not be responsible for creating the lack that needs fulfillment. In pure pleasure, the soul is responsible neither for generating the deficiency nor for inducing a self-unawareness of deficiency (whether bodily or psychical) that is becoming filled. It is not destroying itself or blinding itself.[70]

Even so, the account also shows us that it is not enough for the soul simply to avoid self-destruction or to maintain itself in its present condition. For learning, as we have seen, also requires an openness to being defined or redefined anew in the very experience of the lesson. Learning therefore definitely does not involve merely a kind of *conatus*, or self-preservation. For the soul must be prepared not only to incorporate a new lesson into itself as it presently is but also to actively enable the lesson to define the soul anew. The right measure—or "norm"—for soul is thus different from bodily states like health. For health can indeed be attained through the bringing of a body "back" to a previously established order of health, as when a cut heals. Healing can be interpreted as self-preservation. By contrast, soul's being in a state of good order must mean this: soul actively engages in a self-ordering of itself in light of the good order it learns. Soul thus appropriates the lesson actively and shares in changing its own existing order.[71] Only a soul that self-orders itself in this way—and thus originally institutes for itself a norm by appropriating for itself the measure it learns—can truly overcome an alienated and self-destructive psychical condition. In effect, this means, however, that even the drive to self-preservation is revealed here as optional. For the original learning experience—the experience of coming to psychical order—is also soul's emergence beyond the extant self into the power of the new, that is, into νοῦς (intellect), that is, into the noetic, creative power that, by definition, always brings order and defines itself strictly in light of the measure itself.[72] This is the original "turning" of which the *Republic* 518d speaks.

Thus, in effect Socrates allows that souls are microcosmic participants in what it is to be a cause. Soul's pure pleasures emerge from an autonomous psychical activity occurring when the psyche originally accesses and originally establishes-into-becoming a measure and source of fulfillment. This activity establishes-into-becoming the very norm relative to which the fulfillment to that norm progresses. The lack of this measure in the emergent world was previously necessarily unnoticeable because this mode of measure truly was never-yet-present in the world of becoming. Only now (i.e., now that soul is in fact instituting this norm) is it even possible for one to infer that the norm was previously lacking. Thus, the pleasure of the fulfillment is "pure." It is pure not merely because the lack was de facto unnoticed; it is pure because the lack was impossible to notice, since no living being capable of recognizing the lack had ever yet accessed and instituted-into-becoming the norm relative to which the lack could be measured-as-lack or felt-as-needed.

This account of the learning experience would have the effect of explaining, in turn, why the *political* art of "legislation" in the *Gorgias* (465 ff.) is called the art of "caring for soul" and why this art is also associated with self-control and moderation (ἐγκράτεια or σωφροσύνη). Legislation, there, means accessing measure and instituting for the soul an order according to that measure. Unlike the art of justice, the art of legislation does not set out to correct a lack. The effect (though not the goal) of legislation would then be to preempt the emergence of a lack as much as possible; it preempts the emergence of a lack whose very possibility is comprehended for the first time only due to the possible arrival of this new institution-into-becoming of the eternal law or measure. The possible arrival of the law into the world of becoming, or into soul, makes possible the soul's subsequent recognition of a possible world lacking that law. This recognition of a possible world lacking the law then makes possible the desire for the law. A good increase of desire—even though all desire still depends on there being a yet-filled lack in soul—can thus be envisioned here, so long as we envision it as following from the prior notice of the arriving measure (not merely from a sensation of lack). In learning, therefore, the soul is not politically irrelevant. It is actively involved in the world as a contributor to a community, and it is practically generative of a whole harmony of life. For this reason, I think, Socrates treats pure pleasure as having not merely a passive role to play in the good life. Rather, he describes its active contribution due to the way it signals the arrival of true measure but also makes possible a good and true increase in drive and motivation. It is thus not merely an ingredient of the good life; it causes the good life to emerge as good. This is because soul, when it can experience pure pleasure, is emerging into an active state of self-control that shares in the overall instituting or constituting of the whole; and its desire here helps it persevere in this contribution.

Thus, Socrates's description of the principle guiding the second list (in the table in the introduction to chapter 3) reveals that pure pleasures must be included. They share in causing the overall order to emerge with measure. Two of his statements in particular emphasize the way the final list's content is indeed concerned with ranking the extent to which the members share in causality. First, at 64c5–d9, Socrates states:

> But it is certainly not difficult to see what factor [αἰτίαν, i.e., cause] in each mixture it is that makes it either most valuable or worth nothing at all. . . . That any kind of mixture that does not in some way or other possess measure or the nature of proportion [μέτρου καὶ τῆς συμμέτρου φύσεως] will necessarily corrupt its ingredients and most of all itself. For there would be no blending in such cases at all but really an unconnected medley, the ruin of whatever happens to be contained in it (64d).

Here, Socrates says that the "cause [αἴτιον]" in the mixture that makes the mixture (of the good life) valuable is what is responsible for the measure and measuredness in it.[73] But Socrates has already argued at length in the fourfold classification (23c2–27c7) that measure, or limit, does not just "happen" to show up in mixtures. Rather, measure emerges because limit is introduced to the unlimited by some "cause." Thus, in the passage 64c5–d9, when Socrates asks which candidate in the mixture is "more closely related [προσφυέστερον]" to this cause, he is asking about the extent to which things are causes of, or share in causing, the presence of measure in mixtures.

Second, additional evidence for this conclusion that the final order ranks participation in "causality" lies in the fact that Socrates's statements above align perfectly with 22c8–e2. There, the entire competition was reoriented to the new prize of being "more like" the cause that "makes [the good life] choiceworthy and good" (22d9).[74] The use of the comparative in each of these passages is remarkably consistent. Both passages state that the competition concerns measuring each candidate's relative share in causation. Thus, the final list expresses the results, and pure pleasure is indeed listed as one of the things that is to some extent "of a kind" with the cause. We should expect this outcome, since we have seen that pure pleasure imports its own specific kind of measure, that is, the distinctively emerging measuredness. And thus the pure pleasures can be ranked, finally, as the fifth factor responsible for goodness.

Before looking more closely at the principle of the ranking, we must first regather a sense of why the importation of measure is so important in the first place. That is, since we are concerned with what imports goodness, it has become important that we explore once again the very nature of "the good" that the cause imports. What does "the good" mean to us, now that we have found its presence in many places and even as something imported by the emerging goodness of pure pleasure? Socrates poses this question directly at 64a4. And, just as we saw in chapter 1, he explores the good not as one idea alone but rather as a one that emerges in plurality:

> SOCRATES: Well, then, if we cannot capture the good in one form
> [μιᾷ . . . ἰδέᾳ], we will have to take hold of it in a conjunction
> of three [σὺν τρισὶ]: beauty, proportion, and truth [κάλλει καὶ
> συμμετρίᾳ καὶ ἀληθείᾳ]. Let us affirm that these should by right
> be treated as a unity [ὡς τοῦτο οἷον ἕν] and be held responsible
> [αἰτιασαίμεθ᾽] for what is in the mixture, for its goodness is what
> makes the mixture itself a good one [καὶ διὰ τοῦτο ὡς ἀγαθὸν ὂν
> τοιαύτην αὐτὴν γεγονέναι].
>
> PROTARCHUS: Very well stated.
>
> SOCRATES: Anyone should by now be able to judge between plea-
> sure and intelligence, which of the two is more closely related
> [συγγενέστερόν] to the supreme good [ἀρίστου] and more valuable
> [τιμιώτερον] among gods and men. . . . So, now let us judge each
> one of the three in relation to pleasure and reason. For we have
> to see for which of those two we want to grant closer kinship [ὡς
> μᾶλλον συγγενὲς] to each of them (65a–b6).

The good is here tracked down as the threefold of "beauty, symmetry, and truthfulness [κάλλει καὶ συμμετρίᾳ καὶ ἀληθείᾳ]." We can consider these three "as if they are one [λέγωμεν ὡς τοῦτο οἷον ἕν]." This threefold should be compared to the other threefold (of the sufficient, the complete, and the choice-worthy) we explored in chapter 1. There, the "learning procedure" demanded the pluralization of the posited one-good into a manifold, so that each life could be compared with the good itself in its own way and revealed as good in its own way. Here, by contrast, the divisions of each kind have already been completed by the interlocutors (though *we* must still examine the actual division of knowledge in chapter 4), and they are thus at the point of "gathering" together the many instantiations of goodness that we have found. Thus, while this new threefold emerges with terms that are different, these different terms appropriately meet the same demand to determine κατὰ δύναμιν (according to what is possible) the "intermediate" number of any form we seek.[75] Only, here we are expressing an understanding of the good that preserves the good's presence within the kinds, that is, within multiple strata of experience we have explored. The good expressed in this way thus allows us to seek within each kind the comparative extent to which that kind imports this measure. If previously we measured each kind externally by the standard of the good, here we measure each kind internally.

Thus, whatever exhibits this threefold character of the good can now be taken to have some responsibility (αἰτία) for the mixture's having "emerged as good [ὡς ἀγαθὸν . . . γεγονέναι]." Thus, we can ask, which kind does a better job in this role? Comparatively, pleasure, as a kind, must be judged inferior to knowledge: "the good and the pleasant have a different nature, and that intelligence has a greater share in the good than pleasure" (60a5–b5). To be inferior to knowledge *as a kind*, however, does not mean that the good examples of pleasure will be inferior to the good in knowledge. Rather, it will mean that whereas all kinds of knowledge are good (as I will explain further in chapter 4), only some pleasures are good, that is, only the pure pleasures we have just examined. Some pleasures are even harmful (66a). The pure pleasures, as we have seen, transcend these difficulties with their kind in general, however, for they imply that we are already involved in the mode of life that shares measure with the whole living being.

Thus, the larger strategy of the dialogue since 22d, which is the strategy of discerning what shares in the cause, is fulfilled in the dialogue's final two lists (see the table above). And we now see why there must be two lists. (i) The first list reflects Socrates's discernment of the different kinds of pleasure and knowledge. He has undertaken this task in order to decide whether all or some of each candidate's sub-kinds (i.e., the sub-kinds of knowledge and of pleasure) are even admissible as *ingredients* in the mixture. (ii) The second list reflects Socrates's actual discernment of which things (within each of the two kinds of candidates) are more closely related to the very *cause* of the mixture.

With respect to (i), the task of discerning the different kinds of knowledge is important; but it does not factor into the decision about what knowledge to include in the good life. For all kinds of knowledge are included (see chapter 4). The discernment of different kinds of pleasures, however, does factor into the decision on the inclusion of ingredients. Some pleasures, as pleasures, are explicitly not included (because, for example, they accompany vice). Many kinds of pleasure are included even though they are not the intrinsically good ones. But not all pleasures can be included.

With respect to (ii), the ordering of the causally contributing factors according to their relative likeness to the cause of the emergence of goodness is vital for understanding pure pleasure. For it tells us what order, or rank of orders, a good life will establish. Pure pleasure has a place in this order because it itself emerges with order and it brings a unique kind of order to the overall order. Even so, the second list also shows that pure pleasure still depends for its emergence on the establishment of the prior elements.[76] It depends on a psychical condition in which the constitutive elements of knowledge are already present. It depends on a life of measure, reason, and right opinion, and so on. This is precisely why, even though pure pleasure is a vital and wholly good contributor in the good life, it cannot take first place in the order. It depends ontologically for its very emergence on the other factors; for its very emergence must follow those factors: pure pleasure, as we have seen, "follows sciences and certain sense perceptions [ἐπιστήμαις τὰς δὲ αἰσθήσεσιν ἑπομένας]."[77] In this sense, reason certainly is "more akin to the cause" than any pleasure is insofar as, ontologically, reason must be mixed into the good life before pure pleasure can emerge. But pure pleasure too must be classed as "of a kind" with the cause, since it expresses intrinsic goodness, even though its emergence is dependent on prior contributors.

Thus, the final order of the good-making factors in the good life is not at all a ranking of things as more or less good. Each has a goodness proper to the kind of thing it is. Each kind enters into the good life in its proper way. Each imports beauty, symmetry, and truth to the whole; but each does so in its own kind. While pleasure's kind admits only rarely of good versions— for pure pleasure requires a whole set of preconditions if it is to emerge as pure—this rarity of pure pleasure does not mean that it is any less good when it emerges.[78] Thus, the final order is not a rank of more or less goodness but rather a ranking of ontological conditions of possibility of the mixture's emergence as a good whole, that is, as a mixture with multiple strata of complete expressions of good measure. The higher does not give to the lower the special goodness proper to the lower, for the lower's goodness must emerge as specific to the lower's own ontological kind (i.e., the emergent kind). But the lower could not occur at all without the prior integration of the higher.

Thus, while pure pleasure may be an uncommon, a highly dependent (ontologically), and indeed a very rare example of pleasure, it can still be understood, just like the other goods in the order, as good in itself. That is, pure pleasure is as an intrinsic good.[79]

Conclusion. Ontology and the Account of the Good Diverge

When perfectionist readers of the *Philebus* assume that the perfect condition without becoming would be better than the mixture of the good life, and when they suggest that the *Philebus*'s good life is a "second-best" mixture, they are saying this because they notice that good life includes emerging goods like pure pleasure.[80] But they are in essence also suggesting that it would be best if all becoming and emergence were to end. Through an examination of pure pleasure, however, I have argued that we can challenge the perfectionist strand of *Philebus* interpretation both textually and conceptually. Perfectionist readers presuppose that an ontological deficiency, which is a prerequisite of any fulfillment, indicates that such a process of fulfillment is something we ought to try to exclude (even though we perhaps cannot exclude it and we must settle for "second best").[81] They interpret the pure pleasures either as not intrinsically good because they become, or as not becoming because they are intrinsically good. But this dilemma arises, as I have argued, only if we fail to grasp the nature of the experience of pure pleasure and the way it reveals the good's transcendence of being. The good's scope in truth extends to some nonbeing, and this truth comes to light for each person who experiences the pleasure of learning.[82] Direct textual evidence in the *Philebus* challenges the strict alignment of being and goodness. Equally powerful conceptual evidence challenges the claim that good becoming could emerge as good only if it were to cease becoming, that is, if it were strictly to be. Such an argument would ignore the possibility of a goodness proper to some cases of becoming. It would ignore the possibility of a goodness proper to the journey itself, as they say.

In defense of the possible goodness of the journey, I have argued that all pleasure becomes and never fully is. This means that pleasures are "ontologically dependent," that is, dependent on the ongoing fulfillment of a deficiency of being. But I have also argued, based on the evidence of pure pleasure, that ontological dependency is not the same thing as deficiency in goodness. While the final order in the good life ranks the conditions of possibility of the whole mixture's emergence as good, and while each member conditions the being or emergence of those below, nevertheless each also manifests sufficient and unique goodness and participates in causing the emergence of a good mixture as a whole. But this means that the pure psychical pleasures—whether strictly psychical or psycho-bodily—can be understood as intrinsically good even though their emergence is dependent on other things such as reason, right opinion, and so on. Their ontological dependency does not demean the intrinsic value of their emergence. For while pleasures are good only if there are other conditions in place—that is, good pleasures only emerge under certain conditions—it is also the case that pure pleasure has its own value as pleasure and as becoming. Something is intrinsically valuable in the positive sense, as I have argued, if its goodness (and its causal contribution of goodness to the good life) cannot be reduced to other sources. While we may therefore "rank" the measure itself, the measured, reason, opinion, and pleasure accordingly in an order of ontological priority and posteriority, nevertheless the intrinsic goodness of each stratum is not subject to a value-ranking according to this ontological ordering. Each has its own goodness. Of course, nothing in the final order is identical to the good itself by itself. Each of the intrinsic goods in the mixture is sufficiently good by participation in the good.[83] In the good life each stratum of life reveals the good in a distinct way.

Thus, as I understand the *Philebus*, the dialogue suggests that we should be wary of pretending that a perfect state—defined as a state of complete being-without-becoming—is something "better" than the good life, which is a mixture. The perfect state, if there were such a thing, would have to measure its own *worth* over and against the standard of the good itself. But the standard of goodness, as Socrates has shown, extends also to some becoming. And thus the command "Do good!"—as distinct from and prior to any supposed command of "Be!"—does not even demand the perfect state. For by what standard would perfection-without-becoming ever judge itself to be better than good? Evidently not by the standard of goodness, since, as we have seen, the good itself allows for a good becoming as becoming, which is something that a perfectionist must decry as an "imperfection."

We should therefore, in my view, take a wholly different approach to Plato and to value theory more broadly. By admitting that some pleasure exemplifies the goodness of which becoming is capable as becoming, we can come to recognize the good's manifestation in becoming as well as in being. The good's manifestation in and as an exemplary case of becoming thus reveals to us that the good itself transcends being. In turn, good's transcendence of being guarantees for us that good becoming is always a possibility. We must therefore be open to change, to fulfillment from out of ignorance into knowledge, and to emergence from out of nonbeing into being. We should always in particular be open to experience of a lesson (μάθημα). For learning is not itself an unfortunate necessity; it is an intrinsic good that brings intrinsically good pleasures that could not occur if there were only things in a perfect state.

We set out to ask: how can a pleasure retain the generic attributes that are shared with all pleasures and at the same time contribute an intrinsic goodness to the good life, a contribution that would seem to transcend the possibilities inherent within that kind? I have argued that pure pleasure indeed belongs to the "kind" of pleasures generally, for it is an example of pleasure among others: it depends on deficiency-fulfillment; it is a becoming; and it is psychically dependent. Yet, I have also argued, in effect, that pure pleasure is a special instance. It stands for the good possibilities of the whole class of pleasures, since it is itself both purely pleasure and something purely unmixed in its goodness. For this reason, pure pleasure can be called a paradigm of goodness. It not only stands for the hopes of all pleasures but also for the hopes of all things that *come to be*.

Purity and the Sciences

The discovery of pure pleasure shows us that our needs are truly fulfilled only when what meets those needs is at the same time what informs our desires. Sadly, we are often motivated by our felt need for fulfillment rather than by the truths whose arrival reveals genuine needs only by first fulfilling them. We thus create a hell for ourselves, defining what we think we desire from within our corrupted state. We pursue more numerous or more intense pleasures and place ourselves into a state of more lack even as we seek to escape it. We fail to accept the arrival of the good we seek; we prefer to keep searching, beyond the good that makes itself available. We in turn miss out on the pure pleasures of a truth-informed progression. These pure pleasures may not be the most intense or the most oft-encountered; but they are pleasure in its purity, better than more numerous or more intense pleasures.[1]

Purity as a concept, however, is difficult to define, if only because it overlaps with the very concept of definition or definiteness. In Greek the term also has many meanings. The term καθαρός not only carries the basic senses of physically clean, free of admixture, of genuine birth, and "free and open space." In its adverbial form, it has pre-Platonic uses meaning to speak plainly or simply, or to show oneself honestly and without equivocation.[2] We have seen that pure pleasures emerge in this way, honestly and without deception, escaping the incessant impropriety and alienation of the indefinite class. They arise for a well-mixed being—for a living being whose structure is analogous to the one-many structure of a true definition—just as the "pure note [καθαρὸν . . . μέλος]" at 51d7 emerges only in a system of relations to other notes.

This sense of purity as existing in and with a manifold, however, is not indicated in all of Socrates's examples. For instance, in linking the concept of "purity" to the concept of "truth," Socrates tries to explain purity through the example of color:

> SOCRATES: Now, can there be purity in the case of whiteness, and what sort of thing is it? Is it the greatest quantity or amount, or is

it rather the complete lack of any admixture, that is, where there is not the slightest part of any other kind contained in this color?

PROTARCHUS: It will obviously be the perfectly unadulterated color.

SOCRATES: Right, but shall we not also agree that it is the truest and the most beautiful of all instances of white, rather than what is greatest in quantity or amount?

PROTARCHUS: Certainly.

SOCRATES: So we are perfectly justified if we say that a small portion of pure white is to be regarded as whiter than a larger quantity of an impure whiteness, and at the same time more beautiful and possessed of more truth? . . . [And] we don't need to run through many more examples to justify our account of pleasure, but this example suffices to prove that in the case of pleasure, too, a very small and insignificant pleasure that is unadulterated by pain will turn out to be pleasanter, truer, and more beautiful than a greater quantity and amount of the impure kind (52d4–53c3).

Here Socrates explores the concept of purity through a kind of *via negativa*. Purity in the case of color tends to mean a state of being completely "not admixed." This refusal of admixture could appear to conflict with the notion of purity of a note as emerging in a mixture. In what sense, we may therefore ask, does the pure emerge in a manifold, and in what sense is the pure not admixed with other things in a manifold? Perhaps Socrates needs a more positive account of the core sense of purity, something more than his *via negativa*, if he is to persuade us that the concept even has a core sense.

Furthermore, without a positive account of purity Socrates could be open to a second objection, stating that that pure pleasures seem to be simply the opposite of what common people enjoy. When, at 52b8, Socrates says that pure pleasures are for the "few" and not for the "many," perhaps Socrates, says the objection, is merely ironically negating what is popular. Maybe pure pleasure is really just the least pleasing of all things, spitefully made out to look like the purest and best pleasure.[3] Indeed, some interpreters of this passage have taken Socrates to mean that pure pleasures are not pleasures at all; they are truly pains.[4] That would indeed be a very deep irony.

As I shall argue, however, the *Philebus* does provide a positive account of what purity means, and it employs a transparent and non-ironical sense of "pure." In one respect, this positive account of purity has already begun. By defining pure pleasure as a case of fulfillment noticed by soul (which was previously unaware of the lack), Socrates established the "positive" conditions that need to be in place for pure pleasure to emerge. It was not achieved through my own act of negating—or reacting in opposition to—feelings of pains or lacks. For I must be aware of the lack in order to negate it, and, if so, then I must be pained. But pure pleasure is free of pain. Thus, Socrates claims pure pleasure is defined not by any reaction but rather by the experience of the arriving of the measure that fulfills and reveals the lack.

Even so, Socrates's account of these "positive" conditions has been largely descriptive. And his arguments against the active pursuit of even the pure pleasures would seem to render pointless this descriptive account. For if we are not supposed to pursue pure pleasure (for to do so is to sustain oneself in a condition of lack), then why explain to us the preconditions of its emergence?[5] The fact that the pursuit of pure pleasure as pleasure would make pure pleasure's very emergence impossible contributes to the anxieties of interpreters. Perhaps purity has only a negative sense? Perhaps it is secretly just an idea of non-admixture? Or perhaps Socrates is engaged in deception or irony?

A response to this line of challenge emerges from 55d1 to 59d9. Socrates's tactic here is ostensibly to judge, not pleasure, but the scientific disciplines according to their own proper purity. While this section is valuable in its own right as a study of scientificity, I aim primarily to discern in it a positive concept of purity. For purity, as Frede has stated well, will provide the common basis for fairly judging our two competitors, knowledge and pleasure.[6] The fact that each candidate can be pure—albeit in different senses—allows us to subject knowledge and pleasure to the same kind of test, that is, to a fair and charitable standard of testing. Indeed, as we recall, Socrates's earlier commitment to testing each kind fairly was precisely what sparked Protarchus's voluntary participation in this whole dialogue (see 1.2). Only now do we finally witness the standard of fairness applied. We learn here that the common standard for judging both knowledge and pleasure is the measuring of each kind by the purity proper to that kind. This test cannot blur their difference in kind, but it must also serve as a truly common standard. We thus need an analogical concept of purity.

This core sense comes to light in two main stages. First, Socrates's account of the nature of science will propose to discover the very element in each and every science (insofar as it is a science) that accounts for its scientificity. Ultimately, this core or "leading" element in any science is the intellection (ἔννοια or νόησις) of a distinctive, real measure. As I shall argue, however, this intellection (which occurs for us in dialectic) is for humans a generative activity. This means that when we engage in intellection, we create or discern examples of the measure with which we are engaging. For example, the intellectual study of number forms (e.g., the three itself) tends to produce a kind of arithmetic—that is, the study of numbers as groups of "pure units"—that differs from the purely intellectual, dialectical arithmetic. Ultimately, I argue that human engagement in any science tends to produce such instances; and this "pure" paradigm serves in each case as the measure of other instances of the same science. Beyond the interest we may have in this vision of science, my aim will be to show, second, that the concept of purity in science also sheds light on purity in pleasure. The purity in pleasure is related both conceptually and experientially to the pure examples generated when we engage in the sciences.

Above all, the *Philebus*'s concept of the purity test, which decides what is included in the good life, cannot be a test applied in the exact same way without distinction across all kinds of things. The purity test must be proper to—and proportionate to—each distinct kind in question. This explains why, in the end, the test includes all sciences but only some pleasures. Even this result should be seen as charitable to pleasure, since, were it assimilated to knowledge or being, pleasure would be destroyed in its nature as becoming. Thus, in the way it demonstrates this nuanced mode of measuring that respects differences in kind, the *Philebus* ultimately teaches us another profound lesson: to understand truthfully is to understand a life in light of the purity and goodness in its own kind.

4.1. The Proposal to Seek Purity in the Sciences

At 55c Socrates approaches the last stage in the account of the elements of the good life. "Now, let us not undertake to give pleasure every possible test, while going very lightly with reason and knowledge. Let us rather strike them valiantly all around, to see if there is some fault anywhere. So we'll learn what is by nature purest in them. And, seeing this, we can use the truest parts of these, as well as of pleasure, to make our joint decision" (55c4–7). Here Socrates appeals to Protarchus's very deep-seated preference for equality. If his candidate, pleasure, has been scrutinized and even chastised at times, so too must knowledge now be scrutinized. We recall that Protarchus was "pleased by the fact that our theses are on the same footing." And only for that reason does he agree that "there can be many and unlike kinds of pleasures" (14a7–9). The name of pleasure has already been shown to apply properly to many things that are not good, that are false or deceptive.

Perhaps the examination of knowledge will prove the same thing of it? Is there bad or false science?

Despite this appeal to fairness, Socrates never promised that fair treatment means that the tests would yield parallel results.[7] Rather, the test must allow for pleasure and knowledge to be treated both equally—that is, by the same kind of test—*and* unequally—that is, as different in kind. One striking similarity between the tests resides in the way the identification of "purity" is not a criterion by which Socrates excludes things—knowledges or pleasures— from the good life. The positively false and bad pleasures were excluded after being examined individually, one by one.[8] They were not excluded due to any lack of purity. Many included were in fact impure. Rather, pure pleasure simply served to reveal the highest possibilities for pleasure's kind more broadly and to reveal that pleasure in general is worthy of a discerning care and attention. Similarly, in the case of purity in knowledge, purity, as we shall see, is not a standard of exclusion but of inclusion. The identification of the pure version of a science will also make possible the inclusion of many additional sciences—eventually all of them—in the good life. Thus, both tests will shed light on the potential goodness in the rest of their kind.

Even so, the candidates are different in kind and the purity test must respect this difference. Protarchus, by contrast, wanted each candidate to receive simplistically equal treatment because he wanted to weaken knowledge's case for being more important (13c ff.). But Protarchus's idea of equal treatment was excessively simplistic, and he had to be corrected by Socrates (14a9 ff.). In truth, it should not be surprising that Protarchus—our defender of hedonism—has a simplistic vision of fairness. Indeed, this was just the problem Plato diagnosed in the soul of the arch-hedonist—corresponding to the democratic soul—in *Republic* VIII. The democratic person cannot effectively treat unequal things as unequal:

> SOCRATES: And I suppose after he [i.e., the democratic youth] spends as much money, effort, and time on unnecessary pleasures as on necessary ones. . . . And so he lives, always surrendering rule over himself to whichever desire comes along, as if it were chosen by lot. And when that is satisfied, he surrenders the rule to another, not disdaining any but satisfying them all equally (*Republic* VIII, 561a2–b5).

Here, the problem in the soul of the hedonist is depicted through his refusal to distinguish kinds of pleasures, that is, the refusal to exclude the bad ones and prefer the good ones. "[He] declares that all pleasures are equal and must be treated equally" (*Republic* VIII, 561c2). Indeed, continues Socrates,

Sometimes he drinks heavily while listening to the flute; at other times, he drinks only water and is on a diet; sometimes he goes in for physical training; at other times he is idle and neglects everything; and sometimes he even occupies himself with what he takes to be philosophy. He often engages in politics, leaping up from his seat and saying and doing whatever comes into his mind. If he happens to admire soldiers, he's carried in that direction, if moneymakers, in that one. There's neither order nor necessity in his life, but he calls it pleasant, free, and blessedly happy, and he follows it for as long as he lives.

ADEIMANTUS: You've perfectly described the life of a man who believes in legal equality (*Republic* VIII, 561c7–e1).

Treating all pleasures equally, the hedonist cannot distinguish between pleasures but simply goes along with whatever happens to please him. Recalling the *Republic*'s running parallel between city and soul, Adeimantus thus immediately associates the hedonistic attitude with someone who is an undiscerning proponent of "legal equality." Taken to excess, this equality rule leads to the idea that chance and lots should determine who, or which activity of the soul, should govern. Socrates, of course, goes to great lengths in *Republic* IX to argue that only when the best aspects of ourselves govern do the pleasures of the choice-worthy life emerge. So too here: only when we can discern equals insofar as they are equal and unequals insofar as they are unequal—that is, only insofar as we do not treat things with a simplistic devotion to simplistic equality—does the more complex truth of fairness and equality emerge.

The *Philebus* is similar to the *Republic* here, but it also has a different purpose. For in the *Philebus* Socrates proposes not only to distinguish between versions of pleasure but also to distinguish pleasure's kind from knowledge's kind. Socrates is arguing that pure pleasure and knowledge can be both intrinsically good and yet unequal in terms of an order of priority of ontological conditions of emergence. To sustain this ongoing argument, Socrates needs to show us how purity in knowledge differs from purity in pleasure. It is therefore unsurprising that Socrates now proposes just this task. We must search for an "analogous" but not identical sense of purity in knowledge:

The aim of our discussion now seems to be, just as it was when we first set out, to find an analogue [ἀντίστροφον] here to the point we made about pleasure. So now we ought to find out [ζητῶν] whether there is [ἄρά ἐστί] a difference in purity [τις ἑτέρας ἄλλη καθαρωτέρα] between different kinds of knowledge in the same way as there was [καθάπερ] between different kinds of pleasures (57a8–b4).

Socrates's invocation of an ἀντίστροφον is important. The term does not merely mean a correlate or a sameness, although these senses are implied to some degree. Rather, it also means a converse, an inverse correlate, a responding movement by a dancer to another dancer's movement, a retort to an accusation, or generally a "turning back against." Frede's translation as "analogue" is therefore effective (though there are Greek terms perhaps more appropriately translated as analogy, such as ἀναλογία and sometimes λόγος). The important idea is the invocation of a correlate that is nevertheless importantly different, even opposite; and to treat things analogously in this sense is thus to treat them in respect of both their similarities and their differences. Thus, the larger question at stake in the forthcoming discernment of the kinds of knowledge—judged according to the standard of their purity—is a question of discerning the core sense of purity by means of discerning the difference in the senses of purity in each kind. Is there an analogy between purity in knowledge and pure pleasure in this way? The question is genuinely posed by Socrates as an ἄρά ἐστί ("Is there . . . ?"); and thus we must conduct a genuine inquiry (ζήτημα) here, a search for the core sense of purity in its different senses.[9]

4.2. Outline of the Division of Knowledge

The search for purity in knowledge begins when Socrates proposes, as his first step, a classification of different particular disciplines that use knowledge. The classification starts with a distinction between the productive and educational kinds: "Among the disciplines to do with knowledge [περὶ τὰ μαθήματα ἐπιστήμης]," says Socrates, "one part is productive [δημιουργικόν], the other concerned with education and nurture [παιδείαν καὶ τροφήν], right?" (55d1–2). Now, as I will argue here, this initial division into productive and educative is not a final separation of two completely different species; it does not disallow overlap. Socrates's point, rather, is to provide a heuristic beginning to a longer classification process. This division is not fully precise; it is a vague division that only subsequently allows us to attain a more precise understanding (57b6–58c5). And thus we begin here merely with a hope of attaining an understanding of what is "more closely related to knowledge itself [τὸ μὲν ἐπιστήμης αὐτῶν μᾶλλον ἐχόμενον]" (55d). This initial classification merely opens up the question of the inquiry: given that we can see a vague difference between these two different kinds of practices, what is the nature of this difference? What is it that makes productive arts specifically productive? Unless we begin with an initial division and a problematic inquiry in this way, no specific discovery can emerge.

The next step focuses specifically on these loosely classified "productive arts" and seeks to make a distinction within that class: "But let us first find out whether [διανοηθῶμεν . . . εἰ] within the manual arts there is one side more closely related to knowledge itself [ἐπιστήμης αὐτῶν], the other less closely; secondly, whether we should treat the one as quite pure, as far as it goes, the other as less pure" (55d3–5).[10] Here Socrates moves forward still in the mode of an inquiry and search; but the inquiry has taken a step toward greater precision. We are not concerned with productive arts per se as much as with what, within them, informs their productivity. Is there a "pure part" of the practice of engaging in productive arts that accounts for and makes possible their productivity? If so, this part will be definitive of what they are.

To clarify what it is he is seeking, Socrates says that this "pure part" will be "the thing that leads" the productivity for each of the productive arts: τὰς τοίνυν ἡγεμονικὰς διαληπτέον ἑκάστων αὐτῶν χωρίς (55d7).[11] This association of "purity" and "leading" could be taken in two different ways. For one, we might conceive of a leading art as itself a particular kind of practice among practices, just as managers have particular practices (e.g., considering the relations of several jobs) that serve to guide the practices of other workers, who have more particular practices. On the other hand, we might conceive of the leading practice as something like a theoretical basis of all the sub-practices of a trade, not a distinct practice in itself. Both the managers and the workers enact different features of one and the same leading plan. Socrates's association of "pure part" and "leading" here seems to forge a synthesis of these senses, for the leading or pure part seems to be a practice in itself and one thing distributed for "each [ἑκάστων]" art. The term "the lead [τὰς τοίνυν ἡγεμονικὰς]" in the passage can be understood as singular or plural, that is, either as what (thing) leads for each or as what (things) lead for each. The pure part can be seen, at once, as *in* all the things we are classifying and as its *own*, distinctive practice.

As Socrates makes his next division, he reveals more clearly a larger principle guiding his whole method of division: what is pure or leading within the initial class of practices is not only what informs those practices as particularly practiced; it must also be what informs our initial classification of them. As we discover the pure part in the initial set, we discover what permits us a precise gathering of the set. I will speak generally of this method momentarily. Here, the method is becoming clear specifically through the way Socrates singles out "building" as the purer part of productive arts. "Let us, then, divide the so-called arts into two parts, those like music, with less precision in their practice, and those like building [τεκτονικῇ], with more precision" (55c5). This building practice is favored, I would suggest, because it always involves to a greater or lesser extent the practices of "counting, measuring, and weighing [ἀριθμητικὴν . . . καὶ μετρητικὴν καὶ στατικήν]" (55e1). If these measuring practices were removed, then each productive art would be left with only "conjecture and training of our senses through experience and routine [ἐμπειρίᾳ καί τινι τριβῇ]," just as musical guesswork involves imprecision (55e2–56a3). Without applied mathematicity, building would be unable to provide productivity to the productive arts. The measures it uses are what informs all productivity in the class.

Now, the best way to explain Socrates's preference for building here is to keep in mind that we began the division with a focus on the productive or manual arts. This residue of this initial, vague, empirical grouping remains. We are seeking and approaching the pure and leading elements of all arts, pure or impure; but we are doing so from out of this impure heuristic starting point, that is, by analyzing what makes productivity specifically productive. And this inquiry takes Socrates to productivity's source in the applied measures used by building. Thus, it seems fair to say that he might have begun the inquiry with a different class than productivity. But, having begun with this class, he must highlight the use of measures as applied by the building practice as the source of the productivity. Without these measures, chaos would ensue.

Momentarily, Socrates will take the division even further, for even applied mathematics has a source of its own power. But first we should pause to make some observations about Socrates's general method. For what is so striking is the way he proposes to arrive at the source of knowledge through a method of division that begins from a particular classification of particular practices. Like an induction, this method begins with particulars and seeks their intelligibility. We use examples of "more or less precise" practices as the starting points for an inquiry about what within them makes them what they are. Yet, this movement is certainly not an induction. For one, Socrates's first step is not to allow his senses to be informed by features of the particulars but, instead, he engages in an active practice of delineating and defining a heuristic class that does not need to be perfectly accurate, since it serves merely as a stepping-stone in the inquiry. Furthermore, Socrates does not move from particular things—presumed to already belong to a genus—to the eventual discovery of their containment in a subspecies of that same genus. This is to say that the division of the sciences here looks much different than the subdivisions of genera in Aristotle.[12] The division proceeds not in the way of discovery of subspecies of a more inclusive genus. Rather, the initial "genus" (i.e., the initial class of "productive arts") will be surpassed later in the division. The beginning carves out a vague, less definite, and empirical classification (i.e., productivity); but we are seeking within this vague and impure class something entirely definite (i.e., the essence of precision and scientificity) that makes it what it is and gives it its character. The subsequent specifications thus do not remain within the initial class; rather, the class serves merely as a "helping" occasion for reflection on what in this group defines this group and transcends its vagaries.

Thus, in rough outline, we may depict the division as taking place in stages ascending from a group that partly contains measure-giving, to a grasp of practices that are more purely measure-giving, and finally to the measure itself that defines that measure-giving:

A ROUGH SKETCH OF THE DIVISION PROCESS

Step n: Arrive at an intellection of the *definiendum* (knowledge itself).

Step 4, 5, 6, . . . to Step [n-1]

Step 3: Next, ask: What is more pure in (a)? = Arithmetical, measuring, and weighing arts.

Step 2: Perform a heuristic classification of the still nominal *definiendum* (i.e., knowledge) according to commonly identifiable classes of instances of what the *definiendum* names. = (a) productive/manual arts versus (b) educational/supporting arts.

Step 1: Propose the nominal *definiendum* = knowledge itself.

While I will modify and complete this sketch momentarily, one bit of evidence can be used now to support it. Step 2 of the procedure involves the rough classification of knowledge into two kinds, (a) and (b). As my figure suggests, this division belongs at the "bottom" because it merely sets the starting point for the regression to the defining essence. It does not yet involve a very precise (ἀκριβής) division or understanding of knowledge as it is in itself, separately from the heuristic starting point. One could argue that the initial subject matter is actually more arbitrarily chosen than not, and that very little understanding of the desideratum (knowledge's essence) is found in this initial classification (productive arts). What is truly important is that one must actively engage for oneself in some initial division or classification, and one must seek the source within that division. The roughness of the initial division is not a problem, since this class is not *what* we are coming to know through the division, and we will not remain within its bounds.[13] This is to say that the very act of beginning must be a self-active measure-giving, and only then can it initiate in us some understanding of the element in the measure-giving practices we are classifying. For only then are we ourselves already sharing in (a still vague and unspecific) intellectual causation-of-measure. Thus, while in the early stages of the division, the standard we are using for the division is not itself very precise and neither is the subject matter we are investigating; by contrast, in the later stages *our* procedure sharpens and the subject matter *itself* becomes the precise standard itself, that is, the measure-giving practice and the measure itself that we seek.

Thus, following the method outlined here, we must once again focus on what is precise within the present class, that is, on what accounts for precise building. This element, as we already noticed, is found in its use of arithmetic, which must now be divided:

> SOCRATES: Let us, then, divide the so-called arts into two parts, those like music, with less precision in their practice, and those like building [τεκτονικῇ], with more precision. . . . And let's take those among them as most accurate that we called primary just now.
>
> PROTARCHUS: I suppose you mean arithmetic [ἀριθμητικὴν] and the other disciplines [τέχνας] you mentioned after it?
>
> SOCRATES: That's right. But don't you think we have to admit that they, too, fall into two kinds [διττὰς], Protarchus? . . . Don't we agree, first, that the arithmetic of the many [τῶν πολλῶν] is one thing, and the philosophers' [τῶν φιλοσοφούντων] arithmetic is quite another? (56c3–d3).

Must there not be some practice, in itself precise, that lies within applied measures and accounts for and enables this applied precision? Socrates responds in the affirmative, and posits that the use of "arithmetic and the other disciplines" all admit of being divided into two distinct kinds. What governs and makes possible the implementation of precise counting and measuring in (1) the various popular building fields is just (2) the more precise art of the "philosopher's arithmetic."

We will return to Socrates's description of this pure, "philosophical arithmetic" momentarily. But we should first examine the implications of this invocation of two kinds of arithmetic for the larger method of division here. For one, the divisions have heretofore been divisions according to which arts are more or less pure *as productive*. If all the subsequent divisions were required to remain within the initial genus of "productive" arts, then one would expect pure arithmetic to be limited to being the purest subspecies of productive activity. Nevertheless, this would be an inaccurate description of Socrates's whole division method. For—and this point gets lost in many interpretations of this passage—we are not ultimately seeking the more pure and leading productive arts, but rather we are using the initial classification merely as a helping aid. We are asking about what accounts for the preciseness of the precision-element in productivity; we are not asking about mere features of particular productive practices. Thus, our next division—which reveals the "pure" kind of arithmetic—clearly is not a subspecies of productive arts. We have rather arrived at a crossroads where the initial empirical classification is transcended and left behind. We have unveiled, later in the division, the element that has guided the classification up to now, insofar as there has been precision in the preceding classifications.

Thus, the larger picture of division developed here is a picture of the way that we as humans lean on empirical classifications and nominal, heuristic divisions. There may even be something "to" these initial classifications, insofar as the items in the class lend themselves imprecisely to our search. But the initial divisions we lean on cannot be allowed to govern our research; for we arrive only later at what is more certain and more clear within the initial, empirical classification. Only the later discovery ought to serve as the true guide. We are thus leaving behind the initial class rather than including the later steps in it. We are originally discovering something in the class that transcends the class but which, in being revealed, shows itself to have been all along the measure of our measuring. Thus, in general outline, the divisions, as they specify the essence of knowledge, will not become less universal but rather more universal.[14]

NARROWING SPECIFICITY (*) AND INCREASING UNIVERSALITY (<< >>)	
`<<        *        >>`	= (arrives at *most universal* and *most specific* art)
`<< * * >>`	= ground of pure arithmetic: [?]
`*<< >>*`	= ground of applied measures: pure arithmetic
`*   <<>>   *`	= ground of productive arts: applied measures
`*      <>      *`	= less universal/specific art: e.g., productive arts

While "mathematics-using (building) arts" is indeed a division of "productive arts," and it is more specific in the Platonic sense, it is nevertheless also at once more universal than the preceding class. It makes itself available even to nonproductive arts like education.[15] But it is only more universal because it is guided by a more specific, more precise science that transcends the vagueness of the original class.

This interpretation allows us to solve an important interpretive problem. For many commentators have complained that Socrates somehow inexplicably divides arts into productive and educative while later arriving at "pure arithmetic" which, they notice, should also have value for educative purposes (as the *Republic* insists), not merely productive purposes.[16] These commentators notice the essential clue in the passages. But they do not see that the initial class of productive arts is not a traditional genus. For to begin with an empirical class does not mean for Plato that one cannot subsequently discover a universal condition in the empirical class that also transcends the empirical and essentially grounds whatever degree of truth may be there in the empirical. The ground of truth in particular productive practices is a ground that also, at once, informs nonproductive practices. Our interpretation of the division can thus account for why Socrates's initial empirical classification is eventually transcended, that is, for why we began with productive as opposed to educational arts all while we arrive at a universal element that is capable of manifestation in both. The initial division is transcended because (i) it is itself a division that is heuristic; (ii) the instances of sciences it classifies have only vague knowledge and so are only quasi-sciences; and (iii) the subject matters that each instance studies are confused, mixed subject matters in themselves.

4.3. Two Kinds of Arithmetic

I have argued that pure arithmetic stands at a "crossroads" between particular scientific practices and the universal in them that accounts for their scientificity. Before examining this universal element we need to examine more closely Socrates's conception of arithmetic. For his distinction between its two kinds sheds light not only on arithmetic but also, as I will argue here, on the possibility that other sciences also admit of both pure and impure versions. The relevant passage that initiates Socrates's argument goes as follows:

> SOCRATES: Don't we have to agree, first, that the arithmetic of
> the many [τῶν πολλῶν] is one thing, and the philosophers' [τῶν
> φιλοσοφούντων] arithmetic is quite another? . . . First there are
> those who compute sums of quite unequal units [μονάδας ἀνίσους],

such as two armies or two herds of cattle, regardless of whether
they are tiny or huge. But then there are the others who would not
follow their example, unless it were guaranteed that none of those
infinitely many units [μονάδα μονάδος ἑκάστης τῶν μυρίων] dif-
fered in the least [μηδεμίαν ἄλλην ἄλλης διαφέρουσάν] from any of
the others (56d5–e4).

The imprecision of the common arithmetic stems from its treatment of
things that are in fact unequals as if they are each in themselves equally a
"unit." The Greek allows that Socrates is speaking of pairs of groups or pairs
of individuals (e.g., see "two oxen [βοῦς δύο]" at 56d9); but a comparison of
a cup and a bicycle could have served equally well. For in all cases of perceptible pairs, the things counted as a two are not each by themselves completely
equal to the other member of the pair; they are rather unequal and yet treated
as equals in being counted as a two. Socrates does not say that this practice is
bad. Rather, he simply suggests here that it is in truth guided by a purer version of the counting science, a counting wherein each member of the count
must be precisely a unit that is equal to each other member of the count.[17]
    In order to explore some of the difficulties in thinking of numbers as
groups of pure units in this way, it will be helpful to address interpretations
of this passage that find hints of the supposedly unwritten doctrines of Plato
in it. Such reconstructions of the unwritten Plato often give supreme importance to number theory; and they draw in particular from Aristotle, who
appears in *Metaphysics* M and N to engage in a fierce debate with something akin to Plato's position in this passage.[18] Succinctly, we may note that
there Aristotle creates a kind of dilemma between two possible but, in his
view, equally unacceptable interpretations of number theory. He examines
two distinct ways of interpreting the thesis that numbers consist of "identical units." To paraphrase Aristotle's argument, numbers, on the one hand,
might consist of units that are shared with all numbers alike, and which can
therefore be used in mathematical procedures such as adding: two pure units
plus three pure units equals five pure units. If so, then the units of a number
are not in fact "specific" to that given number. The two units of the two-group
are the same kind of units as the three units of the three-group. Indeed, they
must be the same, says Aristotle, if they are to be added together; otherwise
it is as if we would be adding apples to oranges. If, however, this theory were
true, Aristotle argues—and thus if each number consists of the same kind of
identical units, identical to one another (i.e., the same in kind with all other
units making up each other number)—then the units of "the three itself"
would not be specifically different from the units of "the two itself." But if

this were true, then it would mean that the very specific difference between the form two itself (and its essential evenness) and the form three itself (and its essential oddness) would be abolished, for each would then be nothing but a particular aggregate of the same kind of thing. Each number would be merely a quantitatively different but generically identical number group; and each group would be nothing different in kind from each other group. Formally distinct essences (differing not only as two versus three but also as even versus odd) would thereby be rendered indistinct. If, on the other hand, in order to avoid such a conclusion (which would abolish genuinely distinct forms for the two and the three and, by implication, between dog itself and stone itself, etc.) one were to posit that there are forms for two and for three which either (i) contain no "units" at all, or which (ii) contain only units which are "proper" to each form (i.e., the two units of "the two" are not universal but are particular to "the two"), then those numbers, in either case, could not in fact be used in mathematical procedures such as adding. For the form two itself and the form three itself clearly cannot be added (since they are distinct in kind), since that would be like adding apples to oranges. Nor can a set of "special," two-styled units be added to a set of "special," three-styled units; for then again one would be, so to speak, adding apple-units to orange-units.[19]

The whole dilemma appears specifically designed to point out difficulties with the Platonic position in the "two arithmetics" passage of the *Philebus*. Even so, we may notice that our brief *Philebus* passage does not by itself present a particular interpretation that would lend itself to either of Aristotle's two options. That is, first, Socrates does not say that the three itself (i.e., the form) is identical to the pure unit groups. He does not claim it is the direct study of number itself, such as that study practiced briefly in the *Phaedo*'s final argument (96a–107e). It is much more plausible—and I will defend this position momentarily—that the philosophical arithmetic of pure units is in fact taken by Socrates to be a manifestation or projection—something akin to what Proclus calls a προβολή—that is derived from the philosopher's prior dialectical understanding of separate and distinct number forms, an understanding that has priority over even this pure unit arithmetic.[20] Pure unit arithmetic will remain, while better than common counting, a science that is still derivative of a prior dialectical arithmology. If so, then whatever Socrates is saying about numbers in our passage, we do not need to interpret him to be saying that the form of three itself consists of units of any kind. Thus, he will not fall into Aristotle's problem of having to decide whether those formal units are either, for one, specific to and different for each number form or, alternatively, the same in kind for all number forms. Thus, while I do think Aristotle's point is in conversation with the *Philebus*, I do not think it can be taken as a direct criticism of it. For if the Platonists' numbers are in themselves separate from the units into which they get "projected," then the *Philebus*'s account is not grappling with the problem of units serving as supposed "constituent elements" of numbers themselves. Rather, it is projecting a level of arithmetical science that resides "below" dialectical arithmology and depends on its prior intellectual insights.

Here, I think it is also helpful to recall *Republic* VII's parallel account of arithmeticians who insist that the units of numbers are indivisible and objects of thought (διάνοια), not of sight. For thought itself is said there to be derivative of a higher insight:

> SOCRATES: You know what those who are clever in these matters are like: If, in the course of the argument, someone tries to divide the one itself, they laugh and won't permit it. If you divide it, they multiply it, taking care that one thing never be found to be many parts rather than one. . . . Then what do you think would happen, Glaucon, if one were to ask them: "What kinds of numbers are you talking about, in which the one is as you assume it to be, each one equal to every other, without the least difference and containing no internal parts?"

> GLAUCON: I think they'd answer that they are talking about those numbers that can be grasped only in thought [διανοηθῆναι] and can't be dealt with in any other way (*Republic* VII, 525d3–526a9).

The proponents of arithmetic here insist that their units are "partless," unlike the things of the world of sense. Also, unlike visible things, they are accessible only in thought (διανόησις). Now, *Republic* VI's "divided line" famously places thought (διάνοια) and its objects one step below intellection or reason (νόησις) (509d ff.). Further, book VII later returns to the theme of the divided line and draws out a revealing formal analogy: the (a) "mathematical" disciplines (μαθήματα) are to (b) knowledge of being (or the forms), which is called dialectic or νόησις, as (c) image-thinking (εἰκασία) about shadows or reflections of visible things is to (d) belief (πίστις) about visible things (534a5–7). The forms themselves transcend and ground all other objects of study (476c7 ff.; 509d ff.); and thus dialectic transcends all the other disciplines (μαθήματα), though it is itself the "highest discipline or lesson [τὸ μάθημα . . . μέγιστον]" (519c8). While there is, of course, much controversy concerning the exact status of the "mathematical objects" in the *Republic*,

Socrates's analogy above with belief and image-thinking clearly suggests that, while διάνοια does indeed have some grasp of the forms, nevertheless it studies them in a fashion analogous to the way one might study a physical object by studying or constructing an image of that object. Thus, dialectical science is higher than διάνοια and its objects are higher than the objects of thought; the latter are in some sense derivative of the former. This priority of dialectic follows, as I will suggest momentarily, from the greater justice implied in dialectic's understanding of forms (including the understanding of number forms such as the two itself).

Before turning to dialectic, however, it will help to reflect on another feature of the "two arithmetics" passage in light of this reading of it as derivative. For this passage can be linked to Socrates's claim at *Philebus* 57b4–b9 that the disciplines each have one name that applies to different cases of the discipline: "Have we not discovered before that different subject matters require different arts and they have different degrees of certainty. . . . It is questionable, then, whether an art that goes under one name and is commonly treated as one should not rather be treated as two, depending on the difference in certainty and purity" (57b6–c1). The most evident point here is that we have just called arithmetic by a single name, all while we have also now revealed its nature to be two. That is, arithmetic is a name belonging properly to pure unit arithmetic but it also applies to the common arithmetic. Socrates thus generously allows the name to be applied even to the impure art.

This generosity can be explained, I believe, by the fact that, as we have seen, pure arithmetic is not merely a particular, distinctive practice undertaken by philosophically minded arithmeticians; it is also a pure principle implicitly assumed by and found within all other arithmetical practices insofar as they are arithmetical at all. The impure counter of impure sensible things must posit that the object counted is a unit like the other members of the count. But this positing in fact presupposes a capacity to project a number form, such as the two, as if it is a group of pure units. The impure counter is already doing this when he or she grasps each member as if it is a unit. Because this pure practice of projection—at least its possibility and power—lies within the other impure practices of counting, it follows that the name of arithmetic can indeed be properly applied to both cases, pure and impure. Thus, we can call pure arithmetic paradigmatic: it serves as a kind of advocate for the impure versions of the sciences. The example of pure arithmetic, as sharing its name truthfully with the impure, sheds light on the nature of the impure versions. It shows that there is a pure arithmetical ability implied even in the impure counting of fingers, cups, armies, or flocks. The impure cases simply mix the pure power into the impure.

In this respect, the passage is striking when compared to *Republic* book I's suggestion that the practitioner of an art is only properly a practitioner of that art if indeed he or she fulfills its essential definition (342a ff.). Doctoring, for example, is the bringing of health to deficient bodies. A "so-called" doctor, who actually practices in such a way that harms the patient, would not in fact be a doctor at that instant or in that respect. The proper use of the name "doctor" derives from what it is to doctor, not from a person's or a group's activities. If one takes the name to be derived from a particular person's activities, or takes it primarily to apply to what a particular person does, then one might confuse, as did Thrasymachus, someone who makes a lot of money or looks through a scope into a patient's throat with being "what it is to doctor." In short, a so-called bad doctor is, in respect of the so-called bad doctoring, really just a non-doctor, that is, not a doctor at all in that respect. Only the one who knows health and brings it to a needy body "counts" as doctoring; and this form alone serves as the measure of any "count-as-doctoring."[21] Now, while this passage would seem to imply that Socrates wants to exclude impure doctoring, impure arithmetic, and so on from counting as doctoring or arithmetic, this is not so. For Socrates very soon adds that an art such as doctoring might still mix out of necessity with other practices like moneymaking. But this fact of mixing does not by itself make the moneymaking-doctor into someone who is not a doctor (347a ff.). A person whose practice is firstly to doctor, but who also makes money, is still accurately counted-as-doctor. In short: the impure versions still count, so long as the essence of the practice is indeed still manifest in the activity.

So too in the *Philebus*: in allowing for even impure arithmetic to be properly counted as arithmetic, Socrates allows that the impure practices of arithmetic remain to some degree "just" in treating of their objects. Even in this impure practice an impure counter could always discern, if he or she were attentive, what it would be for the counted members to be true equals. Certainly, the impure counter counts more confusedly; and the counted objects are in truth mixed with their opposites (since each sensible unit is always also a non-unit). But the count still counts as a count; and all the counts are rightly named "arithmetic." So too with every art: the impure building still counts as building, doctoring, or counting, and so on so long as the essence of the practice is still there.

Finally, as I have already hinted with my references to arts like doctoring, Socrates does not think that arithmetic is alone in admitting that one name names two versions. In fact, Socrates explicitly says that several studies will admit of the division into pure and impure instances: "But don't you think we have to admit that they, too, fall into two kinds, Protarchus?" (56d1–2).

The "they" here refers back to "counting, measuring, and weighing." Each of those arts admits, Socrates says, of pure and impure cases. Thus, the case of pure arithmetic is once again a paradigm. It "stands for" a possible pure counting, certainly, but also for more: for a possible pure measuring, and a possible pure weighing.[22] And, if that were not enough, Socrates later adds that just as "there are two kinds of arithmetic and two kinds of geometry," so too are there "a great many other sciences following in their lead, which have the same twofold nature while sharing in one name" (57d5–7). Thus, the example of arithmetic and the other two arts can be applied, analogously, to many others. This means, I would suggest, not that we must simply apply the results of the study of number forms to the study of, say, a lion, as if the latter study were a mode of arithmetic. The lion should not be understood to contain "pure units" in any literal sense. Rather, the point is that we can perform an analogous inquiry in that different scientific field just as we have inquired into the dual nature of arithmetic. For example, there are objects studied by geometry that follow from the forms it studies; these objects are definitely and purely "line" or "plane" (and not indefinitely so as in the empirical measuring of things). Yet both kinds of the science of geometry—pure and impure instances—deserve the name. The same could apply to lion-ology, blue-ology, and quark-ology. Each admits of a pure, intermediate, instantiated version of itself, that is, a version that mediates between mere empirical classifications, on the one hand, and intellectual insight into the forms themselves, on the other hand.

If this is so, then Socrates's purpose is not at all to make all sciences "quantitative." Rather, his thesis is far less modern and far more explosive. For if the division of the arts proceeds upwards toward the more specific and more universal science, then to arrive at the most specific division is also at once to transcend the material containment of the empirical classification performed at the starting point (e.g., the division into "productive" versus "educative"). Now, having attained the standpoint of pure arithmetic in our division, we reach a model that is relevant to and presupposed implicitly not only by production but also by non-production, for example, by education and presumably by other possible heuristic classes. Each art or inquiry can achieve, or derive, this pure, mediating instance that *communicates* the formal with the empirical. Certainly, Socrates does not explain how each case would work. And he clearly wants to contrast favorably the sciences like pure music with, for example, the merely empirical, experimental practice of "guesstimating" in musical composition. (56a2). Yet, Socrates also seems to notice that such impure constructions are always implicitly able to indicate to us that a pure mode of comprehension and construction is possible for them as well.

This thesis explains why the *Philebus* ultimately allows each and every science into the good life, both pure and impure ones. It can do so precisely because every version of each scientific practice worthy of the name shares to some degree in the intellection of appropriate forms. Even the impure instances are "spoken for" by the very possibility of the pure instance. If this is so, then Socrates can be understood to offer a generalizable model wherein the single name of a given science, deriving from the form it studies, always also applies to a possible dyad of science-instances (pure and impure). We might depict this relationship as follows:

The Naming of the Sciences

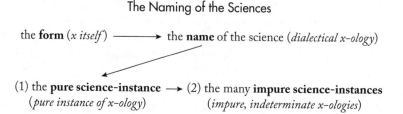

the **form** (*x itself*) ⟶ the **name** of the science (*dialectical x-ology*)

(1) the **pure science-instance** ⟶ (2) the many **impure science-instances**
(*pure instance of x-ology*)　　　　(*impure, indeterminate x-ologies*)

Whether or not the pure instances of each science have yet arisen in this world of becoming is beside the point. We have one such example in the case of pure unit arithmetic, and the possibility of others is enough to encourage us in our scientific practices, even if, at any given stage, we have only so far discovered more or less impure versions. In all cases, this pure possibility is empowering: in arithmetic, we study the relation of seven to odd but we can also project the forms five and seven as units and carry out the pure, a priori synthesis that discovers in this projection the sum number that instantiates the evenness of the twelve. Similarly, one who understands physics projects models from the understanding of certain forms, and these models frame and shed light on the work done in experiments. When the pure instance—as much as we can attain it—shines upon and stands for what is good and true in the many impure sciences, all these remnant sciences can then also be included in the good life. Each is included in its individuality, since each of them is "spoken for" by the pure. The pure version is a distinct practice in itself, different from the impure versions, since it can be conducted purely by itself, for example by a thinker who counts units in thought, not in sight. Yet the pure version also resides as a power even in the many impure versions. For like them it is an instance or example of that science, and it is not dialectical *X*-ology itself. This double heritage allows the pure to stand for and represent the impure.

Before concluding, we must acknowledge a potential drawback to philosophical arithmetic and its analogues for each science, a drawback stemming from their position as non-dialectical. The arithmetic of pure units, which we have called the "pure instance" of arithmetical science, studies innumerable (μυρίος), indistinguishable units.[23] This characteristic perhaps makes this model unsuited, in one respect, to serve as the advocate and representative of the other, impure sciences. For those other instances of a science must grapple with things that are different from one another in infinities of ways, as this cup differs from that army, that cup, or that lion. In this respect, each "pure unit" stands for the impure only insofar as there is indeed purity implied in the impure. Philosophical arithmetic could thus appear to the impure instances as an alienating paradigm. For its presence—while good in itself—is precisely what reveals the lack and impurity in the impure instances. It does not cause them to lack, but it does reveal to them their lack. Thus, philosophical arithmetic and its analogues really reside at a crossroads between being well-suited to stand for and advocate for the goodness of each science and *appearing* as alienating in that role.

Indeed, an argument could even be made that philosophical arithmetic really is different from a truly just "counting." For, first, by treating all things it studies as equally units, it posits that unity is not unique but is rather found everywhere, endlessly (μυρίως). It thereby represents the uniqueness of the unit only in positing it as non-unique. Second, if pure arithmetic is asked what the two itself is, for example, then its practitioner posits (τιθέναι at 56e3) a two-group consisting of identical units. Thus, whatever it studies it always homogenizes; it always treats the distinct form through the medium of a field of "sames." Thus, it cannot be said to be a direct study of forms; it merely represents each form. By contrast, dialectic, as a direct formal study, knows that what is odd cannot be what is even, and that two is wholly even, three wholly odd. Two and three are not the same in kind, even if they can be projected to be as such. There is thus a science superior to this pure unit arithmetic, that is, the science of dialectic, which studies each form as its own kind in relation to others, without treating it as projected into a field of homogeneity.[24]

We should respond to this discovery of the superior science not by abandoning "philosophical arithmetic" and its analogues but by emphasizing their importance in a mediating role. Their arrival reveals to us that the impure sciences are impure, yes. But they also initiate in us a recognition that a higher, dialectical science is possible. Without their presence, we might fall prey to taking the impure, empirical studies of sensuous things to be in themselves definitive of scientific practice. Or, even if we were to recognize the difference between forms and sensuous things, without the mediation of the pure instance we might despair of ever understanding the human import of forms.

In the *Phaedo*, for example, number forms were posited simply as partici-pable, separate essences just like beauty itself. The two itself is neither a unit divided nor a unit doubled.[25] But this positing left those forms seemingly separate and without mediation with instantiations, which were seemingly treated as one and all impure. What is clear in the *Philebus* is that philosoph-ical arithmetic has a special status as a mediator. It offers the opportunity of a shared, common space not only between the heterogeneous forms but also between forms and sensibility. It mediates so well because it never calls attention to itself per se but rather trains us to see beyond itself. By present-ing "partial" sciences in purified form, it reveals itself to be a passage to a more "whole" science. Through it, we glimpse the possibility of dialectic. And certainly dialectic itself must do more than what is done by the pure instance. For dialectic alone knows that while pairs are perhaps countable "as if" they are built of homogeneous units, a science capable of counting them as dyadic pairs, insofar as they are dyadic, is more just. To account for the two as two, being as being, one as one, quark as quark, city as city, and square as square: this is the prerogative, and the goal, of dialectical science. It must always humble and correct the "as ifs" of the very helpful but still limited, projective, pure instances of science. Thus, while philosophical arithmeticians are "infi-nitely superior . . . in precision and truth in their use of measure and number" when compared to the common counting (57d2–3), nevertheless philosophi-cal arithmetic must itself be grounded in a greater and purer understanding of truths. "The power of dialectic," Socrates insists, "would repudiate us if we put any other science ahead of her" (57e6).

4.4. Dialectic as the Leading Science

Dialectic has to be committed to accounting for each thing itself and not only for each as it can be manifest through a pure medium or modeling. While this demand to discern each reality was in chapter 1 expressed in terms of discovering the being for each posited unity by way of discovering an "intermediate," here dialectic is treated in light of the direct intellec-tion (ἔννοια or νόησις) of each being that it affords. The learning procedure remains essential to the dialectical procedure. But we now learn that dialectic takes its meaning first and foremost from the way it harbors intellection.

Socrates's statements on dialectic are sparse, but he is clear in his pre-sentation of dialectic as the superior art or science. The account begins with familiar terms, defining dialectic's object through several related expressions: "[Anyone] with any share in reason at all would consider the discipline con-cerned with being [τὸ ὄν] and with what is really [καὶ τὸ ὄντως] and forever in every way eternally self-same [καὶ τὸ κατὰ ταὐτὸν ἀεὶ πεφυκὸς πάντως] by far the truest of all kinds of knowledge" (58a2–4). Given the continuous and explicative double use of καὶ in line 58a3, it is clear that these various ways of saying "being" gloss one another. Further, the ταὐτὸν in the third expression recalls other explicit forms passages (e.g., the "αὐτὸ ὃ ἔστιν ἕκαστον" of *Republic* 531a8), and it can be taken as an abbreviation of such expressions.[26] The familiar terminology for the forms here thus speaks against any "revisionist" interpretation of these passages.[27] Indeed, the distinction between being and becoming and between knowledge and opinion is as stark here as it is in any dialogue:

> SOCRATES: [Did] you realize that most of the arts [αἱ πολλαὶ τέχναι] . . . and those who work at them are in the first place only concerned with opinions [δόξαις] and make opinions the center of their search? For even if they think they are studying nature, you must realize that all their lives they are merely dealing with this world order [τὸν κόσμον τόνδε], how it came to be [γέγονεν], how it is affected [πάσχει], and how it acts [ποιεῖ]? . . . So such a person assumes the task of dealing, not with things eternal [τὰ ὄντα ἀεί], but with what comes to be, will come to be, or has come to be [γιγνόμενα καὶ γενησόμενα καὶ γεγονότα]?
>
> PROTARCHUS: Undeniably.
>
> SOCRATES: So how could we assert anything definite about these matters with exact truth [τῇ ἀκριβεστάτῃ ἀληθείᾳ] if it never did possess nor will possess nor now possesses any kind of sameness [ταὐτὰ]? . . . And how could we ever hope to achieve any kind of certainty [βεβαιότητα] about subject matters that do not in themselves possess any certainty [βέβαιον]?
>
> PROTARCHUS: I see no way.
>
> SOCRATES: Then there can be no reason or knowledge [οὐδ' ἄρα νοῦς οὐδέ τις ἐπιστήμη] that attains the highest truth [τὸ ἀληθέστατον] about these subjects (58e8–59b6).

Here, dialectic is contrasted with "the many" arts and sciences, which are concerned primarily with opinions. Opinions are concerned with this world order and with its various modes of becoming, that is, "γιγνόμενα καὶ γενησόμενα καὶ γεγονότα." Such a subject matter does not in itself possess any self-identity. It is intrinsically unstable and no knowledge can attain the "highest truth [τὸ ἀληθέστατον]" about intrinsically unstable things. Hardly a clearer statement could be adduced for reconfirming the distinctness of the objects of science from things that become.

Even so, as several commentators have noticed, Socrates says here that reason does not attain the "highest truth [τὸ ἀληθέστατον]" about things that become.[28] This language seems to suggest that truth in becoming can be attained somehow. While this idea coincides with my own argument that pure pleasures become and they attain truth, some commentators take Socrates to be claiming more here, namely that a kind of *knowledge* attains truth about becoming. Indeed, Socrates comes close to suggesting as much in one passage:

> SOCRATES: Either we will find certainty, purity, and truth, and what we may call integrity among the things that are forever in the same state, without anything mixed in [περὶ τὰ ἀεὶ κατὰ αὐτὰ ὡσαύτως ἀμεικτότατα ἔχοντα], or we will find it in what comes as close as possible to it [ἢ δεύτερος ἐκείνων ὅτι μάλιστά ἐστι συγγενές]. Everything else has to be called second-rate and inferior (59c1–6).

Controversy surrounds the way Socrates says that "certainty, purity, and truth" may apply also to what concerns itself with what is "of a like kind [συγγενές]" with being.[29] Now, even if "of a like kind" refers to "true opinions" about becoming, we need not assume Socrates means anything more than that true opinions about becoming follow from the science's presence in soul. Reason can have some relationship with becoming and opinion, that is, a relationship of guide to follower. Measure is imported by intellection-of-being into opinions. Indeed, this presence makes it a "true" opinion, while the changeable nature of the true opinion and its changing object make it "opinion."[30] This certainty in what is "like being" is thus a certainty regarding the trace of measure within the opinion or the trace of being within the becoming. If patterns appear to emerge in the world, for example, then they can only be noticed as patterns if first their measuring ground is grasped by intellect. Thus, Socrates is very clear that "reason and wisdom [νοῦς ἐστι καὶ φρόνησις]" are names most properly applied to "insights into true reality [τὸ ὂν ὄντως ἐννοίαις]" (59c8–d4).[31] And thus, while the term ἐπιστήμη (e.g., at 58c1) may apply broadly and adjectivally to what in effect contains traces of intellection (and we can call this an "epistemic opinion"), there is in fact a more precise name for the insight and the element of knowledge itself.[32] The doctor's art is grounded in a grasp of health, and the term "doctor" should always remind us first of what-it-is-to-doctor (i.e., to know and implement health), not of one who looks through scopes. So too should the term ἐπιστήμη always lead us to recall that science is science only by virtue of a prior intellection-of-being. Precise justice in naming thus demands that, while the name "scientific" can apply to science's effects, we should nevertheless use a precise name for the actual intellectual act: νόησις.

Now this intellection arises for humans as we use reason in dialectic, and dialectic thus remains the first discipline for us because of the intellection it presences (57e6). But intellection is not itself a discipline in competition with the others. Intellection can be separate from the impure sciences which it in effect defines as scientific due to its presence in them. But those disciplines, by contrast, cannot be separate from intellection while remaining sciences. The trace of intellection is what lies within each discipline properly called a discipline, including dialectic. The form discovered thus comes to light for us amidst the dialectical conversations that express the form as a many and find in the many the unity of an intellection. But dialectic does not demand that the name of "science" be given only to itself. Rather, dialectic grasps the way intellection is borne by many bearers, that is, by dialectic, by pure science instances, and even by impure instances. Dialectic is thus the specific method (ἡ διαλεκτικὴ μέθοδος) that can salvage *all* these instances of every science, for it is the practice that can devote itself not only to the study of each form but also to considering every mode of each science. It can do this precisely because it is conscious of the stages of the distribution of intellection in all varieties of fragmentary instances of knowing awareness.[33] It detects a trace of the measure imported by reason in all levels of knowing life. It is therefore most fair and just in its own scientific practice.

This prioritization of dialectic—and its transcendence of the other disciplines—is likewise affirmed in the *Republic*. There, Socrates says, "[Whenever] someone tries through argument and apart from all sense perceptions to find the being itself of each thing [αὐτὸ ὃ ἔστιν ἕκαστον] and doesn't give up until he grasps the good itself with understanding itself, he reaches the end of the intelligible" (*Republic* VII, 532a1–b2). Dialectic grasps "the being of each thing itself." The disciplines of pure arithmetic, pure geometry, pure solids science, and pure science of things in motion, by contrast, were given great honor in the *Republic*, but only as "helpers and cooperators [συνερίθοις καὶ συμπεριαγωγοῖς]" (533d3).[34] They are beneficial only because they turn the soul to the dialectical study of the good. They are conditional supports that dialectic "leans on" for drawing us up to its insight.

In the *Philebus* these helpful, pure instances of science remain at this threshold of communication between realms. Yet dialectical exercise is the basis even of those disciplines. Its priority is in the way it directly harbors the intellection that gives the many sciences their scientific character. Any science can be practiced dialectically because, as a science, it contains a trace of an insight discoverable and rediscoverable in dialectic. This explains why all the sciences must be preserved in the end, for they all are indicators of what dialectic can bring to life. Thus, dialectic is at once informative of and regenerative of other disciplines. This generativity is an essential nourishment for us.[35] Without this support we might fail to recognize the intellectual ability available to each and all. But through this generativity we surprise ourselves by revealing to ourselves the ever-available power to know, even in the impure practices in which we engage. The pure instance reveals to us our prior unawareness of this intellectual power, but only by first bringing us to awareness of it. It reveals to us the limits of our present human knowledge, but only by first offering us a share in the intellection of things themselves.[36]

4.5. The Concept of Purity

We must now collect the senses of "purity" we have explored so far and draw out their core sense. To do so, however, we must first touch on an interpretive issue that arises from the previous section's discussion of dialectic. For I have described philosophical arithmetic as "pure" because its objects are units rather than indefinite things. There is certainly support in Socrates's language for this imputation of purity to pure arithmetic: "It is questionable then whether an art . . . commonly treated as one should not be rather treated as two, depending on the difference in certainty and purity [τὸ σαφὲς καὶ τὸ καθαρὸν]" (57c1–2). Yet, while I have suggested that there is a strong analogy between pure arithmetic and pure pleasure—and others have also noticed this analogy[37]—this claim is complicated by Socrates's use of "pure" when speaking of dialectic as well:

> But as to the discipline I am talking about now, what I said earlier
> [in the account of pure pleasure] about the white also applies in
> this case: Even in small quantity it can be superior in purity and
> truth [καθαρὸν . . . τῷ ἀληθεστάτῳ] to what is large in quantity
> but impure and untrue. We must look for this science without
> concern for its actual benefit or its prestige, but see whether it is by
> its nature a capacity in our soul to love the truth [τις πέφυκε τῆς
> ψυχῆς ἡμῶν δύναμις ἐρᾶν τε τοῦ ἀληθοῦς] and to do everything

for its sake [καὶ πάντα ἕνεκα τούτου πράττειν]. And if thorough
reflection and sufficient discussion confirms this for our art, then
we can say it is most likely to possess purity of mind and reason [τὸ
καθαρὸν νοῦ τε καὶ φρονήσεως]. Otherwise we would have to look
for a higher kind of knowledge than this (59b9–d9).

In this passage, dialectic and not pure arithmetic is the "pure" science. The
analogue or ἀντίστροφον of pure pleasure would therefore be the dialectical
science and not the philosopher's arithmetic. Which science has a claim to
the title of the "pure" science?

In response, I would suggest that there are perhaps two senses of purity
here, with one of them being primary. If we look back at the description of pure instances, Socrates is careful to call them "infinitely superior
[ἀμήχανον . . . διαφέρουσιν] . . . in precision and truth in their use of measure
and number" (57d1–2). This language of differing degrees is also reflected
in all of the other passages in that section: "Have we not discovered before
that different subject matters require different arts and that they have different degrees of certainty?" (57b5–6). And: "We must also ask whether the
art has more precision in the hands of the philosopher than its counterpart
in the hands of the nonphilosopher" (57c3–3). In all cases, the language is
decidedly comparative. Even when the superlative is invoked, it remains a
superlative "in comparison with. . . ."

The passages on dialectic above, by contrast, are more assertive of a positive, non-comparative, and non-superlative (in the sense above) notion of
purity. The comparison with pure white there does not merely express the
idea of "non-admixture" but rather suggests that quantity is irrelevant to
whether something has sufficient truth (58d1). This is to say that dialectic's
purity is not in itself comparative in any way—quantitatively or otherwise—
and it does not need to be measured as the superlative "over" something else.
It differs from rhetoric, for example, not by exceeding it in the same kind of
study but by conducting a wholly different kind of study, that is, the study of
the form itself in its "greatest degree of truth" (58c1–2). The positive notion
of purity in dialectic, therefore, is not arrived at through comparison with
another science, nor is its value measured by calculations regarding its results
or usefulness. It compares itself only with the objects it studies, and only
one who knows those objects can discern where the purity of dialectic is
truly found.

Two senses of purity in science thus emerge. For pure arithmetic emerges
as having a maximal kind of comparative purity; it is "purest" among
instances.[38] The concept of purity in dialectic, however, must be understood

as the source and precondition of any other purity, for it is measured only by the criterion of the unconcealment of what each thing itself really is. Neither the most comparatively great expert, nor the most powerful authority, nor the most experienced practitioner measures this purity. Only the form itself is that measure, and all the instances of study—even the best and purest instances—are judged and measured by the standard of each form in question. This conception of dialectical "purity" thus concludes our search for a conceptual core, for it reveals that dialectical purity contains the core sense we have been seeking. For it harbors for us the intellection of the measure itself and thus serves as the basis for every other sense of purity.

This conclusion allows us to close by collecting three ways in which the use of this core concept of purity differs in the cases of science and pleasure. First, pure pleasure is the pure and true version of pleasure, but not all pleasure contains this purity. The purity of science, by contrast, is the transcendent essence of all sciences that is also immanently present in every science to a degree (if that science is a science). Pure pleasure is decidedly not present in any and all pleasures, simply insofar as they emerge as pleasing. For some of them are utterly false and follow from vice. Rather, pure pleasure distances itself from the rest of the pleasures and stands out as having a character that is not immanent in the rest. Pure pleasure transcends the constraints—that is, the boundless unconstraint—of its own kind, thus emerging as a truly measured and excellent version of a thing of its kind. Other things with its nature are indeed properly called "pleasures"; but they do not have purity or complete goodness in them. Pure intellection, by contrast, is present in any science as science. Otherwise, that science is only falsely called science. However, like pure science, pure pleasure stands for what all pleasures can *potentially* be. It stands for the "highest possibilities" of its class—that is, the possibility of being characterized by order and measure, not the chaotic indefiniteness intrinsic to its natural kind. In short, pure pleasure is a pleasure that is able to be other than what it is as it is given by nature, and that (i.e., not what it is as it is given by nature) is the best thing for it to be. It is an ongoing transformation of a nature, in a nature. It is a becoming that is coming to be more than its own nature. In the case of pleasure, purity thus means being immanent in its class—it, like all pleasures, always becomes and never exactly is—and yet purity of pleasure also means being wholly self-separating from its class, for it is measured and pure. By contrast, in science purity means, primarily, being originally separate from any given kind (as reason/intellection is transcendent of any class) while also at once being manifest in each and every science (if it is a science) as what makes that science scientific.

Second, the discovery of purity in pleasure follows the analysis of various false pleasures which are eventually excluded from the good life because they are positively bad. In science, we also began with examining the impure. But the discovery of pure science reveals here that all sciences, properly so called, are already bound to be included in the good life, precisely because, being sciences, they always already imply the purity required. They all presuppose a prior intellectual power. This source grounds them all and they all have a trace of its purity in them, if they are sciences. By contrast, we have seen why the purity of pleasure does not lead to the inclusion of all pleasures. Pleasure in the dialogue stands for that kind of thing only some of which will join in the measuredness of the good life.

Third, whereas the discovery of purity in science could be conceived as the discovery of the constitutive essence of each and every "scientific" activity, the discovery of purity in pleasure is more akin to a refinement process. Pleasure emerges for the soul when the necessary but non-sufficient conditions for possible anxiety and pain (i.e., lack, need, deficiency, etc.) are removed through fulfillment and the soul is aware of this process. In a measureless world we would find such need, poverty, and lack—as well as responding fulfillments—in boundless and infinite supply. Thus, while pleasures—even the most extreme pleasures—could emerge in such a world, pure pleasure could not emerge there at all. Pure pleasure depends on the prior operation of reason and the presence of the measure it imports into the soul. Without reason, we would endlessly self-propagate our neediness by seeking a "more" that always brings along a "less," and thus we would, in the extreme, become "leaky jars." Pure pleasure, by contrast, occurs only when reason offers measure to the lowest strata of the psyche, even to what would otherwise be a completely indefinite nature buried deep within the overall mixture of the soul. Only some of this indefinite nature in fact follows measure and thus emerges into the definition offered it. Thus, the discovery of pure pleasure is the discovery—or the creation for oneself—of a refined, exemplary case unlike the rest, that is, one that, in its exemplarity, invites the remnant to follow as well. It therefore is not the essence of pleasure; it shines forth as what, in its difference from the type, invites the type to become a good version of itself.

Thus, we have indeed discovered in the sciences an analogue (ἀντίστροφον) of pure pleasure, but not an identical sense of purity. These different senses arise due to the fact that knowledge and pleasure are ontologically distinct in kind. The major effect of this difference is manifest here: while there is no science—only non-science—where intellection is absent, by contrast only some of what is properly called a pleasure really manifests the purity of the measure imported by intellect. The other pleasures please us impurely or falsely. While the senses are thus different, both senses are grounded in measure, or the good itself, and thus they are not equivocal.

Finally, we must close by showing that there is in fact more than a merely *conceptual* link between pure pleasure and purity in science. There is also a real, *experiential* link between them. For just as pure arithmetic is a manifestation of intellection into an immanent field of identical units, so too is pure pleasure something that emerges from soul's experience with such a pure manifestation, that is, with something that draws the soul to intellection. Evidence for this link between pure pleasure and expressive encounters can be found in a passage we have yet to analyze where Socrates describes the sensible pure pleasures as arising from "figures" constructed purely:

> PROTARCHUS: But, Socrates, what are the kinds of pleasures that one could rightly regard as true?
>
> SOCRATES: Those that are related to so-called pure colors and to shapes and to most smells and sounds and in general all those that are based on imperceptible and painless lacks, while their fulfillments are perceptible and pleasant. . . . What I am saying may not be entirely clear straightaway, but I'll try to clarify it. By the beauty of a shape [σχημάτων], I do not mean what the many might presuppose, namely that of a living being or of a picture. What I mean, what the argument demands, is rather something straight or round and what is constructed [γιγνόμενα] out of these with a compass, rule, and square, such as plane figures and solids. Those things I take it are not beautiful in a relative sense [πρός τι καλὰ], as others are, but are by their very nature forever beautiful by themselves [ἀεὶ καλὰ καθ᾽ αὑτὰ πεφυκέναι]? (51b1–c9).

The pure pleasures taken in the visible world arise from σχήματα made from the use of precision instruments. Why would Socrates find such beauty in these schemata? This passage can be explained, I think, if we understand them to symbolize, in sensuous format, the very idea of the actual importation of measure. They emerge as a public, sensuous fact offering a trace of evidence of prior intellection. Such an introduction of measure—as we saw when analyzing the precision in productivity—presupposes that a prior grasp of the source of that precision is possible. Thus, we need not assume that Socrates finds beauty in these sensuous schemata because he passively experiences better vibes from them than he does from, say, a sunset. Rather, he judges them purely and sensuously pleasant just insofar as they exhibit the idea and the very possibility that measure can come to be in descending strata of existence and that we too can share in generating this emergence. The sensuous schemata thus convey and symbolize this love of measure, this love of the good's power to bring-to-presence each thing's own proper measure.

This power is, I think, most purely experienced in the case of the pure pleasures of learning (i.e., of a psychical rather than a psycho-somatic pleasure). For in learning, we experience—in the course of a dialogue with others— the emerging lesson as our own emerging-into-knowledge or as knowledge's emerging-to-define-us-anew. This direct learning experience is not beautiful due to its symbolic nature as standing for the possibility that measure can emerge. Rather, it is measure's very emergence, or our own coming-to-measure. Indeed, this experience, I would argue, precedes and makes possible any sensuous, symbolic pure pleasure. For the measure in the sensible world can only have meaning for us as an exemplar of measure's emergence if we ourselves are first persons for whom the eternal measure itself emerges, that is, if we are first and foremost learners. If we have not engaged in learning, the symbolism of the sensuous world goes unrecognized. Thus, learning itself—the life of a mind open to measure—must be distinct from and prior to any learning "through" sensuous things, for example, prior to any meaningful epistemic engagement with technological productions, textbooks, art, natural things, and so on. Only for learners does the sensuous world speak. And when the dialogue goes well, we move ourselves to a shared, common measure, and we demonstrate this measure in our own becoming new.

This interpretation explains why a diversity of human activities—from producing and educating, to writing books, to building cities, to playing music, to conversing or disputing seriously—can all have a unified sense of epistemic value. They may all be the expressions and the bearers of the lesson. And the true philosopher, if he or she is properly named, attempts nothing more than to bring an actual learning into such manifestations, or to show how the learning in them can be relearned. Fortunately, some helpful remnants of this life of learning are available to us (such as Plato's dialogues). And we can be grateful for their survival. We ignore so many of them until one day a learning experience surprises us and opens our eyes to them. Similarly, we even surprise ourselves at times with performative evidence of our own progress, for example in having written something containing more than we ourselves could honestly confess to have provided from ourselves. We thus have a twofold duty to protect and value both our own creative expressiveness *and* the manifest historical-intellectual artifacts of learning. Why would we desire to try to activate or reactivate an original learning experience without these aids, when we could just as well lean on them? There is no good reason to adopt an iconoclasm that would reject such materializations and institutionalizations of learning. Rather, we must simply recall that a real dialectical engagement with them is what gives them intellectual life.

Dialogue harbors learning experiences that culminate in intellection of the beings themselves. If we appropriate this learning actively, the insight bears down on all our faculties of awareness. In addition to the pure pleasures that emerge in this direct learning, soul's active self-appropriation of experience in learning enables even our senses to share in a higher purity. Thus, even the modes of life that can never attain being itself are able to share in the goodness of measure. With this ennobling of the emergent strata of our lives, we arrive at the central message in the *Philebus's* concept of purity. Purity is manifest in each kind of thing differently, as our two examples—of pure pleasure and of pure science—have exhibited. The senses of purity in them are connected conceptually by measure and experientially by learning, and thus they are not radically equivocal. But they are also very different senses because they preserve the basic truth of differences in kind. The *Philebus* thus exhibits a remarkable method of charity in the way it treats each kind fairly by the standard proper to it. It engages with each thing itself, not by any external standard nor by any deficient version of it, but rather charitably, that is, in the light of its purity. This charitability reveals the way an intrinsic relation to the good can always be found in any kind of life either as an essential element or at least as an exemplary instance of its kind. Thus, we learn from the dialogue that the burden of proof stands against anyone who would generically exclude any kind from the good life. Each kind and its opposite must be explored in the mode of a search for its good version; and the responsibility is on us to discover it or to bring it about.

Conclusion. Mixing the Elements

Socrates's investigation of the elements of the good life is thus complete, and he must now carry out the actual mixing. A parallel passage in *Republic* VII can help foreground this discussion, for Socrates is concerned there to list the disciplines (μαθήματα or τέχναι) that "turn the soul" to the most important study (τὸ μάθημα . . . μέγιστον), that is, the dialectical grasp of the forms (519c8; 532b ff.). As H. Lang has clarified, the μαθήματα there are not ordered or listed randomly but appear in a determinate order.[39] We begin with the arithmetic of pure units, which can then unfold into the more complex geometry of lines and planes, then into the study of depth, and finally into the study of solids in motion. This ordering from simple to more complex is essential. And when Glaucon hopes to leap directly from geometry to the study of the visible stars in motion, Socrates famously corrects him and says that the pure study of circular motion precedes and grounds any empirical observations (529c7 ff.). Proper ordering requires that the pure in the sciences, and then the purer kinds of sciences, must come before anything impure.

Now, the *Philebus* will confirm this emphasis on order; but it also adds a new clarification. For, as I have argued, pure "unit arithmetic" has no ultimate priority for Socrates. Rather, it is the science that exemplifies the pure possibility of an unfolding that is available to be actualized by *any* science of any form, whether it is the science of the beautiful, the even, or the quark. Each science will know a different form (and its relations to other forms), and therefore each science's proper unfolding must be different in the details of its unfolding. But the science, if it is to be a science, must unfold first from its original νόησις. The *Philebus* thus clarifies the way this unfolding must happen equally for each distinct science. For each science, a true intuition cannot be derived from the market of opinions about instances of the object, nor from the traditions of study that have studied mere instances of those forms, nor from the pseudo-authority of supposed expert scholars who would dictate what can be said about a form. Authority in science derives only from what is being studied. We must only prepare ourselves to study it through leaning on the historical supports available to us, by appealing to persons who can dialectically correct us, and by embracing the eternal and undying power already inherent in each of us to grasp reality when we engage dialectically with others.

Indeed, that this undying power always already belongs to each of us was indicated at the height of the *Republic*. Socrates there claims that "the instrument with which each learns [τὸ ὄργανον ᾧ καταμανθάνει ἕκαστος]" is a power that is "present in everyone's soul [ἑκάστου δύναμιν ἐν τῇ ψυχῇ]." Indeed, "the other so-called virtues of the soul . . . really aren't there beforehand but are added later by habit and practice. However, the virtue of reason [φρονῆσαι] seems to belong above all to something more divine, which never loses its power [δύναμιν] but is either useful and beneficial or useless and harmful, depending on the way it is turned" (*Republic* VII, 518c2–519a1). The *Philebus* differs in no way on this point, adding only that dialectic is "the capacity in our soul to love the truth and to do everything for its sake" (58d2–3). Each of us has this a priori ability to allow reason to be informed by measure, to self-appropriate measure, and to allow measure to generate virtue. This means that the good life is available to everyone.

Yet, just as the *Republic* emphasizes, the whole cannot be mixed all at once. We must respect the preconditions that make possible not only a mixed life, but a "well-mixed" life (61b3). To begin by mixing opinions or pleasures without first aiming at their preconditioning measures is self-defeating. And to mix corrupted versions of each before the pure versions would only lead to confusion. We must therefore consider the "pure" and "true" parts of each candidate first:

> SOCRATES: Didn't we find that one pleasure truer than another, just as one art was more precise than the other? . . . But there was also a difference between the sciences, since one kind deals with a subject matter that comes to be and perishes [τὰ γιγνόμενα καὶ ἀπολλύμενα], the other is concerned with what is free of that, the eternal and self-same [κατὰ ταὐτὰ δὲ καὶ ὡσαύτως ὄντα ἀεί]. Since we made truth our criterion, the latter kind appeared to be the truer one. . . . If we took from each sort the segments [τμήματα] that possess the most truth and mixed them in together, would [not] this mixture provide us with the most desirable life? (61d5–e3).

Importantly, pure pleasure and pure knowledge are not actually mixed at this point. They are merely considered for inclusion, with the "pure segments [τμήματα]" considered first, before the impure. Socrates includes pure pleasures only later, after he has included every kind of knowledge. The admission of all knowledge preconditions the possibility that anything else could emerge well in the soul. Thus, we must introduce the pure knowledge first, but we can also admit even those ones that are only impurely and loosely called "scientific":

> SOCRATES: Suppose, then, there is a person who understands what justice itself is [αὐτῆς περὶ δικαιοσύνης ὅτι ἔστιν], and can give appropriate definitions [καὶ λόγον ἔχων] and possesses the same kind of comprehension about the rest of what there is [περὶ τῶν ἄλλων πάντων τῶν ὄντων]. . . . Will he be sufficiently versed in science [ἱκανῶς ἐπιστήμης ἕξει] if he knows the definition of the circle and of the divine sphere itself [κύκλου μὲν καὶ σφαίρας αὐτῆς τῆς θείας τὸν λόγον ἔχων] but cannot recognize the human sphere and these our circles [τὴν δὲ ἀνθρωπίνην ταύτην σφαῖραν καὶ τοὺς κύκλους τούτους ἀγνοῶν], using even in housebuilding those other yardsticks and those circles?
>
> PROTARCHUS: We would find ourselves in a ridiculous position if we were confined entirely to those divine kinds of knowledge, Socrates!

SOCRATES: What are you saying? Ought we at the same time to include the inexact and impure science of the false yardstick and circle, and add it to the mixture?

PROTARCHUS: Yes, necessarily so, if any of us ever wants to find his own way home (62a2–b8).

Socrates here contrasts divine knowledge with knowledge of the distinctively "human" (ἀνθρώπινος) things. Strikingly, he suggests that some people among humans can indeed grasp the divine thing, for example, "what concerns justice itself [αὐτῆς περὶ δικαιοσύνης]." Since the ὅτι that follows here is best translated as "that" rather than "what," we can understand Socrates to be attributing to humans some understanding "concerning Justice Itself, that it is" (even if we still lack a complete grasp of what it is).[40] Humans can also have an "account" of all such realities. But humans need even more. For what happens if such a person fails to also grasp the distinctively "human" versions of the forms? In response, Socrates thus allows the mixture of impure sciences that are "lacking [ἐνδεεστέραν]" and that use the false yardstick and circle and guesswork in music (62c1).[41] Socrates can only make this admission because he has previously discovered and admitted reason into the mixture. Reason's intellection is a purity found in any science actually worthy of the name, even when it mixes with the impure. Evidence that only the prior inclusion of intellection allows for the inclusion of the others is found at 62c7–d2:

SOCRATES: Do you want me, then, to yield like a doorkeeper to the pushing and shoving of a crowd and to throw open the doors and let the flood of all sorts of knowledge in, the inferior kind mingling with the pure?

PROTARCHUS: I for my part can't see what damage it would do to accept all the other kinds of knowledge, *as long as* we have those of the highest kind [my emphasis].

Without Protarchus's qualification of "as long as," some things falling under the name of science would not have been actual sciences. With this qualification, however, the required intellection is understood to be already present in soul, and thus even the impure sciences that follow for such a soul will be practices and opinions that do indeed contain fragments of this intellection. Socrates's earlier, stark separation between science and non-science (e.g., mere opinion) thus still holds here. There he was making a distinction between taking opinion and becoming first to be one's goal versus taking truth first: "[Most] of the arts and sciences and those who work in them are in the first place [πρῶτον] only concerned with opinions and make opinions the center of their research [συντεταμένως]" (58e3–59a1). Here, however, our "mingling of the glens" has already included into the soul the required intellection. Thus, it follows that the "well-mixed" life can admit all of the other sciences, for they will all make reference to some extent to an implied (if not always exercised) capacity to conduct that practice of science purely.

Thus, all knowledge is admitted before any pleasure. At this moment Protarchus proves dramatically that his unqualified hedonism is finally unseated. For after the inevitable or necessary pleasures are admitted (which are not intrinsically good, but which are not bad), he expresses uncertainty about whether any more pleasures should be admitted. He thus consents to allow the pleasures and knowledges themselves to decide the question of whether any more pleasures should be included, beyond the inevitable ones (63a5–9). To exhibit this deferral, Socrates humorously personifies each candidate as a different kind of character. The pleasures are personified as deeply needful and desirous of knowledge. When asked if they should be included, they unhesitatingly insist that they are nothing without knowledge: "It is neither possible nor beneficial for one tribe to remain alone, in isolation and unmixed. We would prefer to live side by side with that best kind of knowledge, the kind that understands not only all other things but also each one of us, so far as that is possible" (63a5–c2). The pleasures are now utterly persuaded they need knowledge first. For "without the true opinion that he enjoys it, without recognizing what kind of experience it is he has, without memory of this affection for any length of time," pleasure is utterly worthless (60e1–4).[42] Thus, for pleasure to be intrinsically good, all the kinds and all the elements of knowledge (measure, the measured, reason, etc.) are necessary.

Humorously, knowledge does not have equal confidence that it should in turn desire pleasures. Eventually, however, it capitulates and admits that it would indeed voluntarily choose to live with at least some pleasures, even some pleasures beyond those that are strictly inevitable in life.[43] Socrates depicts this point by asking personified knowledge,

> "Do you have any need for any association with the pleasures?"
> That is how we would address reason and knowledge. "What kinds
> of pleasures?" they might ask in return. . . . Our discussion would
> then continue as follows: "Will you have any need to associate
> with the strongest and most intensive pleasures in addition to the

true pleasures?" we will ask them. "Why on earth should we need
them, Socrates?" they might reply, "They are a tremendous impediment to us, since they infect the souls in which they dwell with
madness or even prevent our own development altogether. Furthermore, they totally destroy most of our offspring, since neglect
leads to forgetfulness [λήθην]. But as to the true and pure pleasures
[ἡδονὰς ἀληθεῖς καὶ καθαρὰς] as you mentioned, those regard as
our kin [σχεδὸν οἰκείας ἡμῖν]. And besides, also add the pleasures
of health and of temperance and all those that commit themselves
to virtue as to their deity and follow it around everywhere. But to
forge an association between reason and those pleasures that are
forever involved with foolishness and other kinds of vice would
be totally unreasonable. . . . This is particularly true if he wants to
discern [μαθεῖν] in this mixture what the good is in man and in the
universe [τ᾽ ἀνθρώπῳ καὶ τῷ παντὶ] and to get some vision of the
nature of the good itself" (63c5–64a7).

Socrates has already shown that pure pleasure emerges when truth defies
ignorance in the soul. The contrast of soul's state of λήθη (forgetting) with the
ἀλήθεια (truth or unconcealment) of pure pleasure here thus reconfirms this
idea. These true pleasures both depend on reason and contribute originally to
the overall experience of the learner. They are thus welcomed, along with all
the pleasures that follow the virtues that emerge in the soul that prioritizes
measure. While reason itself is nowhere said to "need" these pleasures—they
are not pragmatically necessary for a soul, nor are they inevitable occurrences
for a living being—reason still welcomes them superfluously. For reason,
here, has been "humanized" and depicted as a person, that is, as a self who
is related to a life other than the self alone, and as a self who offers up a
self-expression for all of life. Because reason is thus engaged in this commu-
nicative dialogue, reason can accept the pure pleasures that follow from this
dialogue as pleasures near to its own heart.

If the *Philebus* could be said to propose an "anthropology," I submit that
it is found precisely in this personified meeting of reason and pleasure. We
are this welcoming of life into reason and this communication of reason
with life. We witness here the process by which humanity itself emerges
into definition only by sharing in the self-defining of its own constitution.[44]
The complete life for humans thus emerges only as this mixing activity, as
an activity that also includes an ever-ongoing completion process. We must
assume our part as discerning co-causes of this mixture. But we must also
welcome the other kind, that is, the emergents that follow from the embrace

of reason and measure. Thus, the *Philebus*'s anthropology does not define humans. Rather, it shows us that humanity is found precisely in the different ways we each share in reason, and in the ways this sharing in reason constitutes our continued becoming.

This is why Socrates's final addition of "truth" to the mixture is not an afterthought as it might appear.[45] As Socrates says: "Wherever we do not mix in truth [ἀλήθειαν] nothing could truly come to be [γίγνοιτο] nor remain in existence once it had come to be [γενόμενον]" (64b1–2). The fact that the inclusion of truth is said to make possible a "becoming" is a testament to truth's source as first stemming from the good itself. The good, as we have emphasized, transcends being. And truth's very source is in the good-beyond-being before it is in being. If truth's first source were not transcendent of being then it would be impossible to attribute genuine truth to any becoming as becoming.[46] Instead, here Socrates says that truth and goodness make possible "truthful becoming." A mixture conceived without this coming-to-completion, without this remnant of nonbeing, would be conceived insufficiently, not because there cannot be knowledge, truth, goodness, or being without becoming but rather because there cannot be a whole mixed life that includes all truth and all goodness unless that life also includes the goods that come to be.

Why Should the Good Come to Be?

I examined in part I the basic dialectical concepts underlying the *Philebus*'s conception of the good life. I defended an interpretation of dialectical practice as a learning procedure that, through a process of positing and searching for the metaphorical number of something through discourse, ultimately leads to a discovery of what each reality is. What we will discover through the learning procedure cannot be decided in advance. Yet in each process of learning, it is clear that what comes to light is the limit, the standard, or the measure of what each revealed reality is. This discoverable measure is what becomes manifest in perceptible examples of those realities. I then argued that whether or not limit is manifest in becoming depends on whether or not a cause brings the limit proper to each thing into the unlimited, thus causing a mixture to emerge. The cause, of course, remains always potentially independent of this mixture-becoming, given that its essential object—that is, each reality itself in its own proper limit or measure—is itself independent of mixture. Since the object is definitive of the content of causation, the cause, insofar as it is a cause of limit's emergence in the mixture, is independent of the mixture it causes.

In part II, then, I argued that living beings like us partake of such causality. Since this causality is determined in its content toward the limit which it brings to presence, this causality is itself what is meant by intellection. Thus, we are intellectual living beings, and this means that we have at least some responsibility over what emerges in this world order, that is, responsibility for helping what emerges to emerge well.

This possibility for causing the emergence of a well-ordered mixture is exemplified, in the *Philebus*, through the account of pure pleasure. For, as something wholly good that also becomes, pure pleasure stands for the general possibility of good becoming. As something for which we humans have a responsibility, it stands for the specific possibility of a good dependent on our freedom. Pure pleasure is within the realm of distinctively human caretaking because we are the living beings who share in both intellectual causation and inevitable becoming. Accompanying experiences like those of coming to know, this pleasure is itself an emergent phenomenon, a phenomenon partly dependent on us. But pure pleasure's psychical dependency, its becoming, and thus its ontological dependency detract in no way from its intrinsic goodness.

Finally, I argued in chapter 4 that the learning process, or the process of being raised up to dialectic and intellection, is aided by "mathematical" lessons. It is aided by such lessons because those lessons contain, in manifestation, the fragmentary traces of an intellection of forms. Thus, for humans, the encounter with a μάθημα or lesson, or also with a perceptible instance of "beauties themselves," provides an opportunity for us to enact or to reenact the learning experience, that is, to move dialectically toward an always-original intellection. We can enact or reenact the originary becoming-present of measure—that is, the original learning, or the original experience of coming to the intelligible world—that underlies those lessons. In this way, pure pleasure—accompanying our psychical or sensible coming-into-the-presence-of-measure—is itself able to be "pure." It can be pure, on the one hand, because it accompanies the process of coming to dialectical intellection, which intellection is itself the pure constitutive essence of each science (because the objects of intellection "truly are"). On the other hand, pure pleasure is different in kind from such intellection itself, since it is bound to what "becomes and never is." The purity in pure pleasure thus applies not to all but only to some pleasures.

As a result of these considerations, I have argued that we can take from the *Philebus* an expansive and important thesis. The good itself in no way precludes becoming. Indeed, some becoming is intrinsically good. Good is manifest in becoming and in pleasure in the way proper to them, not in the way proper to being or to knowledge. While some goods depend on others in the order of conditions of possibility (as pure pleasure can only emerge in a life already endowed with reason and measure), nevertheless each good in the final analysis is just as good, in terms of containing a proper goodness, as each other heterogeneous good. Regardless of any consideration of the extent to which an intrinsic good is common or uncommon in certain kinds of reality, we can say that whenever and wherever the good is present it makes that kind in which it is present properly good in its own proper way.

Now, I have reviewed my main claims because I want to ask in closing: why should the good itself emerge in the generally unstable realm of becoming, where good and bad can both be found? After all, the good itself does not need its opposite, the limit does not need to become manifest in a mixture, and the measure itself is not bound to unmeasuredness. In response to this question, I would like to suggest, in closing, two possible argumentative strategies that might be adduced to account for why the good should become. Only the latter strategy is acceptable, in my view.

The first argumentative strategy for explaining why the good should emerge, which I would call the subjective argument, would say that the good should come to be because beings like us need the emergence of the good. For example, we, as living beings, are inevitably bound to choose pleasure. We are bound to seek what fulfills our needs, without necessary regard for measure or right proportions. Thus, if the good were not to emerge in this world order (as a good pleasure), then we would inevitably be bound to choose what is not the good when we inevitably choose pleasures. Thus, precisely because we are always driven by our needs and always seeking the fulfillments of pleasure, the good should emerge as pleasure and need-fulfillment for us (and for beings like us in this respect). Indeed, other animals are like us in pursuing pleasure; and unless what they inevitably seek—pleasure—is also a good for them, then the good will not be attained by them. Thus, says this subjective strategy, because there are living beings of this kind who subjectively need the emergence of the good, it follows that the good should come to be.

This strategy, I think, provides no reason for why the good itself should emerge, but only a reason why it would be better for beings like us if the good would emerge for us. In response, an objector might argue that, rather than accommodating needy beings, the good truly demands that the needy beings themselves should be destroyed or transcended. To eliminate needy beings is, after all, to eliminate their needs. If we cannot become flawless, then perhaps the best option would be to abort the project of humanity.

In response to such an objector I would defend the descent, the immanentization, and the humanization of the good. I would defend it not from the standpoint of the subjective neediness of the human kind but from the objective standpoint suggested by the *Philebus*. It is true that humans inevitably fail to live up to the standard of deficiency-free being. Yet the human definition for Plato stems first from the good itself and not first from being. And the good itself has a power and dignity beyond being. If this is so, then both in our being and in our nonbeing we humans can attain our own proper goodness. This is so because the human definition, as the *Philebus* argues, is not merely given to us but is a self-determination, determined through our participation in the cause. But the cause is the cause of the emergence of goodness in becoming, or nonbeing. Thus, if humans share in this causation, then this sharing makes possible the emergence of at least one good that would not emerge without our causation. And this possibly emergent good *should* objectively emerge.[1] Furthermore, because we can understand that the good itself transcends being and its scope extends beyond being, we are uniquely suited (as intellectual beings) to discover the genuine importance of our own position as co-causes. We are uniquely suited to serve knowingly and gladly as the cocreators of the goods that become. We therefore have an objective reason—the reason being the possible emergence of these goods themselves—to persevere in our pursuit of the good even as beings-who-become. Because the good can come to be for us, we are obligated to take up and appropriate actively our own becoming in a way that yields its proper goodness.[2] Our goal is thus not to eliminate our becoming but to bring goodness from out of such a condition. We should have the courage to accept this risk and to embrace the resulting emergence of the good.

This response works, however, only if the good transcends being. For if goodness does not transcend being, then our becoming, far from making possible a unique goodness in the journey itself, would only be a moral weakness. The *Philebus*, however, steps in as becoming's advocate. It reveals a sufficiency among us that, in its pure immanence, imports the hope of the transcendent. By awakening us to these pure pleasures of learning in the here and now, the *Philebus* draws us to share in an eminent goodness beyond being.

NOTES

Introduction

1. Damascius, *Lectures on the "Philebus,"* trans. Leendert Gerrit Westerink (Chelmsford, Eng.: Prometheus Trust, 2010), 1–6. See also Gerd Van Riel, *Pleasure and the Good Life: Plato, Aristotle, and the Neoplatonists* (Leiden, Neth.: Brill, 2000), 134–76.

2. See, for example, Reginald Hackforth, *Plato's Examination of Pleasure: A Translation of the "Philebus" with an Introduction and Commentary* (Cambridge: Cambridge University Press, 1945), 12. For a view similar to my own, see Sylvain Delcomminette, *Le "Philèbe" de Platon: Introduction à l'agathologie platonicienne* (Leiden, Neth.: Koninklijke Brill NV, 2006), 36–39.

3. I will often translate variants of γένεσις as "emergence." For a precedent using the term "emergent" in a Platonic context, see Plotinus, *The Enneads,* trans. John Dillon and Stephen MacKenna (London: Penguin Books, 1991).

4. I will examine false pleasures only briefly due to concerns with space. They often receive a lot of attention not only because they take up a lot of space in the dialogue but also because of a perceived scandal in the *Philebus*'s ostensible claim that false pleasures are indeed pleasures. I do not find this ostensible claim to be scandalous, either empirically or textually, as chapter 3 clarifies. Even so, I hope my focus on true pleasure may indirectly contribute to the debate on false pleasures.

Chapter 1

1. Galen reported on the awkwardness of these topical transitions. See Edward Poste, *The "Philebus" of Plato, with a Revised Text and English Notes* (Oxford: Oxford University Press, 1860), 105.

2. Compare to Aristotle, *Metaphysics* Z, 12–17 and H, 6.

3. See the introduction to chapter 3 and the conclusion to chapter 4 for the results.

4. Translations are from Plato, *Complete Works*, ed. John M. Cooper and D. S. Hutchinson. (Indianapolis, Ind.: Hackett, 1997) unless I state that they are my own, in which case they are translated from John Burnet, *Platonis Opera: Recognovit Brevique Adnotatione Critica Instruxit* (Oxford: Oxford Classical Texts, 1900–1907).

5. At the start of the dialogue, Socrates lists the several candidates he supports and does not literally list ἐπιστήμη here. In this chapter, I will often refer to Socrates's candidates under the single heading of "knowledge," however, simply in order to avoid relisting them all. The distinction only becomes vital for us in chapter 4.

6. Compare here the claim that Philebus has "given up [ἀπείρηκεν]" with the description of the ἄπειρον in 2.3.

7. See 4.4 where the power of intellect is shown to be available to every person. For an account of the impact of intellect on other-than-human lives, see Luc Brisson, "Le Continuum de la vie chez Platon, des dieux aux plantes," in *Lire Platon*, 2nd edition (Paris: Presses Universitaires de France, 2014); and Amber D. Carpenter, "Embodied Intelligent (?) Souls: Plants in Plato's Timaeus," *Phronêsis* 55 (2010): 281–303.

8. Notice that Philebus's account is given by proxy, by Protarchus, who speaks for the unspeaking Philebus. Waterfield notices this problem: "Protarchus is only a stand-in for Philebus, the dramatic idea being that because pleasure is irrational, a hedonist is unimpressed by Socratic reasoning, and an amenable interlocutor must be found" (Robin Waterfield, trans., *Philebus* [New York: Penguin Group, 1982], 10).

9. See René Girard, *The Girard Reader*, ed. James G. Williams (New York: Crossroad, 1996), chaps. 1–3. See also Sherwood Belangia, "Metaphysics Desire in Girard and Plato," *Comparative and Continental Philosophy* 2 (2010): 197–209.

10. Contrast this approach with the Aristotelian route of narrowing our inquiry from what is common to the vegetative, to the appetitive, and only then to the specifically human (see, e.g., Aristotle, *Nicomachean Ethics* I, 13). In these passages we begin with the good itself (which is the only worthy source of humanity) and only then discern how the good is manifest in human capacities. In this way, the good is invited to define humanity and our happiness. See Delcomminette, *Le "Philèbe,"* 1–19. See also the conclusion to chapter 4.

11. See Plato, *Cratylus*, 400e–401a for a parallel passage.

12. On elenchus, see Richard Robinson, *Plato's Earlier Dialectic* (Oxford: Clarendon, 1953). He argues that Socrates (fallaciously) takes the method of elenchus to demonstrate which of the contradictory beliefs should be rejected. See also Gregory Vlastos, "The Socratic Elenchus," *Oxford Studies in Ancient Philosophy* 1 (1983): 27–58, which uses this understanding of elenchus to explain why Plato "abandons" the method later. For a challenge to the view that it is abandoned, see Donald Davidson, "Plato's Philosopher," *Apeiron* 26 (1993): 179–94. See also Delcomminette, *Le "Philèbe,"* 171.

13. For accounts of bad pleasures, see especially *Gorgias*. While the *Protagoras* (351 ff.) entertains the "pleasure is the good" thesis, this is not really counterevidence. For there Socrates is merely showing that two commonly held positions are inconsistent with one another: (a) the claim that "pleasure is the good," and (b) the many's claim that "pleasure overcomes knowledge" in cases of incontinence. Socrates can easily be interpreted as rejecting either or both of these theses. See also Joe Sachs, "Introduction," in *Socrates and the Sophists* (Newburyport, Mass.: Focus, 2011).

14. Socrates himself will soon admit even (2), that is, the possibility of unlikeness, for his own candidate of knowledge. See chapter 4.

15. See Mary McCabe, *Plato's Individuals* (Princeton, N.J.: Princeton University Press, 1994), 4–5 for a fruitful distinction between the "austere" and the "generous" individual in Plato.

16. Socratic dialogue cannot be based in mere assertions but must involve a willingness to ask oneself whether the good is truthfully such as one proclaims it to be. See Nicholas Rescher, "Kant's Neoplatonism: Kant and Plato on Mathematical and Philosophical Method," *Metaphilosophy* 44 (2013): 69–78, which distinguishes between the mathematical and the philosophical by a similar distinction.

17. Contra Waterfield, trans., *Philebus*, 39. See 4.1 and 4.5 for more on "equality" as a central theme.

18. This passage constitutes not the first but the second "reflective" turn the dialogue has taken. The initial "account summaries" (11a ff.) reflectively summed up the prior, basic accounts. This second reflective turn notes that the discussion has up to now exhibited a somewhat predictable structure.

19. Compare Plato, *Republic* VII, 523b.

20. See 4.3.

21. Features typically indicative of Platonic forms—namely the use of ἀεὶ εἶναι X and αὐτὸ τὸ X—are not found in this passage. Instead, this passage hinges on the term ἕν as combined with the thing in question: "καὶ βοῦν ἕνα καὶ τὸ καλὸν ἓν καὶ τὸ ἀγαθὸν ἕν" (15a7). Likewise, this passage does not use εἶναι even in a weak copulative sense to speak of each item. This fact implies, I suspect, that in our subsequent discussion we must be prepared to *learn* the "being" or "number" of each posited unity; it is not presumed to be a given at the start.

22. See 4.3 on monads as, by contrast, each absolutely partless and identical to one another.

23. Σωκράτης. πρῶτον μὲν εἴ τινας δεῖ τοιαύτας εἶναι μονάδας ὑπολαμβάνειν ἀληθῶς οὔσας· εἶτα πῶς αὖ ταύτας, μίαν ἑκάστην οὖσαν ἀεὶ τὴν αὐτὴν καὶ μήτε γένεσιν μήτε ὄλεθρον προσδεχομένην, ὅμως εἶναι βεβαιότατα μίαν ταύτην; μετὰ δὲ τοῦτ᾽ ἐν τοῖς γιγνομένοις αὖ καὶ ἀπείροις εἴτε διεσπασμένην καὶ πολλὰ γεγονυῖαν θετέον, εἴθ᾽ ὅλην αὐτὴν αὑτῆς χωρίς, ὃ δὴ πάντων ἀδυνατώτατον φαίνοιτ᾽ ἄν, ταὐτὸν καὶ ἓν ἅμα ἐν ἑνί τε καὶ πολλοῖς γίγνεσθαι. ταῦτ᾽ ἔστι τὰ περὶ τὰ τοιαῦτα ἓν καὶ πολλά, ἀλλ᾽ οὐκ ἐκεῖνα, ὦ Πρώταρχε, ἁπάσης ἀπορίας αἴτια μὴ καλῶς ὁμολογηθέντα καὶ εὐπορίας ἂν αὖ καλῶς.

24. Frede's translation treats the passage as containing *two* questions. Fowler's translation reflects the *three* questions I find in the passage. See also Amber D. Carpenter, "Nevertheless: The Philosophical Significance of the Questions Posed at *Philebus* 15b," *Logical Analysis and History of Philosophy* 12 (2009): 103–29.

25. This interpretation raises the difficulty of how we are to deal with someone who posits "the one-being" as a distinctive *henad*. This posit is unlike the others insofar as it already appears to posit "being" initially. This problem might lead one to prefer interpretation kind (2) explored below, wherein each posited *henad* contains an implied being. Alternatively, one might argue that "the one-ox" and "the one-being" do not differ fundamentally: the "being of ox" comes to light in its being unfolded as a plurality, and likewise the "being of being" comes to light in such an unfolding.

26. Socrates is trying to show that despite their non-becoming, it is still difficult to conceive of how these unities can both "be" and be "one," while remaining one and not becoming indefinitely many. The *Parmenides* also notices this danger in saying that a "unity is." For this saying risks multiplying the unity into an indefinite many. See Francis M. Cornford, *Plato and Parmenides: Parmenides' "Way of Truth" and Plato's "Parmenides"* (London: K. Paul, Trench, Trubner, 1939). See also Carpenter, "Nevertheless," for an efficient solution.

27. Aristotle tries to "explain away" the kind of problem Plato dwells on here. If we are talking about something, he suggests, then it is silly to ask "whether" it *is* or is *one*, since this is implied already. See Aristotle, *Metaphysics*, Z, 12–17 and H, 6. See also 4.1, n. 9.

28. The third question follows this whole line of inquiry by asking *whether* the *henad* loses its self-identity in its expression as multiple. We will approach this problem in the next section. See also 4.1, n. 9.

29. See A. G. Long, *Conversation and Self-Sufficiency in Plato* (Oxford: Oxford University Press, 2013), 138 on the inability of interlocutors to participate in dialogue as a major concern of Plato. See also Gregory Kirk, *The Pedagogy of Wisdom: An Interpretation of Plato's "Theaetetus"* (Evanston, Ill.: Northwestern University Press, 2015), for a helpful account of similar dynamics in the *Theaetetus*.

30. We may wish to link the ἀεί to ὄντων rather than to λεγομένων; but it does not follow that the term λεγομένων can therefore be ignored. We are dealing here with a

discussion of "accounts of being," that is, with accounts that reveal being and with being coming to light in accounts.

31. We will return to this point in chapter 2, where it becomes clear that a cause always generates definite multiplicities (one-many structures).

32. See *Gorgias* on art versus knack at 448e ff.

33. For a fruitful discussion of this principle of accounts, see Hans-Georg Gadamer, "Plato's Unwritten Dialectic," in *Dialogue and Dialectic: Eight Hermeneutical Studies of Plato*, trans. P. C. Smith (New Haven, Conn.: Yale University Press, 1980). Gadamer (a) interprets the logic of the written dialogues as expressions of a living dialogue. He then (b) interprets the living dialogues' logic as manifesting the structure (*Struktur*) of number. That is, members of a dialogue express through multiple perspectives the whole of the thesis that is coming to light. Gadamer then argues, following Léon Robin and others, that (c) the core of Plato's supposed "unwritten doctrines" resides in the interpretation of forms as numbers in some sense (Aristotle, *Metaphysics* I, 6). Thus, he concludes that (d) the core of the "unwritten doctrines" is really the same as the core of the written dialogues: a certain logical structure that is discernible in living dialogues—a whole account is attained only through multiple contributing accounts that can go on endlessly—thus parallels the way numbers are each one-many structures and the whole number line can continue indefinitely.

34. One drawback of this interpretation is its implication that the form "dyad" also gets posited as "the one-two" (like "the one-ox"). Thus, the two gets posited as a *unity* at the start of an inquiry rather than discovered as part of the unfolding of another *henad*. A response to this problem here could note that the terms "one" and "many" as used in the learning procedure are simply examples or models for explaining *a* way of carrying out the procedure. Just as not all "intermediates" are literally "numbers" (as I argue below), so too is the study of the "two" not literally a study of a "one-two." On the inverse problem, not of depicting the two as as *henad*, but of projecting the two as consisting of units or monads, see 4.3.

35. Notice that, on this second interpretation, the ultimate how-many of the original idea is the ultimate how-many of that original idea as constituted by the determinate how-many of each of the "others." The original *henad* would have, so to speak, "open doors and windows," offering itself to a nexus of relations that literally co-determine it to be what it is. The procedure would thus be recursive.

36. See the solution of Carpenter, "Nevertheless," 125.

37. Socrates continues with his example of sound: "But you will be competent, my friend, once you have learned how many intervals there are in high pitch and low pitch, what character they have, by what notes the intervals are defined, and the kinds of combinations they form. . . . For when you have mastered these things in this way, then you have acquired expertise there, and when you have grasped the unity of any of the other things there are, you have become wise about that" (17c8–e2).

38. See Anaximander (per Aristotle, *Physics* II, 203b6–10) on the indefinite as the sourceless source.

39. The examples of letters goes as follows: "[Theuth] was the first to discover that the vowels in that unlimited variety are not one but several, and again that there are others that are not voiced, but make some kind of noise, and that they, too, have a number. As a third kind of letters he established the ones we now call mute. After this he further subdivided the ones without sound or mutes down to every single unit. In the same fashion

he also dealt with the vowels and the intermediates, until he had found out the number for each one of them, and then he gave all of them together the name 'letter.' And as he realized that none of us could gain any knowledge of a single one of them, taken by itself without understanding them all, he considered that the one link that somehow unifies them all and called it the art of literacy" (18b9–d2).

40. "[Music] is parasitic upon structure. . . . [The] mere highs and lows of sound have no intrinsic structure of their own. Musical sound itself is built up from a set of mathematically expressible relations between higher and lower sounds defining musical intervals. . . . These intervals are the basis of the scale, and it is only with reference to this organization of a series of intervals that one can identify musical notes as such" (Verity Harte, *Plato on Parts and Wholes: The Metaphysics of Structure* [Oxford: Clarendon, 2002], 204). See also Andrew Barker, *Greek Musical Writings II: Harmonic and Acoustic Theory* (Cambridge: Cambridge University Press, 1989), 63–65. For more on the metaphysical implications, see McCabe, *Plato's Individuals*.

41. Harte, *Plato on Parts*, 206–7.

42. Harte, *Plato on Parts*, 205, n. 344.

43. See 2.3–2.5.

44. See 2.4, n. 28 on Gadamer.

45. This is not to say that other living beings do not share in causation, for Plato indicates in places that they do. See Brisson, "Continuum," as well as Carpenter, "Embodied."

46. See 2.2 and 2.5.

47. See John Russon, "We Sense That They Strive," in *Retracing the Platonic Text*, ed. John Sallis and John Russon (Evanston, Ill.: Northwestern University Press, 2000), 78–79 for an account based in the *Phaedo* of why we must "specify conditions of realization" for any posited form. The good is realized in "giving light to differences" and "determinateness."

48. In chapter 3 I show that Socrates fulfills this demand for pleasure (at 34e ff.), and in chapter 4 he fulfills it for knowledge (55c2 ff.).

49. See 4.5.

Chapter 2

1. See 3.3 and 4.5 on coming-to-completion.

2. This appeal to a simplistic "equality" of each candidate is a common theme in Plato's depiction of hedonism. See especially 1.2, 4.1, and 4.5.

3. The previous mentions of νοῦς at 13e6, 19d6, 21b8, 21d7, and 22a3 have been more loosely equated "reason," "knowledge," and "right opinion." Here, reason is used more specifically. See also 4.4 and 4.5.

4. See the introduction to chapter 3 for the final results.

5. This is not to say that good pleasure is less good than good knowledge. See chapter 3.

6. See Plato, *Phaedo*, 96a–107e.

7. The "more and less" is not just one example, while hot/cold is another. Rather, what we mean by the term "the more and less" is just what is contained in each example-pair here.

8. This passage is consistent with *Phaedo*, 102 ff., where Socrates speaks of the greater as sharing in "the great itself." Likewise, here, we have no reason to believe that the *words* "more" and "less" cannot be used in different contexts to signify *either* the concept of the unlimited *or* the concept of the definite. Socrates uses the comparative language of "more and less" as his vehicle for signifying the intrinsically "relative-to-its-opposite" character

of the unlimited here. But nothing prevents him from using the same word in a different context to refer to a definite form.

9. 24b8–10 uses the term γίγνεσθον (dual of γίγνομαι): "And since they are endless, they turn out to be [γίγνεσθον] entirely unlimited." (a) I modify Frede's translation to reflect that they "become [γίγνεσθον] unlimited." Similarly at 24d7–8 Frede's translation might not allow us to recognize the terminology of "becoming." (b) Also, Plato's language here binds the content of the topic—that is, the pair "more and less"—to the grammatical dual in a way we miss if we lack the dual.

10. For parallel passages see Plato, *Timaeus*, 27e and Plato, *Parmenides*, 152a.

11. See Kai Hauser, "Cantor's Concept of Set in Light of Plato's *Philebus*," *Review of Metaphysics* 63 (2010): 783–805. See also Cornelius Castoriadis, "The Logic of Magmas and the Question of Autonomy," in *The Castoriadis Reader*, ed. David A. Curtis (Malden, Mass.: Blackwell, 1989), 290–318.

12. Number means for Socrates definite number (see 16c6 ff., 18a7, 19a2, and 25e2). Whatever is strictly more-or-less never arrives at any such "how many."

13. See Plato, *Statesman*, 284a1–b1 where the indeterminate commits the violence against the determinate. It is destructive of the measure required in all crafts. See also the discussion of χώρα at Plato, *Timaeus* 52a ff.

14. Plato, *Statesman*, 268 ff. mythologically depicts only the "Age of Chronos" as a time when things are utterly sortable and determinate, divided into species and kinds in a completely neat way. Yet, this is not the age in which we "presently" live. To live in the present is to be subject to some indefinition.

15. Nichomachus maps the Aristotelian distinction between multitude and magnitude onto this passage. That distinction seems to me to be logically subsequent to Plato's distinction of limit and unlimited, since conceiving of it would require these concepts. See Nichomachus of Gerasa, *Introduction to Arithmetic*, trans. Martin Luther D'Ooge (London: Macmillan, 1926), 184.

16. On a closely related issue, Theon of Smyrna, as noted in Joseph D. Macadam, "Theo Smyrnaeus: On Arithmetic" (M.A. thesis, University of British Columbia, 1969), 86 distinguishes intervals from ratios. 1:2 and 2:1 have the same interval, while they are different ratios. Theon notices that the order of the terms determines the ratio symbol to mean either half-ratio or double-ratio. Interestingly, Theon argues that a grasp of specific ratios must precede a grasp of mere intervals. If true, this would lend support to my view that ideas like double and equal should be understood first as separate and nondependent on one another, even though we can also understand them as manifest together. See also Nicomachus, *Introduction to Arithmetic*, 237, n. 3.

17. If this is so, then something can be both double and non-double (e.g., equal) at the same time and in the same respect. For when we speak about it as both double and equal, we are speaking about the phenomenon in the respect of "being an octave," which in that respect can always be both or either.

18. This is not to deny that this generated octave participates in a distinct form of "the octave." It is to say that double and equal can each be used to comprehend or express it.

19. Likewise, "to be double" is perhaps always to be able to be the doubling *of* some thing or another. Yet, "to double" is independent of any particular thing that is doubled. For any doubled-thing is not in every way "double" like the double itself is. Rather, the doubled-thing is also other things, for example, it is a doubled *length*. But a doubled length is thus a mixture, that is, it is not double itself by itself.

20. For another helpful interpretation on music, see Harte, *Plato on Parts*, 177–211 and my comments in 1.4. See also McCabe, *Plato's Individuals*. These views emphasize that a melody is only what it is by virtue of the notes; yet the notes are defined through their contribution to the melody. The system would be neither the notes alone, nor the system alone without the notes, but the whole that they constitute, that is, a whole which also constitutes them as notes. The very idea of there being such a mutually determining system seems to me to be implied in Socrates's examples of the limit class, at least insofar as these limits are able to be manifest in mixtures. The idea of this system's actual emergence in sounds (i.e., in unlimited pitch) seems to me to be what Socrates means by mixture.

21. Andrew Barker, *The Science of Harmonics in Classical Greece* (Cambridge: Cambridge University Press, 2007), 2–32.

22. See Andrew Barker, "Plato's *Philebus*: The Numbering of a Unity," *Apeiron* 29 (1996): 143–64.

23. See 3.2 on Bossi and our contribution to an ongoing mixture.

24. Kenneth Sayre, *Plato's Late Ontology: A Riddle Resolved* (Princeton, N.J.: Princeton University Press, 1983) argues persuasively that not all mixtures, as mixtures, are perfect mixtures. For the opposing view, that is, that supposed imperfect mixtures are in truth not even mixtures at all, see Harte, *Plato on Parts*. In addition to reiterating Sayre's arguments, I would suggest that the *Philebus*'s distinction between (a) ingredients in a good life and (b) the order of causes (see the introduction to chapter 3) shows that the good life both (i) is a mixture and (ii) includes some imperfect (i.e., never-perfectly-mixed) elements. In general, I argue (see chapter 3) that we do not need to eliminate all imperfection in mixtures. Indeed, to demand that any mixture should be as mixture a perfect mixture can be dangerous. For, first, a mixture as mixture cannot be perfect (if by "perfect" one means "not lacking in being"); for to be a mixture is to contain an element incapable of totally "being itself." And, second, to try to make a mixture perfect (i.e., to try to make it "be itself perfectly") would in fact always yield a less-than-good mixture. For one would then exclude certain permissible things (such as the imperfect things Socrates does include in the good life). Thus, instead of seeking perfection in mixedness, Socrates in fact has us aim first at the good itself, which—as more inclusive and permissive than the "perfect"—in effect allows for a sufficiently good mixture to emerge as "better" than an ontological perfection (see the conclusion to chapter 3). In short: any mixture will be ontologically complete as a mixture only κατὰ δύναμιν; but this does not mean that it lacks a complete intrinsic goodness proper to its own kind.

25. See the "Conclusion," where I argue that the goodness of the whole good life depends not on a once-and-for-all causation by a single cause, but rather on descending levels of ongoing, responsible causation.

26. See 17c7 on "high and low" in the domain of pitch. See also chapter 3 on how something can be both complete in value (as are some things in the final mixture) and incomplete in being (as are all mixtures).

27. See the conclusion to chapter 4 on why the inclusion of complete truth and goodness into the good life requires that we admit even goods—such as pure pleasure—that are emerging. The complete good life thus includes some elements that bring an emerging-completeness.

28. Evidently, an intellection of limit by means of making a mixture can only be attained if the mixture is produced and understood *from* limit into the mixture, not understood *from* any extant mixture or the unlimited. This point becomes clear in the forthcoming

discussion of cause. By contrast, Gadamer gives priority to the mixed class as the single source of limit and unlimited. Gadamer concedes that "it is possible to *disregard* this connection of number and measure [i.e., limit] to things [i.e., mixtures]" and then to define them "in this detached state" (Hans-Georg Gadamer, *Plato's Dialectical Ethics: Phenomenological Interpretation Relating to the "Philebus,"* trans. Robert M. Wallace [New Haven, Conn.: Yale University Press, 1991], 134–38, my emphasis). But his language of "disregard" appears to mean that he thinks limit and unlimited belong *originally* together in the mixture, and we can simply ignore this fact and create an "abstraction" that separates limit and unlimited. Thus, he says limit and unlimited are "existential moments [*Seinsmomente*]" of mixture (137). By contrast, I think that for Plato a mixture as mixture is impossible without the original separateness of limit from unlimited or any mixture. See 2.2.

29. For the view that mixture is not equivalent to emergence, see Sayre, *Late Ontology*, 174–86; and Constance C. Meinwald, "Plato's Pythagoreanism," *Ancient Philosophy* 22 (2002): 87–101. Both see the forms as mixtures of limit and unlimited but not as emergent things. I see the balance of evidence (especially "the genesis of the third kind" at *Philebus*, 26d1 ff.) as suggesting that all mixtures become. For a mixture never reaches a point at which it can be guaranteed, if left to itself, not to devolve and differ from the status it attains when measured. By contrast, a form cannot fail to be what it is even if all by itself. Thus, forms are not mixtures, though they are mixable.

30. A "helping condition" is a condition with which something else can be done. But it is not the same as a "necessary condition," without which something else cannot be done. See Plato, *Phaedo*, 96a ff. for the latter. To say that "the present" has been a helping condition is just to say that another phenomenon could have occasioned our study of the kinds.

31. We find an agreement on this point in Immanuel Kant, "What Does It Mean to Orient Oneself in Thinking?" in *Religion within the Boundaries of Mere Reason and Other Writings*, trans. Allen Wood and George di Giovanni (Cambridge: Cambridge University Press, 1999), 7.

32. See also Plato, *Republic* V, 476c ff. on opinion's object as being and nonbeing.

33. Even if this passage is not already stating that the limit and unlimited in themselves are distinct from the cause (which is clearly stated later), it could, instead, be read as making a distinction between limit itself and limit-as-employed-in-mixing, or between the unlimited and the unlimited-as-employed-in-mixing. These "subjected" version limit and unlimited would then be said here to be different from the cause. Either reading makes possible a distinction between the product/process and the "subject."

34. If mixtures are thus explicable as coming from limit and unlimited, we do not thereby reject the idea that each mixture is unique and in some sense can be said to be original as mixture or even created ex nihilo. For the unlimited becoming from which any mixture must emerge never in itself attains "being itself." It is rather an incessant becoming, and it no more "is" than it "is not." Only in this sense can we say that mixtures come from nonbeing, that is, only if by nonbeing we mean "not-itself-being" or "not-itself-limit." Compare to Aristotle, *Physics* I, 8-9.

35. See Robert Bolton, "Plato's Distinction between Becoming and Being," *Review of Metaphysics* 29 (1975): 66–95; as well as Eugene E. Benitez, *Forms in Plato's "Philebus"* (Assen/Maastricht, Neth.: Van Gorcum, 1989), 92–108 for problems arising from the fact that becoming is sometimes spoken of as "never being" and other times is spoken of as "a kind of being." The former I take to refer to the unlimited flux. The latter refers to a mixture, which emerges with some measure. Furthermore, see Plato, *Statesman*, 283a for a

parallel treatment of measure as the necessary condition for the "emergence" of something. I do not take the latter passage to state that all kinds of becoming are mixtures. Rather, the *Statesman* is talking about the things with which a *craft* deals (e.g., health-in-bodies), and it is supposing that measure is the necessary condition for the generation of *those* beings. The *Philebus* would refer to those beings as mixtures having some definiteness. Thus, measure is a necessary condition for the emergence of mixed things; measure is nowhere found in the indefinite becoming itself. See also 2.3 and especially 3.2.

36. For the full argument see Plato, *Gorgias*, 488e ff.

37. See also 1.1–1.3.

38. For more detail on the way intellect is instantiated in varieties of living beings, see Brisson, "Continuum," as well as Carpenter, "Embodied."

39. On the oddness of Socrates's use of the terminology of "king," see Cornelius Castoriadis, *On Plato's "Statesman,"* trans. David A. Curtis (Stanford, Calif.: Stanford University Press, 2002), 34 ff.

40. Socrates makes three jokes indicating that the discussion of divine intellect is "playful" (28c7, 30e9, and 34d7).

41. This placement of one example beside another is explored at Plato, *Statesman*, 278a8 ff., where a "paradigm" is generated when a simple instantiation of something stands "beside" and helps us grasp a more complex instantiation. On παράδειγμα as signifying both sensible examples and perfect instances of forms, see Victor Goldschmidt, *Le Paradigme dans la dialectique platonicienne* (Paris: Presses Universitaires de France, 1947).

42. See Cornelius Castoriadis, *Philosophy, Politics, Autonomy*, trans. David A. Curtis (Oxford: Oxford University Press, 1991), 163: "Tradition means that the question of the legitimacy of the tradition cannot be raised." See also the famous line from Al-Ghazali: "[The] essential condition in the holder of a traditional faith is that he should not know he is a traditionalist."

Chapter 3

1. Daniel Russell, *Plato on Pleasure and the Good Life* (Oxford: Clarendon, 2005), 21–27. Russell, following Korsgaard in part, defines (i) an intrinsic good as something "valuable in its own right" (versus an extrinsic good for which "value must be brought about in it"). He argues that all intrinsic goods are also (ii) unconditional goods, meaning they "bring about value in other things" (versus conditional goods in which "something else brings about value"). Russell also distinguishes (iii) final goods (versus instrumental goods) and argues that this distinction is not the same as either of the others. He ultimately concludes that no pleasure is intrinsically or unconditionally good, not even "pure pleasure." I will argue, by contrast, that pure pleasure shares in causing value to emerge, is a valuable "possession" in its own right, and is completely good (though it is not an end-goal).

2. The second list speaks of "causes." See 3.3.

3. Paul Shorey, *The Unity of Plato's Thought* (Chicago: University of Chicago Press, 1903), 22–25. Shorey speaks here about pleasure generally in Plato.

4. Gadamer, *Dialectical Ethics*, 192–94; Gabriella R. Carone, *Plato's Cosmology and Its Ethical Dimensions* (Cambridge: Cambridge University Press, 2005), 108–9; and Francisco Bravo, "Genesis of Pleasure and Pleasure-Genesis in Plato's *Philebus*," in *Inner Life and Soul: Psyche in Plato* (Sankt Augustin, Ger.: Academia Verlag, 2011), 61 all argue that when pleasure is understood properly as it *is*, rather than as *becoming*, pleasure can be understood as good. I argue that all pleasures become, including good ones (see 3.3).

Similarly, some have argued that anything that pleases us counts as a pure pleasure; false pleasures simply do not please us. I argue that such a view misses the sense of "pure" at work in the dialogue (see 4.5). For this debate, see, for example, J. C. B. Gosling, "False Pleasures: *Philebus* 35c–41b," *Phronêsis* 4 (1959): 44–53; Anthony Kenny, "False Pleasures in the *Philebus*: A Reply to Mr. Gosling," *Phronêsis* 5 (1962): 45–52; Terry M. Penner, "False Anticipatory Pleasures: *Philebus* 36a3–41a6," *Phronêsis* 15 (1970): 166–78; Dorothea Frede, "Rumpelstiltskin's Pleasures," *Phronêsis* 30 (1985): 151–80; and Sylvain Delcomminette, "Appearance and Imagination in the *Philebus*," *Phronêsis* 48 (2003): 215–37.

5. Against the intrinsic value of pleasure, see, for example, Dorothea Frede, "Life and Its Limitations: The Conception of Happiness in the *Philebus*," in *Plato's "Philebus": Selected Papers from the Eighth Symposium Platonicum*, ed. John Dillon and Luc Brisson (Sankt Augustin, Ger.: Academia Verlag, 2010), 3–16; Russell, *Plato on Pleasure*; Catherine H. Zuckert, *Plato's Philosophers: The Coherence of the Dialogues* (Chicago: University of Chicago Press, 2009), 409–10; and Joachim Aufderheide, "An Inconsistency in the *Philebus*?" *British Journal for the History of Philosophy* 21 (2013): 817–37. Aufderheide distinguishes the "two lists" as I have. Nevertheless, he argues that "nothing insofar as it is a *genesis* is good in its own right" (835). Thus, while he says pure pleasure is good (in its own right), he also argues it is not good insofar as it still comes-to-be. See my counterargument in 3.2.

6. Emily A. Austin, "Fools and Malicious Pleasure in Plato's *Philebus*," *History of Philosophy Quarterly* 29 (2012): 125–39 argues that "mixed" pleasure-pain experiences belong in the sixth "empty" position in the final list of goods. For a counterargument, see Beatriz Bossi, "How Consistent Is Plato with Regard to the 'Unlimited' Character of Pleasure in the *Philebus*?" in *Plato's "Philebus": Selected Papers from the Eighth Symposium Platonicum*, 123–33, which offers excellent reasons for not including mixed pleasure-pain events in the final order.

7. Russell, *Plato on Pleasure*, 27 denies this possibility. His argument would be correct if ontological dependency implied, for Plato, a lack of value. See 3.2.

8. See *Plato, Republic* VI, 509b10.

9. Per the *Gorgias*, pleasure is not the good. Pleasures are like the case of, for example, recovery from a painful lack of nourishment (e.g., 494c ff., 496e ff.). The pleasure in "eating" can occur only if a lack of nourishment is presently in process of being filled. Thus, the pursuit of pleasure cannot be the pursuit of the good. For the presence of a good, like health, is not conditioned upon ongoing filling and thus on lingering, yet-filled deficiency (494c2). Health endures even when sickness departs completely.

10. Socrates uses ἀπιέναι, ἀπόδοσις, or, most generally, simply πλήρωσις, without any connotation of *re*-turn, for the motion involved in various pleasures. This passage shows that "fulfillment [πλήρωσις]" cannot be taken literally since the "coagulation" of freezing counts here as an emptying, while the "redistribution" counts as the fulfillment. We can thus take πλήρωσις generally to mean a coming-to-a-norm; and κένωσις is used for any move away from the norm. Contrast my view that πλήρωσις is the general term for the motion in pleasure with David Wolfsdorf, *Pleasure in Ancient Greek Philosophy* (Cambridge: Cambridge University Press, 2012), 43, 77, and 97–99. He takes the general term to be *re*storation. See my review of his book: John V. Garner, "David Wolfsdorf: *Pleasure in Ancient Greek Philosophy*," *Ancient Philosophy* 34 (2014): 462–67.

11. At 31d8 Socrates says this initial account of pleasure works "if we must pronounce only a few words on the weightiest matters in the shortest possible time."

12. Socrates refers to the "natural condition [τὴν αὐτῆς φύσιν]" (31d9) as a mixture or harmony (ἁρμονία), established by a cause (αἰτία) (26e). Socrates later suggests that at least some souls participate in this causality. See 3.3.

13. See 3.3 for pleasures not involving *bodily* motion.

14. Socrates establishes several levels. First, for the gods, something like a natural condition (which mortal animals do not finally attain) is without any becoming and thus would be a condition also neutral with respect to pleasure and pain (see 21e, 27b1, 32e1–33b7, 44b–d, 55a5). Second, for most mortal beings, it is probably the case that the soul is largely or entirely bound to bodily motions, meaning that the ability for it to attain the psychically neutral condition is impossible or rare (i.e., only when the body is briefly [if this is even possible] not in flux). However, third, for mortal living beings like humans, a neutral condition of soul is indeed possible through non-perception (as I argue below). (Pure pleasure is not a neutral condition, since it involves awareness of fulfillment.) Carone, *Plato's Cosmology*, 262–64 argues that gods experience pleasure, against the straightforward reading of 33b6, which states that the gods do not experience pleasure (and she does this only by implausibly denying that all pleasures are lack-fulfillments). Her conclusion is also challenged, in part, by the absence of the term ἡδονή in her supporting passages. See also Suzanne Obdrzalek, "Next to Godliness: Pleasure and Assimilation in God in the *Philebus*," *Apeiron* 45 (2012): 1–31, 213–14 for a cogent objection to Carone.

15. The psychical state alone does not determine whether there is a *bodily* pleasure, since bodily motions are also a factor. But psychical awareness of bodily motion is sufficient for bodily pleasure.

16. See Theodore J. Tracy, *Physiological Theory and the Doctrine of the Mean in Plato and Aristotle* (Chicago: Loyola University Press, 1969), 123–36.

17. Socrates does not overlook the distinction between non-perception and forgetting. It is Protarchus who responds by saying that the flux is "forgotten," thus confusing non-perception and forgetting. Alternatively, it is possible that λανθάνειν is here used nontechnically to mean "overlook." The term was used nontechnically at 33d9, before Socrates corrected himself and introduced the term's technical sense.

18. At 32a ff. and 51a ff. Socrates refers to unperceived motions without specific reference to the magnitude of bodily impacts being small or light. Contrast Van Riel, *Pleasure and the Good Life*, 24–25.

19. Not all psychical pleasures involve *bodily* motions. The point here is that pleasure is not taken in the bodily motion unless that motion is also shared with soul (e.g., in perception). See Carpenter, "Embodied."

20. Van Riel, *Pleasure and the Good Life*; and especially Kelly Arenson, "Natural and Neutral States in Plato's *Philebus*," *Apeiron* 44 (2011): 191–209 have definitively established the distinction between the "neutral state" and the "natural condition" based on these passages.

21. Pleasureless pains are mentioned at Plato, *Timaeus* 65b but not in the *Philebus*.

22. Pleasures can emerge only where there is soul. For even at 21b ff., when pleasure is considered "by itself," soul's sensation is present. Thus Socrates implies that the "mollusk" (a) might be pleased to a degree and (b) has a psychical motion and bodily motion which are all but indistinct (21c7). Generally, this near-indistinguishability of soul's self-motion from bodily (other-generated) motions is an important factor distinctive of nonrational (or less-rational) animals. See Brisson, "Le Continuum."

23. See Benitez, *Forms in Plato's "Philebus,"* 92–108.

24. See note 9. The *Gorgias* does not clarify the psychical precondition for pleasure and thus suggests that pleasure cannot outlast "pain" (496e5). Once the psychical condition for pleasure is established in the *Philebus*, however, it becomes clear that both dialogues really imply that no pleasure can outlast deficiency-fulfillment (while some pleasures can still be painless).

25. Thus, even the experience of pure pleasure will preclude the pursuit of the experience of it, for the pursuit implies one is motivated by one's notice of one's own deficiency.

26. Whatever is unlimited "becomes unlimited" (24b). See 2.3.

27. See note 9. See also Plato, *Phaedo*, 60b5 where Socrates says pleasure and pain are "joined at the head." Only the common pleasures are bound to prior or subsequent pain. Contrast *Philebus*, 51b.

28. See 2.5.

29. "When the natural combination of limit and unlimitedness that forms a live organism . . . is destroyed, this destruction is pain, while the return towards its own nature, this general restoration, is pleasure" (32b1–4). These pleasures are defined relatively to the established structure of the living beings (mixtures) for which they emerge. Thus, these pleasures are no longer defined in the "purely relative" sense like the unlimited. See also 2.3.

30. Bossi, "How Consistent Is Plato."

31. Bossi, "How Consistent Is Plato," 130 argues that once pleasure is "limited" by the cause (here personified as a goddess), thus creating natural harmony, pleasure does not easily remain within those limits. There always remains the potential for "unlimitedness to develop beyond the natural limits she herself sets." Thus, "ordering action is not finished [by the goddess] but *requires our subsequent government* to subdue pleasure to its measure and proportion with regard to other desires" (130, my emphasis). Bossi's explanation captures the way humans participate essentially in an ongoing establishment of measure.

32. See Donald Zeyl, "Plato and Talk of a World in Flux: *Timaeus* 49a6–50b5," *Harvard Studies in Classical Philology* 79 (1975): 125–48 and Bolton, "Plato's Distinction" for accounts of flux in general in Plato.

33. See Bravo, "Genesis of Pleasure," and Gadamer, *Dialectical Ethics*, 192–94 for more refined defenses of this view.

34. Since for Aristotle process is subordinated to the actuality of a being and pleasure is also an end-goal, he argues that pleasure is or belongs to the actuality of a being, which determines the end-goal. See Aristotle, *Nicomachean Ethics* VII and X.

35. Amber D. Carpenter, "Pleasure as Genesis in Plato's *Philebus*," *Ancient Philosophy* 31 (2011): 73–94.

36. Cynthia Hampton, *Pleasure, Knowledge, and Being: An Analysis of Plato's "Philebus"* (Albany: State University of New York Press, 1990) and J. C. B. Gosling and C. C. W. Taylor, *The Greeks on Pleasure* (Oxford: Clarendon, 1982) argue that not all pleasures require fulfillment. I would direct the reader to the arguments of Dorothea Frede, "Disintegration and Restoration: Pleasure and Pain in Plato's *Philebus*," in *The Cambridge Companion to Plato*, ed. Richard Kraut (New York: Cambridge University Press, 1992): 425–63; Thomas Tuozzo, "The General Account of Pleasure in Plato's *Philebus*," *Journal of the History of Philosophy* 34 (1996): 495–513; Van Riel, *Pleasure and the Good Life*, 21–22; Carpenter, "Pleasure as Genesis"; and James Warren, *The Pleasures of Reason in Plato, Aristotle, and the Hellenistic Hedonists* (Cambridge: Cambridge University Press, 2014), 21–51 (among others), all of which defend general "fulfillment" conditions as holding for all pleasures. Also, Mitchel Miller, "The Pleasures of the Comic and of Socratic Inquiry:

Aporetic Reflections on *Philebus* 48a–50b," *Arethusa* 41 (2008): 263–89 has provided a cogent argument showing how the fulfillment model applies to the difficult case of 47e ff.

37. Aufderheide, "Inconsistency in the *Philebus*?" states this problem clearly. However, he argues that pleasure's ontological dependency is evidence that it has lesser value. See Warren, *Pleasures of Reason*, 21–51 for an objection similar to my own.

38. See note 9. See also Bravo, "Genesis of Pleasure." Bravo rightly argues that pleasures generally are becoming. Yet Bravo's solution to subtlers' problems is to posit that good pleasure uniquely escapes becoming and attains being. His argument thus in effect accepts the subtlers' identification of being and goodness.

39. Warren, *Pleasures of Reason*, 21–51 summarizes the problem.

40. Plato, *Gorgias*, 499e–500a can be read as saying that by choosing to live for the good, and to live a life of "sound jars," we are merely *in effect* "choosing and acting to have" the "beneficial pleasures." He is not committing to the idea that we should choose to live for any pleasure as an end-goal, for that would require seeking the prerequisite lack. He can be understood instead to be saying that the choice for sound jars is in effect the choice for the life that good pleasures themselves follow. See notes 41 and 42 below for more on Plato's conception of an end-goal.

41. Plato, *Gorgias*, 470a9 suggests that if one acts or rests for the sake of a genuine good end-goal (and therefore one is doing what one truly wants), then "acting as one sees fit follows [ἕπηται] acting beneficially" (470a9). Thus, the seemingly ascetic *Gorgias* leaves space for just pleasures. See also at 499d and 500a7. See note 42.

42. Even good pleasure is not for Plato a final goal in Aristotle's sense of an end-goal. A final goal for Aristotle is valuable for its own sake *and* other things are valued for *its* sake (e.g., *Metaphysics* B, 994b9–16). Pure pleasure here, by contrast, can be complete (τέλεος) in goodness without being pursued as an end-goal in the latter sense. Thus, when *Republic* II, 357a ff. says some pleasures are "welcomed [ἀσπαζόμενοι] for themselves," Socrates is only saying that given our condition of lack, they are welcomed, not that we should pursue their emergence (and thereby seek to create or sustain a lack). Further, when Socrates there denies that harmless pleasures are good merely for "what results from them [οὐ τῶν ἀποβαινόντων ἐφιέμενοι]," he is also careful not to deny there that pleasure is in itself still an "effect" or γιγνόμενον.

43. It is not wrong to say becoming "is" in some way; but it is wrong to say that it "is" completely and independently. See Benitez, *Forms in Plato's "Philebus,"* 92–108.

44. Socrates continues by saying that, according to the subtlers, nobody would choose destruction instead of a "neutral life." Recall that Socrates himself distinguishes (a) the "neutral life" of unperceived flux from both (b) the "natural condition" without fulfillments or lacks (which is probably unattainable for animals) and (c) the good life, involving pure pleasure fulfillments.

45. Socrates's agreement with this idea does not commit him to the badness of becoming. He is only committed to saying that it is not good to *pursue* a becoming, since that requires also pursuing the prerequisite deficiency of being. Thus, Socrates only needs to say that "all being is some good," not "less being entails less goodness."

46. Gosling and Taylor, *Greeks on Pleasure*, separates the subtlers from the anti-hedonist "naturalists" mentioned at 44b. Some evidence supports the idea that they are the same persons, since they both prefer reason alone without pleasure. See Plato, *Republic*, 505b–c and *Gorgias*, 493a.

47. For Christine Korsgaard, "Two Distinctions in Goodness," *Philosophical Review* 2 (1983): 169–96 there are final goods that are not intrinsic goods. Here, I argue in effect that there are also intrinsic goods that are not final goods. See note 1.

48. Van Riel, *Pleasure and the Good Life*, 40 argues that each and every pleasure "tends towards its own destruction, since it is directed to a condition beyond all lack (and thus beyond replenishment)." This means pleasure, as becoming, is directed to *being* (i.e., non-becoming). In my view, Socrates rejects this argument (i.e., the subtlers' argument) identifying the goal of pleasure with being. Rather, good pleasure can achieve its proper goodness in *becoming well*.

49. See Helen S. Lang, "On Memory: Aristotle's Corrections of Plato," *Journal of the History of Philosophy* 18 (1980): 379–93.

50. Satoshi Ogihara, "The Contrast between Soul and Body in the Analysis of Pleasure in the *Philebus*," in *Plato's "Philebus": Selected Papers from the Eighth Symposium Platonicum*, 215–20 catalogs many ways soul is independent of body in the *Philebus*.

51. For categorizations of false pleasures, see Gosling and Taylor, *Greeks on Pleasure*; Wolfsdorf, *Pleasure in Ancient Greek Philosophy*; and Warren, *Pleasures of Reason*. See also "Introduction," note 4.

52. That is, soul can access a coming bodily fulfillment that has never yet been encountered by body. Memory accounts for this ability to access (desire) such a fulfillment. Thus, memory cannot be restricted to memory of prior perception in time. Indeed, Socrates explicitly says memory is preservation of either (a) a perception or (b) a lesson (μάθημα), the source of which can be unrelated to body. See Benitez, *Forms in Plato's "Philebus,"* 114.

53. Protarchus thinks being thirsty is a pain and so is the hope for a non-present fulfillment. That is, he thinks hoping adds a second level of pain, making for "double pain." Socrates disagrees, since hoping for non-present fulfillment is a psychical pleasure (not a pain) that mixes with the present psycho-bodily pain of thirst. The experience of despair (or unhope) during a bodily destruction is in fact the true "double pain." Socrates here provides a powerful defense of hope, though he implies that it would be better not to have to hope. For a related defense of hope, see Augustine of Hippo, *The City of God against the Pagans*, ed. and trans. R. W. Dyson (Cambridge: Cambridge University Press, 1998), book XIX.

54. Plato, *Phaedo*, 60b, implying that Socrates's pleasure ceases before pain arrives (and vice versa), does not imply that mixtures of pleasures and pains are impossible. Socrates's death was a mixed pleasure-pain for Phaedo.

55. Ludwig Feuerbach, *Lectures on the Essence of Religion* (New York: Harper and Row, 1967), 276–85.

56. Freedom from pain is not a sufficient criterion for pure pleasure but only a "mark of similarity" (44a5 and 51e3). A person free of pain or distress could be in the neutral, pleasureless condition. Thus, we can contrast Plato's pure pleasures with Epicurean katastematic pleasures.

57. See Plato's *Timaeus*, 64a ff. for an account of the physiological side of this psychosomatic experience.

58. See McCabe, *Plato's Individuals*, 251–53; and Harte, *Plato on Parts*, 27–28, 162, and 200. See also 2.4 and 1.4.

59. Hence, there is a πλήρωσις here in the general sense of coming-to-a-norm. See note 10.

60. See 2.4 on the completeness of music as something expressible as a process of coming-to-completeness.

61. See 1.4 on the importance of determining the "how-many" for learning. See also 4.5.

62. See also Plato, *Republic*, 585b1–6 where true pleasures of soul are also called fulfillments of soul's ignorance. Importantly, the term πλήρωσις, used in both cases, might refer either to a "process" or to a "completion of a process." Even if the latter is right, the completion should be understood as an ongoing *coming-to-completion* in these cases. Carone, *Plato's Cosmology* and Bravo, "Genesis of Pleasure" argue implausibly that πλήρωσις implies a completed state of being.

63. Forgetting or ignorance either may presently condition learning's possibility or may be presaged, by a learning experience, as a potential future loss that might follow for the soul later in time. In either case the lack cannot be noticed without prior, actual learning itself.

64. Warren, *Pleasures of Reason*, 25 seems correct in arguing that pains of ignorance have these necessary conditions: (1) "the lack of knowledge must be noticed or reflected upon"; and (2) "the knowledge that is lacking must be recognized as needed or necessary in some way." However, my view is that the second criterion also demands a third, which makes the other two possible: (3) to notice a lack or to recognize some knowledge as needed already requires and implies that the soul is engaging in a prior learning (or relearning), and this learning is *separable* from any such notice of lack or of a need for knowledge.

65. I would only tentatively suggest the possibility of distinguishing *alethic* pure pleasures, which recover from forgetting, from *anagnostic* pure pleasures more generally, which move out of a general agnostic condition.

66. Learning can occur without prior recognition of ignorance; but recognition of ignorance cannot occur without prior learning. A reconciliation of my account with depictions of learning as painful or as preceded by aporia could focus on the way "originary learning," as pure, is separate from, prior to, and implied as possible in all those mixed cases of learning that involve aporia and pain. But learning itself must not be confused with such cases of mixed learning. See also Warren, *Pleasures of Reason*, 37–50.

67. Memorials, as expressions of human life, may therefore offer a remnant of past events of human perception (αἴσθησις) or, more powerfully, they may offer a remnant of a (re)newable process of learning (μάθησις). Thus, we need not posit a complete dis-analogy between material memorialization and human practices of memorization.

68. See 4.4.

69. See chapter 4, note 1.

70. The *Philebus* thus clarifies that any supposed demand for "assimilation to God" does not mean humans are to strive for a "neutral state" by eliminating our awareness of bodily or psychical processes. Augustine, challenging Stoics, argued similarly against pursuing desensitization in *City of God* XIX.

71. Admittedly, the *Philebus* never uses the phrasing we find in the *Phaedrus* or *Laws* X where soul is called "self-moving motion." Even so, we have seen that some psychical fillings are not merely re-turns to a pre-given natural harmony but are rather original turnings. Thus, something like self-moving motion is implied and indeed required in the *Philebus*. This is also suggested by the priority of πέρας relative to any mixture made from it and by the flexibility of the concept of filling (πλήρωσις), which involves no "re-." These concepts allow us to see that psyche can access and can even institute-into-becoming a measure which has never yet come to be until now. Of course, this does not imply that the measure has no *being* before it is brought to *become* by the soul.

72. On this power of intellection, see the conclusion to chapter 2 and 4.4.

73. Hence, reason will still be ranked only third, because its value comes from the way it brings measure and measuredness (first and second rank) into the mixture.

74. See 2.1.

75. See the conclusion to chapter 1.

76. See Philippa M. Lang, "The Ranking of the Goods at *Philebus* 66a–67b," *Phronêsis* 55 (2010): 153–69; and Aufderheide, "Inconsistency in the *Philebus*?" See also note 37.

77. Pure pleasure's status as "following" from the sciences does not mean that the pure pleasure is the pleasure of knowledge. For knowledge, in its essence, is unchanging (see 4.4). Rather, it means that learning can only occur if there is a knowledge to attain; and it is in the *attaining* of that knowledge that the pleasures follow. Also, the claim about "following" is coordinate with the argument against pleasure-seeking. See note 9. Also, while the term for "following" (ἕπειν) here is different from the term analyzed in 2.5 (ἐπακολουθεῖν), it is nevertheless important that pure pleasure cannot exist without prior causes in the mixture taking the "leading" role. It always "follows" in this sense, even though it also "leads" insofar as it brings a unique kind of emergent-measure into the order. Compare this difficulty of a leading-following with the concept of self-moving motion, for example, at Plato, *Phaedrus*, 245c and *Laws* X.

78. See 52b7 on the rarity of pure pleasures.

79. See note 1.

80. See 2.4.

81. See Frede, "Disintegration and Restoration."

82. See the conclusion to chapter 4. See also Russon, "We Sense That They Strive," 79 on the "space of the *not*" as the "space of the *good*."

83. "[Both] reason and pleasure had lost any claim that one or the other would be the good itself, since they were lacking in autonomy and in the power of self-sufficiency and completeness" (67a5–8, translation modified). See also Aufderheide, "Inconsistency in the *Philebus*?" 826.

Chapter 4

1. Intensity of pleasure is almost always the surest sign of extreme lack, for example, of disease of soul or body. See 66a and 63d. Further, the violent pleasures belong "to the class of the unlimited, the more and less, which affects both body and soul," whereas pure pleasure "we will assign to the class of things that possess measurement" (52c1–d8). Importantly, these latter pleasures "possess measurement [ἔμμετρος]" and belong to the mixed class; they are not limits themselves belonging in the class of limit (πέρας). Contrast with Eva Brann, *Feeling Our Feelings: What Philosophers Think and People Know* (Philadelphia: Paul Dry Books, 2008), 48.

2. See Plato, *Cratylus*, 426a.

3. See Simone de Beauvoir, *Ethics of Ambiguity*, trans. Bernard Frechtman (New York: Citadel, 1949), part 2 on the dangers of delusional nihilism.

4. Seth Bernadete, *The Tragedy and Comedy of Life: Plato's "Philebus"* (Chicago: University of Chicago Press, 1991), 209–12 argues implausibly that the Socratic irony here implies that pure pleasure is in truth a pain.

5. There is nothing wrong with the prediction or hope that pure pleasure will emerge when the purity-conditions are in place. The problem is with the pursuit of pleasure's emergence or the establishment of the preconditioning lack. See 3.3.

6. Dorothea Frede, "Introduction," in *Philebus: Translation with Introductory Essay* (Indianapolis, Ind.: Hackett, 1993), lviii.

7. Socrates will not discover bad or false knowledges as he discovered bad and false pleasures. See Frede, *Philebus*, 67.

8. As for what must be excluded, Socrates either examines kinds of false and bad pleasures one by one (36a–50e), or he notes that some pleasures are necessarily associated with bad or harmful things, such as a vicious character or a disease (e.g., at 63e). Such pleasures exclude themselves. This self-exclusion is dramatically represented by Philebus's self-exclusion from dialogue.

9. The ἆρά ἐστί is the question of "whether there is . . . ?" It is not a "how there is" or "why there is." For these latter presuppose a fact but do not question the fact. The ἆρά ἐστί allows for genuine surprise such as the surprise in learning. This sense of the ἆρά ἐστί is related to the difference between a "problem" and a "theorem" as explored by Proclus, *A Commentary on the First Book of Euclid's "Elements,"* trans. Glen R. Morrow (Princeton, N.J.: Princeton University Press, 1992), 65: "When, therefore, we propose to inscribe an equilateral triangle in a circle, we call it a *problem*, for it is possible to inscribe a triangle that is not equilateral. . . . But when a man sets out to prove that angles at the base of an isosceles triangle are equal, we should say that he is proposing a *theorem*, for it is not possible that the angles at the base of an isosceles triangle should not be equal." In both the ἆρά ἐστί and in a problem, something different than what is proposed is always presumed possible.

10. The "productive" and "manual" arts may not be exactly synonymous terms. But since the initial classes are heuristic, and the point is to discover the basis of any science, deciding this issue is not vital.

11. See 2.5 where the cause is defined as bringing limit and as leading.

12. If we were dividing a genus, the division might include art => productive art => building productive art => arithmetical building productive art => purely arithmetical building productive art. Notice that the initial genus would never be transcended.

13. "But let us first find out whether within the manual arts there is one side more [μᾶλλον] closely related to knowledge itself, the other less [ἧττον] closely related" (55d5). This invocation of the "more and less" in the beginning of the division process indicates the indefinitude still present in the initial starting point. See 2.3.

14. Contrast with Aristotle, *Metaphysics* Z, 12–17 and H, 6, where all the subdivisions of a genus, and the genus itself, telescope into the last division; they approach prime substance, which is never predicated of another. Lower divisions are thus less universal.

15. My reading owes a debt to Frede, *Philebus*, lix. Also, Gadamer rightly noticed this increase in universality of understanding as we "divide." But he does not mention the necessity that the discovered universal must be in itself independent of the division's heuristic starting point. See Gadamer, *Dialectical Ethics*, 202–3.

16. See, for example, Hackforth, *Plato's Examination*, 114, which expresses confusion over why the *Philebus*'s division arrives at a later science (pure arithmetic) which then has relevance to something outside (educative arts) the initial class. See also Benitez, *Forms in Plato's "Philebus,"* 126.

17. Socrates may call pure unit arithmetic "philosophical" because it can be traced back to the Pythagoreans, whose notion of number is precisely an aggregate of identical units. See Nichomachus, *Introduction to Arithmetic*, 190. Even so, the Pythagorean tradition seems to have counted sensible things as in essence reducible to these units, while Socrates allows that sensible things are not simply units or reducible to units. See 2.4.

18. My view on this issue accords broadly with Gadamer's claim that there is an "unwritten dialectic" rather than, strictly speaking, an "unwritten doctrine," at the basis of the dialogues. Gadamer, in "Plato's Unwritten Dialectic," avoids two competing options. The first group consists of views taking dialogue as secondary to an underlying doctrine. See, for example, Hans J. Krämer, *Plato and the Foundations of Metaphysics: A Work on the Theory of the Principles and Unwritten Doctrines of Plato*, trans. John R. Catan (Albany: State University of New York Press, 1990); Giovanni Reale, *Toward a New Interpretation of Plato*, trans. John R. Catan and Richard Davies (Washington: Catholic University of America Press, 1997); J. N. Findlay, *Plato: The Written and Unwritten Doctrines* (London: Routledge and Kegan Paul, 1974); and Léon Robin, *La Théorie platonicienne des idées et des nombres d'après Aristote: Étude historique et critique* (Paris: Félix Alcan, 1908). Gadamer also avoids complete skepticism concerning the possibility of undercutting the dialogue by unwritten doctrines, as we find in Harold Cherniss, *Aristotle's Criticism of Plato and the Academy* (Baltimore: Johns Hopkins University Press, 1944) and, to an extent, in Gerald Press, *Who Speaks for Plato? Studies in Platonic Anonymity* (Lanham, Md.: Rowman and Littlefield, 2000). Gadamer's position instead defends a distinctive third way: "I would hold that the essential core of Plato's doctrine was presented in ongoing didactic discussion which engage the participants for whole days at a time and establish a living community among them" ("Plato's Unwritten Dialectic," 126). Further, he argues, "[It] is vital to read Plato's dialogues not as theoretical treatises but as mimêsis (imitation) of real discussions" (Hans-Georg Gadamer, *The Idea of the Good in Platonic-Aristotelian Philosophy*, trans. P. C. Smith [New Haven, Conn.: Yale University Press, 1986], 97).

19. See the "Introduction" to Julia Annas, *Aristotle's "Metaphysics" M and N* (Oxford: Oxford University Press, 1976).

20. See Proclus, *Euclid*, 3–69 on the "projection" following from and/or presaging a complete understanding of the forms. With Plato he rightly implies that it is psychically necessary for us, but not metaphysically necessary, for knowledge to become manifest in such projections. Also, the following reconstruction of Plato's arithmetic owes greatly to Anders Wedberg, *Plato's Philosophy of Mathematics* (Westport, Conn.: Greenwood, 1955).

21. If for Aristotle the "measure" of any number of things is what is being counted, then for Plato by contrast the measure is the form itself (e.g., the two, or the doctor). Thus, if I count (a) a "pair" of unequal things, then the counting of them is grounded in the projection of (b) a prior, pure group of "two pure units." But the latter is in turn grounded in (c) a prior intellectual grasp of the two itself, absent any units. The "measure" of the count-as-two is thus the form "two itself." Interpreters, however, sometimes say that the thing counted is the measure of the number in Plato, distinguishing Aristotle from Plato only in that the former employs units abstracted from sensible things while the latter employs posited pure units. Jacob Klein, *Greek Mathematical Thought and the Origin of Algebra*, trans. Eva Braan (Cambridge, Mass.: MIT Press, 1968) is instead correct when he notices that (a) depends on (b). Yet, while Klein also rightly notices that the "eidetic numbers" in turn ground the pure unit groups, he then turns and argues that this ground, that is, the "eidetic Two," really just "represents the *genos* of 'being' as such, which comprehends the two *eide* 'rest' and 'change.'" While I think Klein is right to ground (a) and (b) in the eidetic numbers, I suspect, contra his reading, that the form of being and the form of the two must be more rigorously distinguished. The two itself does not simply "represent" being. It is a distinct form for itself. That is, the two itself grounds the *count-as-two*, while being itself grounds the *count-as-being*. In short, we must conceive of the nature of the eidetic numbers differently than Klein conceives of them.

22. Furthermore, there need not be any essential hierarchy among sciences. Nichomachus, *Introduction to Arithmetic*, 188 notices that the needs of learning require a proper ordering: "Hence arithmetic abolishes geometry . . . but is not abolished by it, and while it is implied by geometry, it does not itself imply geometry." But we should not for that reason conclude that the study of one form is in itself better than the study of another. Dialectic can study each form arch-originally.

23. The prospect that there are myriad realities each having exactly all the properties of each other one violates the law of the indiscernibility of identicals. That the dialogues are not committed unequivocally to Leibniz's Law is also evident at Plato, *Cratylus*, 432c4–6.

24. See Plato, *Republic* VI, 511c9–d1 where dialectic makes use "only of forms themselves, moving on from forms to forms, and ending in forms."

25. See Plato, *Phaedo*, 96a ff.

26. See Plato, *Phaedo*, 74a9 ff.; *Phaedo*, 100b6 ff.; *Phaedo*, 101c5; Plato, *Republic* V, 476b7 ff.; *Republic* VI, 510d8; and *Republic* VII, 531a8 which extends dialectical knowledge to "each itself." See also "αὐτὸ τὸ ἀγαθὸν" at *Republic* VII, 534c4.

27. Roger Shiner, *Knowledge and Reality in Plato's "Philebus"* (Assen, Neth.: Van Gorcum, 1974) argues that the textual evidence here is compatible with the view that separate forms are abandoned by Plato. Shiner admits that he does not provide decisive evidence in favor of such revisionism, however. For a non-revisionist standpoint, see Cynthia Hampton, "Overcoming Dualism: The Intermediate in Plato's *Philebus*," in *Feminist Interpretations of Plato* (University Park: Pennsylvania State University Press, 1994), 225 and her *Pleasure, Knowledge, and Being*, 105, n. 30; as well as George Harvey, "The Supremacy of Dialectic in Plato's *Philebus*," *Ancient Philosophy* 32 (2012): 279–301. Also, Robert Fahrnkopf, "Forms in the *Philebus*," *Journal of the History of Philosophy* 15 (1977): 202 says "the Forms receive no explicit mention in these passages." By contrast, I take the present passages to use form-indicating expressions (see above). Furthermore, see also 2.4, since the fate of separate forms, I think, goes hand in hand with the fate of separate limit. To reduce limit to something else (whether to the mixture, the cause, or the unlimited) is, on my reading, tantamount to rejecting forms as well. In my view Socrates maintains the separation of both in the *Philebus*.

28. See Harvey, "Supremacy of Dialectic."

29. See Hampton, *Pleasure, Knowledge, and Being*, which devotes its primary thesis to this problem.

30. The Stoics appear, by contrast, to assert that the sage's knowledge excludes his having opinion. See A. A. Long and D. Sedley, eds., *The Hellenistic Philosophers, Volumes I and II* (Cambridge: Cambridge University Press, 1987), 249–53. Socrates allows by contrast that knowledge grounds, makes possible, or even generates right opinion (when reason is present in souls like ours). For a dissenting opinion about how to read Plato on opinion, see Katja M. Vogt, *Belief and Truth: A Skeptic Reading of Plato* (Oxford: Oxford University Press, 2012).

31. Thus, the *Philebus* does not make science itself a kind of process, contra A. P. David, *Plato's New Measure: The Indeterminate Dyad* (Austin, Tex.: Mother Pacha, 2011), 85–104. For νοῦς as such does not depend on becoming or soul. Yes, without some soul as a source of motion (i.e., a self-moving source of motion) νοῦς would not be able to become (see *Philebus*, 30c8: "σοφία μὴν καὶ νοῦς ἄνευ ψυχῆς οὐκ ἄν ποτε γενοίσθην.") But this is not to say that νοῦς must indeed become. This independence of νοῦς from becoming explains why an intellective soul can self-move itself even if other sources of motion are absent (see

Plato, *Laws* X, 895b ff.). See also Carpenter, "Embodied" and Stephen P. Menn, *Plato on God as Nous* (Carbondale: Southern Illinois University Press, 1995). Menn rightly notes that intellection cannot "become" without soul, and this does not mean intellect in itself is soul-dependent or dependent on motion. Also, Delcomminette, *Le "Philèbe,"* 477 tends, like David, to assimilate our knowledge as such to an ongoing learning process; but Warren, *Pleasures of Reason*, 37 ff. rightly distances himself from these views. See also 3.2 on process in general.

32. This loose reference to knowledge is also reflected in the *Seventh Letter*, 343d1 ff., where "knowledge [ἐπιστήμη]" is ultimately transcended by a "fifth," higher cognition. Presumably, this "fifth" could refer to intellection or to the unity of the account with the thing itself. See Giorgio Agamben, "The Thing Itself," *SubStance* 16 (1987): 18–28.

33. Intellect can be called an "element" here so long as we understand it in Proclus's sense of a *causal* element, as when "what proves is an element of what is proved by it," as opposed to a *material* element, such as the letters of a word. See Proclus, *Euclid*, 59–60.

34. "[Dialectic] gently pulls it [i.e., the soul] out and leads it upward, using the crafts we described to help it and cooperate with it in turning the soul around" (Plato, *Republic* VII, 533d3). Here, dialectic leans on disciplines like arithmetic. While dialectic and unit arithmetic both "make their claims for the sake of" the forms (510d9), the non-dialectical arithmetic relies on unquestioned assumptions. Dialectic, by contrast, seeks the grounds of any and all assumptions and "raises them up" to truth. "Therefore," concludes Socrates, "dialectic [ἡ διαλεκτικὴ μέθοδος] is the only inquiry that travels this road, doing away with [ἀναιροῦσα] hypotheses and proceeding to the first principle itself" (533c8–9).

35. Projections may be necessary consequences that human reason generates, and humans may need these projections; but neither projections nor material supports are necessary conditions for reason itself (e.g., for a possible divine reason). Contrast my view with the idea of the emergent "categorial novum" as elaborated by Nicholai Hartmann, *New Ways of Ontology* (New Brunswick, N.J.: Transaction, 2012). Contra Hartmann, I take it that for Plato the "higher" levels like reason in soul are not dependent for their reality on "lower" faculties like perception. Rather, the higher make the lower possible in their true versions.

36. Hence, knowledge is not restricted by preestablished limitations or human capacities (e.g., sensibility). Rather, the descent of reason, in its self-revelation to unreasoning and sensuous things, in effect generates and defines the power of a distinctively human sensibility.

37. See Robert S. Brumbaugh, *Plato for the Modern Age* (Lanham, Md.: University Press of America, 1991), 176.

38. Thus, any supposedly pure instance of science might be shown later, for us, to not have been the completely pure instance, as when a model in physics must be modified. Instances can progress indefinitely in purity. In this way, so-called progress in science can be accounted for as a progress in the instantiations of the science from impure to purer.

39. This order of disciplines in the *Republic* is definitive of what we call the three "dimensions" rather than guided by or adapted to a presupposed notion of space as having three dimensions. See Helen S. Lang, "Plato on Divine Art and the Production of Body," in *The Frontiers of Ancient Science: Essays in Honor of Heinrich von Staden*, ed. K.-D. Fischer and B. A. Holmes (Berlin: Walter de Gruyter, 2015).

40. The proximity of the term "beings" to "justice itself" should lead us to interpret "divine circle and sphere" as referring to the invisible form of circle itself.

41. "False" should not be applied to science directly. Strictly speaking, false science is just nonscience. Here, Socrates evidently means that the measure used is impure, thus yielding an impure science (as the reference to "lack" clarifies).

42. We recall that there are several classes of false pleasures, and those associated with false beliefs are only one class. See Warren, *Pleasures of Reason*, 1–9 and 41.

43. Gods, we recall, are not subject to pleasure (see 3.1). Likewise, intellect is not necessarily instantiated in a soul subject to undergoing lacks (which are necessary conditions for pleasures). But for animals like humans who do suffer lacks, the mere fact of remaining alive will involve us in some necessary pleasures.

44. See Christine Korsgaard, *Self-Constitution: Agency, Identity, Integrity* (Oxford: Oxford University Press, 2009), on the shared vision of a constitutional model of soul in Kant and Plato.

45. See Delcomminette, *Le "Philèbe,"* 556–58.

46. See 3.2 and 3.3. Also, notice that Socrates here says truth and goodness are "as it were, an incorporeal order which shall rule nobly over a living body" (64b6). The living body cannot fail to be something evolving, changing. The dialogue thus makes a special effort here to depict the good as shared with bodies. The whole truth thus involves, in addition to the self-motion of the incorporeal soul, also in effect the becoming of the psycho-bodily whole.

Conclusion

1. Nothing prevents a reformulated version of the Kantian dictum from holding true as well: what should come to be, can come to be.

2. The "begetter of this universe" in the *Timaeus* charges the created gods with the crafting of mortals: "It is you, then, who must turn yourselves to the task of fashioning these living things, as your nature allows. This will assure their mortality, and this whole universe will really be a completed whole." Notice that the whole is completed through the production of these mortals. Furthermore, the god continues the command and indicates that the mortals also share in the immortal: "Imitate the power I used in causing you to be. And to the extent that it is fitting for them to possess something that shares our name of 'immortal,' something described as divine and ruling within those of them who always consent to follow after justice and after you, I shall begin by sowing that seed, and then hand it over to you" (Plato, *Timaeus*, 41c). Perhaps, similarly, these created mortals like us also have a charge to create further emergent goods and to add to the complete whole by cultivating things that are ever coming-to-completion.

Agamben, Giorgio. "The Thing Itself." *SubStance* 16 (1987): 18–28.

Annas, Julia. *Aristotle's "Metaphysics" M and N.* Oxford: Oxford University Press, 1976.

———. *Platonic Ethics: Old and New.* Ithaca, N.Y.: Cornell University Press, 2000.

Anscomb, Elizabeth. "The New Theory of Forms." *Monist* 50 (1966): 403–20.

Arenson, Kelly. "Natural and Neutral States in Plato's *Philebus.*" *Apeiron* 44 (2011): 191–209.

Aristotle. *The Complete Works of Aristotle: The Revised Oxford Translation, Volumes I and II.* Edited by Jonathan Barnes. Oxford: Oxford University Press, 1984.

Aufderheide, Joachim. "An Inconsistency in the *Philebus?*" *British Journal for the History of Philosophy* 21 (2013): 817–37.

Augustine of Hippo. *The City of God against the Pagans.* Edited and translated by R. W. Dyson. Cambridge: Cambridge University Press, 1998.

Austin, Emily A. "Fools and Malicious Pleasure in Plato's *Philebus.*" *History of Philosophy Quarterly* 29 (2012): 125–39.

Badham, Charles. *The "Philebus" of Plato.* London: J. W. Parker, 1878.

Barker, Andrew. *Greek Musical Writings II: Harmonic and Acoustic Theory.* Cambridge: Cambridge University Press, 1989.

———. "Plato's *Philebus*: The Numbering of a Unity." *Apeiron* 29 (1996): 143–64.

———. *The Science of Harmonics in Classical Greece.* Cambridge: Cambridge University Press, 2007.

Beauvoir, Simone de. *Ethics of Ambiguity.* Translated by Bernard Frechtman. New York: Citadel, 1949.

Belangia, Sherwood. "Metaphysics Desire in Girard and Plato." *Comparative and Continental Philosophy* 2 (2010): 197–209.

Benitez, Eugene E. *Forms in Plato's "Philebus."* Assen/Maastricht, Neth.: Van Gorcum, 1989.

Bernadete, Seth. *The Tragedy and Comedy of Life: Plato's "Philebus."* Chicago: University of Chicago Press, 1991.

Bobonich, Christopher. "Plato's Theory of Goods in the *Laws* and the *Philebus.*" *Proceedings of the Boston Area Colloquium in Ancient Philosophy* 11 (1995): 101–39.

Bolton, Robert. "Plato's Distinction between Becoming and Being." *Review of Metaphysics* 29 (1975): 66–95.

Bossi, Beatriz. "How Consistent Is Plato with Regard to the 'Unlimited' Character of Pleasure in the *Philebus?*" In *Plato's "Philebus": Selected Papers from the Eighth Symposium Platonicum,* edited by John Dillon and Luc Brisson, 123–33. Sankt Augustin, Ger.: Academia Verlag, 2010.

Boussoulas, Nicolas-Isidore. *L'Être et la composition des mixtes dans le "Philèbe" de Platon.* Paris: Presses Universitaires de France, 1952.

Brann, Eva. *Feeling Our Feelings: What Philosophers Think and People Know.* Philadelphia: Paul Dry Books, 2008.

————. *The Music of the "Republic."* Philadelphia: Paul Dry Books, 2004.

Bravo, Francisco. "Genesis of Pleasure and Pleasure-Genesis in Plato's *Philebus*." In *Inner Life and Soul: Psyche in Plato*. Sankt Augustin, Ger.: Academia Verlag, 2011.

Brisson, Luc. "Le Continuum de la vie chez Platon, des dieux aux plantes." In *Lire Platon*. 2nd edition. Paris: Presses Universitaires de France, 2014.

Brogan, Walter A. "Figuring and Disfiguring Socrates: A Gadamerian Reflection on the Relationship of Text and Image in Plato's Philosophy." *Philosophy Today* 52 (2008): 144–50.

————. "Gadamer's Praise of Theory: Aristotle's Friend and the Reciprocity between Theory and Practice." *Research in Phenomenology* 32 (2002): 141–55.

————. *Heidegger and Aristotle*. Albany: State University of New York Press, 2005.

————. "Plato's Dialectical Soul: Heidegger on Plato's Ambiguous Relationship to Rhetoric." *Research in Phenomenology* 27 (1997): 3–15.

Brumbaugh, Robert S. *Plato for the Modern Age*. Lanham, Md.: University Press of America, 1991.

Burnet, John. *Platonis Opera: Recognovit Brevique Adnotatione Critica Instruxit*. Oxford: Oxford Classical Texts, 1900–1907.

Burnyeat, Miles. "Plato on Why Mathematics Is Good for the Soul." In *Mathematics and Necessity*, edited by Timothy Smiley, 1–81. Oxford: Oxford University Press, 2000.

Bury, Robert G., ed. *The "Philebus" of Plato*. New York: Arno, 1973.

Butler, J. Eric. "Plato's Pyrrhic Victory: An Intellectualist Reading of the *Philebus*." *Oxford Studies in Ancient Philosophy* 33 (2007): 89–123.

Carone, Gabriella R. "Hedonism and the Pleasureless Life in Plato's *Philebus*." *Phronêsis* 45 (2000): 257–83.

————. *Plato's Cosmology and Its Ethical Dimensions*. Cambridge: Cambridge University Press, 2005.

Carpenter, Amber D. "Embodied Intelligent (?) Souls: Plants in Plato's *Timaeus*." *Phronêsis* 55 (2010): 281–303.

————. "Hedonistic Persons: The Good Man Argument in Plato's *Philebus*." *British Journal for the History of Philosophy* 14 (2006): 5–26.

————. "Nevertheless: The Philosophical Significance of the Questions Posed at *Philebus* 15b." *Logical Analysis and History of Philosophy* 12 (2009): 103–29.

————. "Pleasure as Genesis in Plato's *Philebus*." *Ancient Philosophy* 31 (2011): 73–94.

————. "Putting the *Philebus*' Indispensable Method to Use." *Ancient Philosophy* 27 (2007): 1–20.

————. "What Is Peculiar in Aristotle's and Plato's Psychologies? What Is Common to Them Both?" In *Aristotle and the Stoics Reading Plato: Bulletin of the Institute of Classical Studies*, volume 107, edited by Verity Harte. London: Institute of Classical Studies, 2010.

Castoriadis, Cornelius. *The Castoriadis Reader*, 290–318. Edited by David A. Curtis. Malden, Mass.: Blackwell, 1989.

————. *Ce qui fait la Grèce*, vols. 1–3. Paris: Éditions du Seuil, 2004–2011.

————. *On Plato's "Statesman."* Translated by David A. Curtis. Stanford, Calif.: Stanford University Press, 2002.

————. *Philosophy, Politics, Autonomy*. Translated by David A. Curtis. Oxford: Oxford University Press, 1991.

Cherniss, Harold. *Aristotle's Criticism of Plato and the Academy.* Baltimore: Johns Hopkins University Press, 1944.

Code, Alan. "Reply to Michael Frede's 'Being and Becoming in Plato.'" In *Oxford Studies in Ancient Philosophy,* Supplementary Volume (1988): 53–60.

Cohen, Hermann. "Socrates and Plato: Founders of Ethics." In *Ethics of Maimonides.* Madison: University of Wisconsin Press, 2004.

Cooper, John. *Knowledge, Nature, and the Good.* Princeton, N.J.: Princeton University Press, 2004.

———. "Plato's Theory of the Human Good in the *Philebus.*" *Journal of Philosophy* 74 (1977): 714–30.

Cooper, Neil. "Pleasure and Goodness in Plato's *Philebus.*" *Philosophical Quarterly* 18 (1968): 12–15.

Cornford, Francis M. *Plato and Parmenides: Parmenides' "Way of Truth" and Plato's "Parmenides."* London: K. Paul, Trench, Trubner, 1939.

———. *Plato's Cosmology.* Indianapolis, Ind.: Routledge, 1935.

Crombie, I. M. *An Examination of Plato's Doctrines.* New York: Humanities, 1962.

Damascius. *Lectures on the "Philebus."* Translated by Leendert Gerrit Westerink. Chelmsford, Eng.: Prometheus Trust, 2010.

Dancy, R. M. "The One, the Many, and the Forms: *Philebus* 15b1–8." *Ancient Philosophy* 4 (1984): 160–93.

David, A. P. *Plato's New Measure: The Indeterminate Dyad.* Austin, Tex.: Mother Pacha, 2011.

Davidson, Donald. "Gadamer and Plato's *Philebus.*" In *Truth, Language, and History: Philosophical Essays Volume 5.* Oxford: Oxford University Press, 2005.

———. *Plato's "Philebus."* New York: Garland, 1990.

———. "Plato's Philosopher." *Apeiron* 26 (1993): 179–94.

De Chiara-Quenzer, Deborah. "A Method for Pleasure and Reason: Plato's *Philebus.*" *Apeiron* 26 (1993): 37–55.

Delcomminette, Sylvain. "Appearance and Imagination in the *Philebus.*" *Phronêsis* 48 (2003): 215–37.

———. *Le "Philèbe" de Platon: Introduction à l'agathologie platonicienne.* Leiden, Neth.: Koninklijke Brill NV, 2006.

Desjardins, Rosemary. *Plato and the Good: Illuminating the Darkling Vision.* Boston: Brill, 2004.

Dimas, Panos. "Good and Pleasure in the *Protagoras.*" *Ancient Philosophy* 28 (2008): 253–84.

Dixsaut, Monique, ed. *La Fêlure du plaisir: Études sur le "Philèbe" de Platon,* vols. 1 and 2. Paris: Vrin, 1999.

Dodds, E. R. *The Greeks and the Irrational.* Berkeley: University of California Press, 1951.

Dybikowski, James C. "False Pleasure and the *Philebus.*" *Phronêsis* 15 (1970): 147–65.

Evans, Matthew. "Plato on the Possibility of Hedonic Mistakes." *Oxford Studies in Ancient Philosophy* 35 (2008): 89–124.

———. "Plato's Rejection of Thoughtless and Pleasureless Lives." *Phronêsis* 52 (2007): 337–63.

Fagan, Patricia. *Plato and Tradition: The Poetic and Cultural Context of Philosophy.* Evanston, Ill.: Northwestern University Press, 2013.

Fahrnkopf, Robert. "Forms in the *Philebus.*" *Journal of the History of Philosophy* 15 (1977): 202–7.

Festugière, A.-J. *Contemplation et vie contemplative chez Platon.* Paris: Vrin, 1950.

Feuerbach, Ludwig. *Lectures on the Essence of Religion.* New York: Harper and Row, 1967.

Findlay, J. N. *Plato: The Written and Unwritten Doctrines.* London: Routledge and Kegan Paul, 1974.

Fine, Gail, "Plato on Perception: A Reply to Professor Turnbull, 'Becoming and Intelligibility.'" In *Oxford Studies in Ancient Philosophy,* Supplementary Volume (1988): 15–28.

Foucault, Michel. *The History of Sexuality, Volume 2: The Use of Pleasure.* Translated by Robert Hurley. New York: Pantheon Books, 1985.

Fowler, D. H. *The Mathematics of Plato's Academy: A New Reconstruction.* Oxford: Clarendon, 1987.

Fowler, H. N., trans. *Statesman, Philebus, Ion.* New York: Loeb Classical Library, 1925.

Frede, Dorothea. "Disintegration and Restoration: Pleasure and Pain in Plato's *Philebus.*" In *The Cambridge Companion to Plato,* edited by R. Kraut. New York: Cambridge University Press, 1992.

———. "The Impossibility of Perfection: Socrates's Criticism of Simonides' Poem in the *Protagoras.*" *Review of Metaphysics* 39 (1986): 729–53.

———. "Life and Its Limitations: The Conception of Happiness in the *Philebus.*" In *Plato's "Philebus": Selected Papers from the Eighth Symposium Platonicum,* edited by John Dillon and Luc Brisson, 3–16. Sankt Augustin, Ger.: Academia Verlag, 2010.

———, trans. *Philebus: Translation with Introductory Essay.* Indianapolis, Ind.: Hackett, 1993.

———. "Puppets on Strings: Moral Psychology in *Laws* Books I and II." In *Plato's "Laws": A Critical Guide,* edited by Christopher Bobonich, 108–26. Cambridge: Cambridge University Press, 2010.

———. "Rumpelstiltskin's Pleasures." *Phronêsis* 30 (1985): 151–80.

Frede, Michael. "Being and Becoming in Plato." In *Oxford Studies in Ancient Philosophy,* Supplementary Volume (1988): 37–52.

Gadamer, Hans-Georg. *The Beginning of Knowledge.* Translated by Rod Coltman. New York: Continuum, 2001.

———. *The Beginning of Philosophy.* Translated by Rod Coltman. New York: Continuum, 1998.

———. *Dialogue and Dialectic: Eight Hermeneutical Studies of Plato.* Translated by P. C. Smith. New Haven, Conn.: Yale University Press, 1980.

———. *The Idea of the Good in Platonic-Aristotelian Philosophy.* Translated by P. C. Smith. New Haven, Conn.: Yale University Press, 1986.

———. "Plato as Portraitist." Translated by Jamey Findling and Snehina Gabova. *Continental Philosophy Review* 33 (2000): 254–55.

———. *Plato's Dialectical Ethics: Phenomenological Interpretation Relating to the "Philebus."* Translated by Robert M. Wallace. New Haven, Conn.: Yale University Press, 1991.

Garner, John V. "David Wolfsdorf: *Pleasure in Ancient Greek Philosophy.*" *Ancient Philosophy* 34 (2014): 462–67.

Girard, René. *The Girard Reader.* Edited by James G. Williams. New York: Crossroad, 1996.

Goldschmidt, Victor. *Le Paradigme dans la dialectique platonicienne*. Paris: Presses Universitaires de France, 1947.

Gonzalez, Francisco. *Dialectic and Dialogue: Plato's Practice of Philosophical Inquiry*. Evanston, Ill.: Northwestern University Press, 1998.

Gosling, J. C. B. "False Pleasures: *Philebus* 35c–41b." *Phronêsis* 4 (1959): 44–53.

———, trans. *Plato: "Philebus."* Oxford: Clarendon, 1975.

Gosling, J. C. B., and C. C. W. Taylor. *The Greeks on Pleasure*. Oxford: Clarendon, 1982.

Grams, Laura. "Absolute Pleasure." Unpublished conference paper. International Plato Society Midterm Meeting: "Plato's Moral Realism." Atlanta, Ga., 2015.

———. "The Eleatic Visitor's Method of Division." *Apeiron* 45 (2012): 130–56.

Guthrie, W. C. K. *A History of Greek Philosophy, Volumes I–VI*. Cambridge: Cambridge University Press, 1962–81.

Hackforth, Reginald. *Plato's Examination of Pleasure: A Translation of the "Philebus" with an Introduction and Commentary*. Cambridge: Cambridge University Press, 1945.

Hampton, Cynthia. "Overcoming Dualism: The Intermediate in Plato's *Philebus*." In *Feminist Interpretations of Plato*. University Park: Pennsylvania State University Press, 1994.

———. *Pleasure, Knowledge, and Being: An Analysis of Plato's "Philebus."* Albany: State University of New York Press, 1990.

———. "Pleasure, Truth, and Being in Plato's *Philebus*: A Reply to Professor Frede." *Phronêsis* 32 (1987): 253–62.

Harte, Verity. "The *Philebus* on Pleasure: The Good, the Bad and the False." *Proceedings of the Aristotelian Society* 104 (2004): 113–30.

———. *Plato on Parts and Wholes: The Metaphysics of Structure*. Oxford: Clarendon, 2002.

Hartmann, Nicholai. *New Ways of Ontology*. New Brunswick, N.J.: Transaction, 2012.

Harvey, George. "The Supremacy of Dialectic in Plato's *Philebus*." *Ancient Philosophy* 32 (2012): 279–301.

Hauser, Kai. "Cantor's Concept of Set in Light of Plato's *Philebus*." *Review of Metaphysics* 63 (2010): 783–805.

Heinaman, Robert. "Plato's Division of Goods in the *Republic*." *Phronêsis* 47 (2002): 309–35.

Hopkins, Burt. "The Source of Platonism in the Philosophy of Mathematics Revisited: Aristotle's Critique of Eidetic Numbers." *American Dialectic* 1 (2011): 396–423.

Hyland, Drew. *Plato and the Question of Beauty*. Bloomington: Indiana University Press, 2008.

Ionescu, Cristina. "Hybrid Varieties of Pleasure and the Complex Case of the Pleasures of Learning in Plato's *Philebus*." *Dialogue: Canadian Philosophical Review* 47 (2008): 439–61.

———. "Plato's Understanding of Pleasure in the *Philebus*: Absolute Standards of Repletion and the Mean." *Journal of Philosophical Research* 33 (2008): 1–18.

Irwin, Terrence. *Plato's Ethics*. Oxford: Oxford University Press, 1995.

Kahn, Charles. "Plato on What Is Good." *Veritas* 49 (2004): 627–40.

Kangas, David. "Dangerous Joy: Marguerite Porete's Goodbye to the Virtues." *Journal of Religion* 1, no. 93 (2011): 299–321.

Kant, Immanuel. *Critique of Judgment*. Translated by Werner S. Pluhar. Indianapolis, Ind.: Hackett, 1987.

———. *Critique of Practical Reason*. Translated by Werner S. Pluhar. Indianapolis, Ind.: Hackett, 2002.

———. *Critique of Pure Reason*. Translated by Werner S. Pluhar. Indianapolis, Ind.: Hackett, 1996.

———. *Grounding for the Metaphysics of Morals*. Translated by J. W. Ellington. Indianapolis, Ind.: Hackett, 1993.

———. *The Metaphysics of Morals*. 2nd edition. Translated by Mary J. Gregor. Cambridge: Cambridge University Press, 1996.

———. *Prolegomena to Any Future Metaphysics*. 2nd edition. Translated by J. W. Ellington. Indianapolis, Ind.: Hackett, 2001.

———. *Religion within the Boundaries of Mere Reason and Other Writings*. Translated by Allen Wood and George di Giovanni. Cambridge: Cambridge University Press, 1999.

Kenny, Anthony. "False Pleasures in the *Philebus*: A Reply to Mr. Gosling." *Phronêsis* 5 (1962): 45–52.

Kirk, G. S., J. E. Raven, and M. Schofield. *The Presocratic Philosophers*. 2nd edition. Cambridge: Cambridge University Press, 2007.

Kirk, Gregory. *The Pedagogy of Wisdom: An Interpretation of Plato's "Theaetetus."* Evanston, Ill.: Northwestern University Press, 2015.

Klein, Jacob. "About Plato's *Philebus*." *Interpretation* 2 (1973): 157–82.

———. *A Commentary on Plato's "Meno."* Chicago: University of Chicago Press, 1998.

———. *Greek Mathematical Thought and the Origin of Algebra*. Translated by Eva Braan. Cambridge, Mass.: MIT Press, 1968.

Kolb, David. "Pythagoras Bound: Limit and Unlimited in Plato's *Philebus*." *Journal of the History of Philosophy* 21 (1983): 497–511.

Korsgaard, Christine. *Self-Constitution: Agency, Identity, Integrity*. Oxford: Oxford University Press, 2009.

———. "Two Distinctions in Goodness." *Philosophical Review* 2 (1983): 169–96.

Krämer, Hans J. *Plato and the Foundations of Metaphysics: A Work on the Theory of the Principles and Unwritten Doctrines of Plato*. Translated by John R. Catan. Albany: State University of New York Press, 1990.

Lang, Helen S. "On Memory: Aristotle's Corrections of Plato." *Journal of the History of Philosophy* 18 (1980): 379–93.

———. "Plato on Divine Art and the Production of Body." In *The Frontiers of Ancient Science: Essays in Honor of Heinrich von Staden*, edited by K.-D. Fischer and B. A. Holmes. Berlin: Walter de Gruyter, 2015.

Lang, Philippa M. "The Ranking of the Goods at *Philebus* 66a–67b." *Phronêsis* 55 (2010): 153–69.

Letwin, Oliver. "Interpreting Plato." *Phronêsis* 26 (1981): 187–206.

Long, A. A., and D. Sedley, eds. *The Hellenistic Philosophers, Volumes I and II*. Cambridge: Cambridge University Press, 1987.

Long, A. G. *Conversation and Self-Sufficiency in Plato*. Oxford: Oxford University Press, 2013.

Long, Christopher. *Socratic and Platonic Political Philosophy: Practicing a Politics of Reading*. Cambridge: Cambridge University Press, 2014.

Macadam, Joseph D. "Theo Smyrnaeus: On Arithmetic." M.A. thesis, University of British Columbia, 1969.

McCabe, Mary. *Plato's Individuals*. Princeton, N.J.: Princeton University Press, 1994.

McCoy, Marina. *Plato on the Rhetoric of Philosophers and Sophists*. Cambridge: Cambridge University Press, 2007.

Meinwald, Constance C. "Good-bye to the Third Man." In *The Cambridge Companion to Plato*, edited by Richard Kraut, 365–96. Cambridge: Cambridge University Press, 1992.

———. "The *Philebus*." In *The Oxford Handbook of Plato*, edited by Gail Fine. Oxford: Oxford University Press, 2008.

———. "Plato's Pythagoreanism." *Ancient Philosophy* 22 (2002): 87–101.

———. "Prometheus's Bounds: *Peras* and *Apeiron* in Plato's *Philebus*." In *Method in Ancient Philosophy*, edited by Jyl Gentzler, 165–80. Oxford: Oxford University Press, 1998.

Menn, Stephen P. *Plato on God as Nous*. Carbondale: Southern Illinois University Press, 1995.

Miller, Mitchel. "The God-Given Way." *Proceedings of the Boston Area Colloquium in Ancient Philosophy* 6 (1990): 323–70.

———. "The Pleasures of the Comic and of Socratic Inquiry: Aporetic Reflections on *Philebus* 48a–50b." *Arethusa* 41 (2008): 263–89.

Moravcsik, Jules M. "Forms, Nature, and the Good in the *Philebus*." *Phronêsis* 24 (1979): 81–104.

———. *Plato and Platonism: Plato's Conception of Appearance and Reality in Ontology, Epistemology, and Ethics, and Its Modern Echoes*. Malden, Mass.: Wiley-Blackwell, 1992.

Nichomachus of Gerasa. *Introduction to Arithmetic*. Translated by Martin Luther D'Ooge. London: Macmillan, 1926.

Obdrzalek, Suzanne. "Fleeing the Divine—Plato's Rejection of the Ahedonic Ideal in the *Philebus*." In *Plato's "Philebus": Selected Papers from the Eighth Symposium Platonicum*, edited by John Dillon and Luc Brisson, 209–14. Sankt Augustin, Ger.: Academia Verlag, 2010.

———. "Next to Godliness: Pleasure and Assimilation in God in the *Philebus*." *Apeiron* 45 (2012): 1–31.

Ogihara, Satoshi. "The Contrast between Soul and Body in the Analysis of Pleasure in the *Philebus*." In *Plato's "Philebus": Selected Papers from the Eighth Symposium Platonicum*, edited by John Dillon and Luc Brisson, 215–20. Sankt Augustin, Ger.: Academia Verlag, 2010.

Penner, Terry M. "False Anticipatory Pleasures: *Philebus* 36a3–41a6." *Phronêsis* 15 (1970): 166–78.

Plato. *Complete Works*. Edited by John M. Cooper and D. S. Hutchinson. Indianapolis, Ind.: Hackett, 1997.

Plotinus. *The Enneads*. Translated by John Dillon and Stephen MacKenna. London: Penguin Books, 1991.

Poste, Edward. *The "Philebus" of Plato, with a Revised Text and English Notes*. Oxford: Oxford University Press, 1860.

Press, Gerald, ed. *Who Speaks for Plato? Studies in Platonic Anonymity*. Lanham, Md.: Rowman and Littlefield, 2000.

Proclus. *A Commentary on the First Book of Euclid's "Elements."* Translated by Glen R. Morrow. Princeton, N.J.: Princeton University Press, 1992.

———. *The Elements of Theology*. Translated by E. R. Dodds. Oxford: Clarendon, 1963.

Reale, Giovanni. *Toward a New Interpretation of Plato.* Translated by John R. Catan and Richard Davies. Washington, D.C.: Catholic University of America Press, 1997.

Reeve, C. D. C. "Plato's Metaphysics of Morals." *Oxford Studies in Ancient Philosophy* 25 (2006): 39–58.

Reidy, David A. "False Pleasures and Plato's *Philebus.*" *Journal of Value Inquiry* 32 (1998): 343–56.

Rescher, Nicholas. "Kant's Neoplatonism: Kant and Plato on Mathematical and Philosophical Method." *Metaphilosophy* 44 (2013): 69–78.

Robin, Léon. *La Théorie platonicienne des idées et des nombres d'après Aristote: Étude historique et critique.* Paris: Félix Alcan, 1908.

———. *Les Rapports de l'être et de la connaissance d'après Platon.* Paris: Presses Universitaires de France, 1957.

Robinson, Richard. *Plato's Earlier Dialectic.* Oxford: Clarendon, 1953.

Rockhill, Gabriel. *Logique de l'histoire: Pour une analytique des pratiques philosophiques.* Paris: Éditions Hermann, 2010.

Ross, William D. *Plato's Theory of Ideas.* Oxford: Clarendon, 1951.

Russell, Daniel. *Plato on Pleasure and the Good Life.* Oxford: Clarendon, 2005.

Russon, John. "We Sense That They Strive." In *Retracing the Platonic Text,* edited by John Sallis and John Russon, 70–84. Evanston, Ill.: Northwestern University Press, 2000.

Sachs, Joe. "Introduction." In *Socrates and the Sophists.* Newburyport, Mass.: Focus Publishing Group, 2011.

Sanday, Eric. *A Study of Dialectic in Plato's "Parmenides."* Evanston, Ill.: Northwestern University Press, 2015.

Sayre, Kenneth. *Metaphysics and Method in Plato's "Statesman."* Cambridge: Cambridge University Press, 2006.

———. "The *Philebus* and the Good: The Unity of the Dialogue in Which the Good Is Unity." *Proceedings of the Boston Area Colloquium in Ancient Philosophy* 2 (1987): 45–71.

———. *Plato's Late Ontology: A Riddle Resolved.* Princeton, N.J.: Princeton University Press, 1983.

Schleiermacher, Friedrich E. D. *Introductions to the Dialogues of Plato.* Translated by William Dobson. New York: Arno, 1973.

Shiner, Roger. *Knowledge and Reality in Plato's "Philebus."* Assen, Neth.: Van Gorcum, 1974.

Shorey, Paul. *The Unity of Plato's Thought.* Chicago: University of Chicago Press, 1903.

Szabó, Árpád. *The Beginnings of Greek Mathematics.* Translated by A. M. Ungar. Budapest: Akademiai Kiado, 1978.

Taylor, A. E., trans. *Plato: "Philebus" and "Epinomis."* London: Thomas Nelson and Sons, 1956.

———. *Plato: The Man and His Work.* Abingdon, Eng.: Routledge, 1926.

Tenkku, Jussi. *The Evaluation of Pleasure in Plato's Ethics.* Helsinki: Suomalaisen Kirjallisuuden Kirjapaino, 1956.

Thein, Karel. "Imagination, Self-Awareness, and Modal Thought at *Philebus* 39–40." *Oxford Studies in Ancient Philosophy* 42 (2012): 109–49.

Tracy, Theodore J. *Physiological Theory and the Doctrine of the Mean in Plato and Aristotle.* Chicago: Loyola University Press, 1969.

Tuozzo, Thomas. "The General Account of Pleasure in Plato's *Philebus.*" *Journal of the History of Philosophy* 34 (1996): 495–513.

Turnbull, Robert G. "Becoming and Intelligibility." *Oxford Studies in Ancient Philosophy,* Supplementary Volume (1988): 1–14.

———. *The "Parmenides" and Plato's Late Philosophy: Translation of and Commentary on the "Parmenides" with Interpretative Chapters on the "Timaeus," the "Theaetetus," the "Sophist," and the "Philebus."* Toronto: University of Toronto Press, 1998.

———. "Response to Professor Fine's Critique of 'Becoming and Intelligibility.'" In *Oxford Studies in Ancient Philosophy,* Supplementary Volume (1988): 29–36.

Van Riel, Gerd. *Pleasure and the Good Life: Plato, Aristotle, and the Neoplatonists.* Leiden, Neth.: Brill, 2000.

Vlastos, Gregory. "The Socratic Elenchus." *Oxford Studies in Ancient Philosophy* 1 (1983): 27–58.

Vogt, Katja M. *Belief and Truth: A Skeptic Reading of Plato.* Oxford: Oxford University Press, 2012.

———. "Why Pleasure Gains Fifth Rank: Against the Anti-Hedonist Interpretation of the *Philebus.*" In *Plato's "Philebus": Selected Papers from the Eighth Symposium Platonicum,* edited by John Dillon and Luc Brisson, 250–55. Sankt Augustin, Ger.: Academia Verlag, 2010.

Warren, James. "Plato on the Pleasures and Pains of Knowing." *Oxford Studies in Ancient Philosophy* 39 (2010): 1–32.

———. *The Pleasures of Reason in Plato, Aristotle, and the Hellenistic Hedonists.* Cambridge: Cambridge University Press, 2014.

Waterfield, Robin, trans. *Philebus.* New York: Penguin Group, 1982.

Wedberg, Anders. *Plato's Philosophy of Mathematics.* Westport, Conn.: Greenwood, 1955.

Wolfsdorf, David. *Pleasure in Ancient Greek Philosophy.* Cambridge: Cambridge University Press, 2012.

———. *Trials of Reason: Plato and the Crafting of Philosophy.* Oxford: Oxford University Press, 2008.

Zeyl, Donald. "Plato and Talk of a World in Flux: *Timaeus* 49a6–50b5." *Harvard Studies in Classical Philology* 79 (1975): 125–48.

Zuckert, Catherine H. *Plato's Philosophers: The Coherence of the Dialogues.* Chicago: University of Chicago Press, 2009.

INDEX

abstraction, 30, 50
account (*logos* [λόγος]): xi, 5–9, 15–16, 19–21, 31; principle of, xi, 16, 19, 148n33
affection (*pathêma* [πάθημα]), 74–75, 90, 91
agency, responsible, 38
aggregate, 117, 161n17
alone (*monos* [μόνος]), xi, 5–6, 38, 41; being alone, 85, 89
analogue (*antistrophon* [ἀντίστροφον]), 108–9, 131
animals, ix, 8, 143, 155n22, 165n43
anticipation, 74, 87
argument: love of, 8; subjective, 143
Aristotle, 81, 112, 146n10, 147n27; on end-goal, 156n34, 157n42; on genus, 161n14; on numbers, 116–18, 162n21
Aristoxenus, 52
arithmetic, 106, 113–24, 128–29, 132, 134–35; "philosophical," 113–14, 115, 117, 122–23, 128, 161n17
Aufderheide, Joachim, 154n5, 157n37
Augustine, 158n53, 159n70
Austin, Emily A., 154n6
authority, 130, 135
autonomy, 94, 160n83

Barker, Andrew, 52
beauty (*kalon* [καλόν]), 88, 96, 132, 142
becoming (*genesis* [γένεσις]), x, xii, 46, 55, 157n43; being vs., 80–81, 125–26, 152n35, 157n45; good and, 142–44; pleasure and, 70, 78–86, 130, 157n38, 158n48; truth and, 140. *See also* emergence
being (*ousia* [οὐσία]; *on* [ὄν]), x, xii, 18–19, 23–24, 27, 48, 83, 124–25, 158n48; coming-into-being, 55, 56, 58, 71, 101; goodness and, 85–86, 99
belief (*pistis* [πίστις]), 118–19
Bernadete, Seth, 160n4
body (*sôma* [σῶμα]), 74–78; soul vs., 86–87, 90, 93, 165n46. *See also* pleasure: bodily
Bossi, Beatriz, 80, 154n6, 156n31
Bravo, Francisco, 157n38
building, 111, 113

Carone, Gabriella R., 155n14
Carpenter, Amber D., 81

cause and causation (*aitia* [αἰτία]; *aition* [αἴτιον]), xi, xii, 37–39, 48, 55–66, 95, 141; souls and, 94
chance, 63, 108
chaos, 60, 63, 111
choice-worthiness, 34, 39, 78, 82, 85, 108
Code, Alan, 81
collecting (*sunagôgê* [συναγωγή]), 43–44, 50–51
coming-into-being. *See* being
community, 92, 94, 162n18
conatus, 93
condition, helping vs. necessary, 152n30. *See also* natural condition
consequence, 70, 83, 164n35
craft (*technê* [τέχνη]), 22; craftspersons, 56–59

Damascius, ix
deficiency, 70–71, 73, 76, 77–78, 81, 93, 99
"*désirants*" on pleasure, 83–85
desire, 8, 34, 94, 103, 107
destruction, 18, 20, 62–63, 72, 84–85, 93, 156n29, 157n44
dialectic (*dialektikê* [διαλεκτική]), xi, 6, 10, 14, 92, 133–35, 141; *Republic* on, 164n34; superiority (and purity) of, 118–19, 123–30
disciplines, 109, 113, 118–19, 124, 127–28, 134–35
discovery, 29, 30
disintegration, 72–73
division (*diairesis* [διαίρεσις]). *See under* knowledge
double, the, 51–52, 150n19

education, 22, 109, 115, 121
element (*stoicheion* [στοιχεῖον]), 64–65, 164n33
elenchus (*elenchos* [ἔλεγχος]), 10, 146n10
emergence, xi–xii, 10, 18, 22, 30, 46, 47–48, 50, 55, 58–60; of multiple goods, x, 14, 31, 34, 37, 39, 140, 143–44; of pleasure, 71, 79, 108, 133, 141–42
empirical classification, 52, 111–12, 114, 121, 135
emptying (*kenôsis* [κένωσις]), 72, 77, 87, 154n10
end-goal (*telos* [τέλος]), 44, 46, 79, 85, 156n34, 157nn40–42
ensouled being (*empsuchon* [ἔμψυχον]), 77, 79

Epicureans, 158n56
equality, 16, 50, 51, 106, 107–8, 116
eristical discourse, 12, 27, 28
even, the, 135
evil, 12, 63, 69–70
exclusion, 107
exigency, 48, 66
experience, ix, 71–72, 74, 77, 86–95, 97, 99–
    100, 111, 132–34, 138, 142, 156n25
expertise, 29, 130, 135, 148n37

Fahrnkopf, Robert, 163n27
fairness. *See* equality
feeling. *See* affections
Feuerbach, Ludwig, 87
flux, 73–78
forgetting (*lêthê* [λήθη]), 75, 89–91, 139,
    155n17, 159n62
form (*eidos* [εἶδος]; *idea* [ἰδέα]), 23, 43–44,
    49, 65, 72, 96, 119, 130, 148n33, 163n27;
    mixture and, 152n29; study of forms,
    134–35, 137
Frede, Dorothea, 23, 70, 105, 109
Frede, Michael, 81
freedom, 141, 158n56
fulfillment (*plêrôsis* [πλήρωσις]), xii, 62, 70–74,
    76–78, 81–88, 90–91, 99, 131; desire and,
    84–85, 87, 94, 103, 143; terminology for,
    72, 154n10, 159n62

Gadamer, Hans-Georg, 148n33, 152n28,
    161n15, 162n18
generation, 18, 83–84
generativity, 50–51, 54, 66, 106, 128
genus (*genos* [γένος]), 7, 11, 43, 49, 111–12,
    161n12, 161n14
geometry, 121, 127, 134–35, 163n22
gods, 9, 12, 38, 40, 62, 80, 155n14, 159n70,
    165n43, 165n2. *See also* pleasure: Aphrodite
good, the (*agathon* [ἀγαθόν]), ix–x, xii, 7, 15,
    31–35, 61, 95–96, 100; becoming and,
    142–43; being and, 85–86, 100, 140, 143–
    44; conditional nature of, 32, 70, 100; final
    vs. instrumental, 153n1, 158n47; *Gorgias*
    on, 71, 82, 154n9, 157nn40–41; intrinsic
    vs. extrinsic, 70–71, 83, 153n1; possessions
    contributing to, 69, 97; reason and, 38–39;
    threefold character of, 33–35, 96–97;
    transcendence of being and, x, xi, xii, 71,
    99–101, 140, 144; unconditional, 153n1.
    See also pleasure: goodness and
good life, xi, xii, 6, 37–38, 60–62, 71, 93, 94–99,
    131, 135, 151nn24–25, 151n27; ingredients
    of, 69–70, 97–98, 106, 134; perfection vs.,

100, 151n24; ranking of causes for, xii,
    39, 63, 69–70, 95–96, 98, 100, 151n24,
    160n73; sciences and, 69, 122, 131. *See also*
    mixture
Gorgias, 71, 77, 78, 82, 94, 154n9, 156n24,
    157nn40–41

happiness, 8–9, 32
harm. *See* pleasures: harmful
harmony, 53, 60, 72, 94, 155n12; "natural,"
    156n31, 159n71
Harte, Verity, 29–30, 149n40
hedonism, 6, 14, 16, 37, 107–8, 138, 146n8,
    149n2
henad (*henas* [ἑνάς]; *henados* [ἑνάδος]), 17–28,
    147n25, 148nn34–35
hope (*elpis* [ἐλπίς]), 9, 87, 101, 158n53
hosautos usage (ὡσαύτως), 25–26

idea. *See* form
ignorance (*agnoia* [ἄγνοια]), 28, 77, 82, 91–92,
    100, 139, 159nn62–64, 159n66
image-thinking, 118–19
imitation, 8, 65
immanent, the, ix, 130, 132, 143
inclusion, 5, 39, 70, 97, 107, 131, 136–37, 140,
    151n27
indefinite, the, 17, 18, 28, 32, 35; pleasure and,
    78–79
indeterminacy, 27, 37, 47, 48, 57. *See also*
    unlimited
induction, 111
instances, xii, 12, 20, 25, 63–65, 72, 112, 115,
    135, 153n41; pure and impure, 120–24,
    127–30, 164n38
intellection (*noêsis* [νόησις]), 105–6, 118, 124,
    127–28, 132, 137, 142, 164n31; capacity
    for, 7, 145n7. *See also* reason
intermediate, the, 27–28, 32, 74, 97, 124,
    148n34
intervals: in mathematics, 150n16; in music,
    29, 148n37, 149n40

joy (*chara* [χαρά]), 7
justice, 94, 136

Kant, Immanuel, 152n31, 165n44, 165n1
kind, class. *See* form; genus
Klein, Jacob, 162n20
knowledge (*epistêmê* [ἐπιστήμη]), 5, 7, 60–61,
    90–91, 126–27, 136–38, 160n77; capacity
    for, 9, 164n36; divisions of, 97, 109–15;
    goodness and, 34, 37, 62, 138; human vs.
    divine, 136–37; pleasure and, 138–39;

productive vs. educational, 109–15, 121;
    purity in, 106–10, 137–38; in *Seventh
    Letter*, 164n32
Korsgaard, Christine, 158n47

lack, 76, 87–88, 90–94, 103, 105, 123, 131,
    157n40, 157n42, 158n48, 159nn63–64,
    160n1, 160n5, 165n41; lack-fulfillment, 78,
    87, 132, 155n14
Lang, Helen S., 134
leading, 110, 114; and following, 58, 160n77
leaky jar scenario, 92, 131
learning process (*mathêsis* [μάθησις]), ix–xii, 6,
    22–23, 25, 28–32, 37, 82, 89–94, 96, 100,
    141–42, 159n66; "original learning," 90–94,
    159n66; pleasures of, xi, 82, 89–92, 133–34;
    psychical experience of, 71. *See also* lesson
legislation, 94
Leibniz's Law, 163n23
lesson (*mathêma* [μάθημα]), ix, xii, 74–75,
    90–91, 100, 118, 134, 142, 158n52
letters, invention of, 29, 148n39
limit (*peras* [πέρας]): mixture and, 50–55, 58,
    95, 151n24, 160n1; pleasure and, 62; and
    the unlimited, 30–31, 40–44, 46–47, 50, 53,
    59–60, 72, 141, 151n28, 152nn33–34

maker (*dêmiourgikon* [δημιουργικόν]). *See
    under* craft
manifestation, xii, 115, 132, 142; of good, 31,
    32, 35, 100; of limit, 54
manual arts, 110–12, 161n10, 161n13
mathematics. *See* arithmetic; geometry
measure, xi–xii, 46, 51, 69, 94–96, 112–14, 126,
    153n35; measure-in-emergence, 71, 93,
    142; pure pleasure and, 132–33
memorials, 87, 92, 159n67
memory (*mnêmê* [μνήμη]), 7, 74–75, 158n52.
    See also recollection
Menn, Stephen P., 164n31
mixture (*mixis* [μίξις]), xi, 5, 34–35, 37–66,
    79, 95–96, 151n24, 151–52nn28–29,
    152nn34–35; "well-mixed" life, 37–38, 61,
    69, 103, 136, 138, 139–40, 151n24
moderation (*sôphrosunê* [σωφροσύνη]), 53,
    69, 94
monad (*monas* [μόνας]; *monados* [μονάδος]),
    27, 106, 115–24
"more and less" characterization, 44–46, 49, 61,
    79, 149–50nn7–9, 160n1, 161n13
motion (*kinêsis* [κίνησις]), 74, 81, 87, 135,
    154n10; bodily, 76, 77, 87, 155n15,
    155n19, 155n22; of soul, 155n22, 159n71,
    163n31

motivation, 95
multiplicity, 5–6, 7, 37, 44, 89
music, 29–30, 51–54, 58, 121, 149n40, 151n20;
    note (*melos* [μέλος]), 88–89, 103

naming, 120–22, 127
natural condition, 72, 73, 155n12, 155n14,
    155n20, 157n44
need, xii, 32, 42, 59, 60, 89, 90–92, 103, 131,
    138–39, 143
neutral state, 76–77, 78, 155n14, 155n20,
    157n44, 159n70
Nichomachus of Gerasa, 150, 163n22
nonbeing, xii, 48, 55, 85–86
non-perception (*anaisthêsia* [ἀναισθησία]),
    75–76, 155n14, 155nn17–18
norm, xii, 53, 72, 93–94; coming-to-a-norm,
    88–89, 154n10, 158n59
now (*nun* [νῦν]), 40. *See also* present, the
number and counting (*arithmos* [ἀριθμός]),
    40–41, 47, 51, 123–24, 148n33, 150n12,
    162n21; music and, 51–52; number theory,
    116–17. *See also* arithmetic

one (*hen* [ἕν]), 17, 18–19
one-many problem, 16–18, 20–22, 24, 30, 44
ontology, x, 37, 48, 55
opinion (*doxa* [δόξα]), 7, 125–26, 135, 138,
    163n30

pain (*lupê* [λύπη]), 61, 71, 72, 73–74, 75–77,
    79, 131, 156n29; "double pain," 158n53;
    Gorgias on, 156n24; learning and, 89–91;
    Phaedo on, 156n27, 158n54
paradigm (*paradeigma* [παράδειγμα]), 64,
    153n41
Parmenides, 147n26
perception (*aisthêsis* [αἴσθησις]), 69, 74–75,
    91
Phaedo, 117, 124, 149n8, 156n27, 158n54
phenomena, 50, 55, 66
Philebus: "anthropology" of, 139–40; drama
    in, xi, 14, 52, 80, 138, 146n8, 161n8;
    playfulness in, 63, 153n40; principal
    themes of, ix–x, 6, 60–61, 134, 142;
    structure of, 5, 146n18; summary
    conclusion to, 69–70
pleasure (*hêdonê* [ἡδονή]): aesthetic, 89;
    alethic vs. anagnostic, 159n65; Aphrodite
    and, 9–10, 14, 20, 38; Aristotle on, 81;
    bad, 12–13, 69, 106–7, 146n13, 161nn7–
    8; becoming and, 70, 71, 78–89, 99,
    158n48; bodily, 8, 71–78, 155n15, 155n19;
    complexity of, 9–10, 77; false, 9, 106–7,

pleasure, *continued*
   131–32, 145n4, 154n4, 161nn7–8,
   165n42; the good, xi, 5–7, 10, 12–15, 20,
   34, 37–39, 61, 69–70, 81, 98–99, 153n1,
   153n4, 154n9; harmful, 78, 97, 139,
   161n8; harmless, 82–83, 157n42; impure,
   86–87, 104, 107, 132; indefiniteness of,
   78–80; intense, 69, 103, 160n1; katastemic,
   158n56; learning and, xi, 82, 89–92, 133–
   34; limits on, 62; mixed, 6, 79; necessary,
   69, 107, 138; opposites in, 10–13, 16;
   plurality of, 10–11; psychical, 71, 74–78,
   86, 99, 133, 155n15, 156n24; pure, x, xi–xii,
   69–71, 77, 78, 82, 86–101, 103–9, 128,
   130–36, 139, 141–42, 154nn4–5; 157n42,
   159n65, 160n77, 160n1, 160nn4–5; pursuit
   of, 78, 83–85, 105, 154n9, 156n25, 160n5;
   soul and, 86–88, 93–95, 155n22; true, 9,
   14, 69, 88, 104, 132, 136, 139; unlimited
   tendency of, 61–62, 79–80
plurality, 5–6, 15, 23
precision (*akribeia* [ἀκρίβεια]), 110–14, 124,
   129, 132
present, the, 39–41, 43, 47, 55, 56, 150n14
procession, 46, 79
Proclus, 117, 161n9
productivity. *See under* knowledge
projection (*probolê* [προβολή]), 87, 117–18,
   162n20, 164n35
proportion, 34, 95–96
Protagoras, 146n13
psyche. *See* soul
purity (*katharos* [καθαρός]), 103–9, 128–34.
   See also pleasure: pure; science: purity and
Pythagoreans, 52, 161n17

quality, 52
quantity and measurement, 44–45, 52, 121

reason (*nous* [νοῦς]), 8, 14, 34, 38, 50, 62–63,
   65–66, 69, 82, 126–27, 131, 160n73,
   163n31; divine, 38, 74, 135, 164n35. *See
   also* intellection
recollection (*anamnêsis* [ἀνάμνησις]), 74, 92
recursive interpretation, 25–26, 148n35
reductionism, 52, 55
Republic, 82, 94, 107–8, 118, 120, 127, 134–35,
   157n42, 164n34
restoration, 72–73, 77, 154n10, 156n29
Russell, Daniel, 153n1, 154n7
Russon, John, 47

Sayre, Kenneth, 151n24
science, x, 66, 69, 82, 126–28; as "epistemic
   learning" (ἐπιστήμη), 126–27; false, 137,
   165n41; purity and, 105–7, 115–16, 119–
   23, 128–38, 164n38; in the *Republic*, 127
self-control (*enkrateia* [ἐγκρατείᾳ]), 94
sensation. *See* perception
separation, 72, 152n28
shapes and figures, 132–33
Shiner, Riger, 163n27
sophistry, 28
soul (*psuchê* [ψυχή]), xii, 53, 71, 72, 74–78,
   155n14, 159n71, 163n31; pure pleasure
   and, 86–88, 93–95, 155n22
sound, 28, 29–30, 52, 148n37
Statesman, 150nn13–14, 152n35
Stoics, 159n70, 163n30
"subtlers" (*kompsoi* [κομψοί]), 81–86, 157n38,
   157n46, 158n48
surprise, 85, 128, 133, 161n9
symmetry. *See* proportion

temperance. *See* moderation
Theon of Smyrna, 150
Theuth (Thoth), 29, 148n39
thought (*dianoia* [διάνοια]), 118–19
Timaeus, 80, 165n2
tradition, 65, 153n42
transcendence, 114–15, 118, 121, 130. *See also
   under* the good
truth (*alêtheia* [ἀλήθεια]), 69, 96, 128–29,
   139–40, 165n46; "highest," 126
two, the (*duas* [δυάς]), 23, 26, 28, 148n34,
   162n21

unit. *See* monad
unity (ὡς εἰς ἓν), 49–50, 147n26. *See also
   henads*
unlimited, the (*apeiron* [ἄπειρον]), 23, 27–28,
   40, 43–49, 53, 57; pleasure and, 61–62, 79.
   See also limit vs. the unlimited
unwritten doctrines, 116, 148n33, 162n18

Van Riel, Gerd, 158n48

Warren, James, 159n64
Waterfield, Robin, 146n8
whole, 140, 165n46, 165n2
wisdom (and the wise), 62, 65, 73, 74, 75–76,
   126
Wolfsdorf, David, 154n10